CULTURAL HISTORIES OF CENTRAL ASIA

CULTURAL HISTORIES OF CENTRAL ASIA

Edited by
Rashmi Doraiswamy

ACADEMY OF THIRD WORLD STUDIES
Jamia Millia Islamia
New Delhi

AAKAR

CULTURAL HISTORIES OF CENTRAL ASIA
Edited by Rashmi Doraiswamy

First published, 2009

ISBN 978-81-89833-76-3

Published by
AAKAR BOOKS
28 E Pocket IV, Mayur Vihar Phase I, Delhi-110 091
Phone : 011-2279 5505 Telefax : 011-2279 5641
aakarbooks@gmail.com; www.aakarbooks.com

Printed at
Arpit Printographers, Delhi-110 032
arpitprinto@yahoo.com

CONTENTS

Introduction

The Central Asian region has, through the centuries, been the hub of vibrant and diverse cultural practices. Situated at a vantage position geographically, it is linked to East, South and West Asia, as well as to Europe. As part of the Silk Route, it was open to a vast spectrum of influences from China to the Mediterranean. Cultural articulations, as a result, were highly syncretic, looking towards the past while creating new vistas for the future.

The Central Asian region has also seen and experienced often contradictory and rapid transitions from one state of political and social being to another: nomadic-sedentary, feudal-socialist, and now socialist-capitalist.... Pre-Islamic religions such as Buddhism and Zoroastrianism transformed and adapted themselves to the advent of Islam in the region; Sufism questioned religious orthodoxy; agrarian societies leap-frogged into socialist production; epical, oral literatures morphed themselves into realist writings. Such radical transformations gave rise to cultural articulations that were innovative, unorthodox, and capable of reinventing their significances through the ages.

There is a need to assess, in 'close-up' as it were, the encounter of West, South and East Asia with Central Asia in pre-modern and modern times and the encounter between Russia and Central Asia in pre-Soviet and Soviet periods. These exchanges are centuries old and have mutually enriched cultural forms in the entire region, including our own subcontinent. To club them under a single, linear history would do no justice to the multifaceted cultural formations of the region. Essentialist readings cannot find a place in critical writing on this region: so diffuse and diverse are the interminglings.

One of the reasons for this tremendous intermingling, no doubt, is the way ideas and images travelled beyond the boundaries of empires and pre-modern states. This travel was due to the nomadic lifestyles of many of the peoples of this region as well as the Silk Route, both of which created forms of cosmopolitanism and vernacularism. The region witnessed a pre-modern globalisation where cosmopolitanism was born as much out of the interaction of traders, craftsmen, and artisans as by conquests. It was this plural nature of cultural formations in Central Asia that was addressed in the seminar, 'Articulating the Modern: Cultural Histories of Central Asia', organised in December 2004 at the Academy of Third World Studies, Jamia Millia Islamia. The participants at the seminar were academics, as well as art practitioners and independent researchers. The seminar included a wide spectrum of disciplines and the participants were eminent people from the area of Central Asian Studies, Russian Studies, Architecture, Ethno-Musicology, History, Painting, Textiles, Literature, and International Relations. This volume, in the main, consists of selected presentations made at the two-day seminar. Professor Devendra Kaushik, who had chaired a session at the seminar, and Dr Dilorom Karomat, who had attended the seminar, gave in their essays at a later date.

There is in the essays in this volume a sense of the outreach of historical and political events, their outward ripples extending geoculturally to places that are distant and far-flung. There is also a zooming in on details of these encounters, of examining exchanges in close-up. As Professor Hari Vasudevan put it in his introductory remarks to the seminar, there was a need to look beyond the boundaries of traditional disciplines, in order to understand these histories: "We were very, very conscious of the fact that there has been an interest in India in Central Asia at two levels. The first, well established, was our traditional interest in the pre-modern and early modern link between South Asia and Central Asia, the very close connections that existed between these regions. We also bore in mind the fact that there was a considerable interest in contemporary geo-politics in the region. Russia is our point of entry in many ways. What we did feel is that what was necessary was a greater, more direct interest in the local cultures of Central Asia today, than has been the case in the past. The intent was to go beyond the standard preoccupation with the geo-political or the medieval or at least while preserving it, to firm it up with, to reinforce it, to strengthen it with a close interest in the literatures and cultures of this particular region, other than that which has been formed through the Russian connection. The other 'level' of interest is that standard disciplines are not the only point of entry in the study of the area. Sociology, anthropology, history, international relations, of course these are well marked out fields through which we come to know the area. In fact each of these produces a particular history, a particular time line, a particular phase of that time line. So what tends to happen is that those who have an intimate personal knowledge of this region, of the connections between this region and South Asia, begin to evolve a very, very deep set of networks with the region, begin to understand things that perhaps escape the standard area of a discipline. In order to go beyond disciplines, we required a broader terrain within which to place our research. And this is what the seminar has set out to do, by dealing with cultural practices as a source of information concerning this region. We are interested in this intimate sense of the region. But there are different ways of going about it rather than the purely disciplinary".

The presentations at the seminar underscored the fact that cultural artefacts of the region are palimpsests: meanings are layered with no 'core'. Whether it is sculpture, painting or music, the form, the representation, the style are all marked by hybridity. The essays examine the relationship of this region with the Indian subcontinent, on the one hand, and with Russia and Europe on the other. The way in which motifs, styles and compositions have travelled back and forth from Central Asia to other regions, point to fluidity in the notion of the 'neighbourhood'.

The timeline of historical and cultural formations covered in the seminar spans the pre-medieval, medieval and modern periods. Epics form an important part of the pre-modern cultural heritage. The Kyrgyz epic, *Manas,* said to be the longest epic in the world, is subjected to a thematic analysis in Neelima Singh's essay. Professor Qamar Rais focuses on the Uzbek epic *Alpomysh,* and compares it to the *Ramayana*. Radha Banerjee's article examines the various religious and political influences that are to be found in the art of the Central Asian region. Representations in sculpture, painting and on coins, point to a composite culture in which Buddhism, Zoroastrianism, Manicheanism, Nestorian Christianity, and Hinduism have mingled freely.

Al Farabi was in many ways a Renaissance man. Known as 'the second teacher' (after Aristotle), Al Farabi was one of the philosophers who heralded the Asian Renaissance, that many Central Asians like the well-known Kyrgyz writer Chingiz Aitmatov (who sadly passed away recently), believe predated the European Renaissance. Al Farabi's views on music, the ideal state, religion, science and mathematics prefigure a 'modern' sensibility in the pre-modern period. The victory of spirit over matter is encapsulated in Kalpana Sahni's tale of the tomb of the Sufi saint, Yasawi, in Kazakhstan who, despite all architectural structures and ideological superstructures over centuries, has survived as a spiritual force to reach out to his followers. The dome as an iconic representational form that travelled all the way from Central Asia and Iran to India, is the focus of K. T. Ravindran's presentation.

The Russian colonisation of Central Asia in the nineteenth century was to impact the region in many ways. While traditional writing, that was rich in poetry and prose, continued to flourish (as outlined in Saifullah Saifi's article), there was a distinct aspiration towards a realistic representation born of the encounter with the Russian tradition of realism that flourished in the nineteenth century. Writers such as Sadriddin Aini from Tadjikistan and Abai Kunnanbai from Kazakhstan (on whose works Professor Abhai Maurya's essay focuses in detail), took up cudgels against all forms of feudal exploitation in their realist works. The Soviet period saw intervention in the cultural sphere in Central Asia on a larger scale and in a more systematic manner. In many ways, this intervention was shaped by the enlightenment project, with education playing an important role. Cultural industries were set up, even as indigenous forms either faced the need to adapt, or transform themselves in accordance with the new historical context. The presentations delineate in fascinating detail the nature of this encounter in architecture, music and cinema. Romi Khosla's essay focuses on the Soviet enterprise of transforming lived architectural spaces into 'heritage' and substituting it with a counter-monumental architecture in Uzbekistan. The 'intimate' details of the encounter between Russia and Central Asia in the field of music, the spectrum of political attitudes to the *Shashmaqom* in the twentieth century, the minute changes that were affected in its composition, performance and reception, are dealt with in Dilorom Karomat's essay on the *Shashmaqom*.

The Silk Road is viewed from three different contemporary viewpoints in this volume: Rajeev Sethi takes a look at the pre-modern connectivity that 'chastens' us to realise that the networking of the internet era is not the only globalisation this world has known. Global trade without boundaries has gone on for centuries, and trade in textiles had sustained the Silk Route for more than a millennium. The fate of the textiles, their industries and the people who work in this field today, as well as what Sethi calls 'the future of human skills', is analysed by both Rajeev Sethi and Rta Kapur Chisti in their articles for this volume. The revival of the Silk Route as transport corridor and its geopolitical implications is dealt with by Meena Singh Roy.

Travellers, making their way through hostile steppes, deserts and mountains, played an important role in the collection of data on the cultural forms of the region, in cataloguing this data and in the construction of an idea of Central Asia, that was very often a discursive construction of the region as the 'Orient' and as the 'Other' of Russia. Arup Banerjee charts the routes and expeditions undertaken by Marc Aurel Stein to discover extant traces of the Silk Route and Ruby

Roy examines the sources that are available on Kyrgyz history and the accounts of Russian travellers on the region.

The essays in this volume present Central Asia as a region that was intensely and intimately networked to its extended neighbourhood for better, rather than for worse. The painter, Gulammohammad Sheikh, evocatively characterises this 'fluidity' as 'travelling cultures'. These cultures are distinctive for not being tied down firmly to the problematics of region, territory or nation-state and for 'overflowing' physical and political boundaries. Several essays underline the fact that the extraordinary vibrancy of cultural forms questions and transgresses any 'limits' that Orientalism, or negative forms of 'Otherness' may lay down. In music, in cinema, in literature and architecture, as well as in the ideas that the region has nurtured, no form of orthodoxy, censorship or repression has succeeded in fully wiping out cultural forms, or completely homogenising them in accordance with a given ideological vision. Put on the backburner of history, they have simmered and kept the flame aglow, to re-emerge later in other forms, styles, and even in other 'scales' elsewhere (to quote Sheikh again).

I am grateful to Professor Mushirul Hasan, Vice-Chancellor, Jamia Millia Islamia and Professor Hari Vasudevan, who was in 2004 the Honorary Deputy Director of the Academy of Third World Studies, for encouragement and support in organising the seminar.

I also wish to express my deep gratitude to Rajeev Sethi for having brought along Professor of Ethnomusicology and a specialist on Central Asian music, Ted Levine, and the well-known Central Asian musician, Abduvali Abdurashidov, to the inaugural session of the seminar. Professor Levine and Abduvali Abdurashidov were in New Delhi for a programme of the Aga Khan Music Initiative. Professor Ted Levine, at the inaugural session, speaking on the reinvention of traditions and the revival of cultural memory, stated: "UNESCO has recently given a large grant to both Uzbekistan and Tadjikistan to revive all sorts of activities connected to *Sashmaqom*, to create a new encyclopedia about it, to create a new critical edition, to create recordings.... There is a lot of demand, there is a lot of interest now among really young children and young families in having their children return to these traditions". He also spoke of the musical instrument, the *sartor*, and how it is being popularised by the musician Abduvali Abdurashidov: "One can think of the *sartor* as perhaps being a kind of a distant ancestor of the *sarangi*. It has a very vocal quality to its sound as does the *sarangi*. Abduvali Abdurashidov has become a very busy man with this soft-spoken instrument. He runs a music academy in Dushanbe, Tadjikistan that is sponsored by my project, the Aga Khan Music Initiative in Central Asia, in which he is training an elite group of graduate students, to master this tradition. Abduvali Abdurashidov is not only a performer, he has a research degree from Tashkent Conservatory. He has put together poetry and music that goes very deep into the past. He is a kind of 'Court Musician' of the President of Tadjikistan. So my point is, this kind of music, in addition to literature and religion, provides another window into this issue of cultural memory. It is evidence of how cultural memory is manipulated, re-established, and made into an important element that is connecting Central Asia to other parts of the world through international initiatives, like the Aga Khan Music Initiative". It was our privilege that Abduvali Abdurashidov very graciously played the *sartor* for the participants of the seminar at the inaugural session. This impromptu recital, for which I am immensely grateful, set the tune literally and metaphorically, for the rich exchange of ideas that followed over the next two days.

I warmly thank all the contributors to this volume for their essays and for the patience they have shown in the wait for this publication to see the light of day.

August 2008 **Rashmi Doraiswamy**
New Delhi.

I. THE ARTS

Architecture

1

Central Asian Architecture: The Persistence of Pre-Modernism

Romi Khosla

Conservation of architecture has become an important issue in Asia as well as Central Asia. The conservation or re-styling of existing monuments and the reconstruction of the remains of old buildings has now become necessary to compete for tourists and pilgrims as well as to give regions a sense of identity linked to an imagined golden past.

Authenticity and Identity

Monumental architecture is a good tool to use if a ruler wants to forge a new identity for his people. It is large, often old and full of imagined references to a glorious past. If it is large and old but lacks grandeur because it is in ruins, then reconstruction can be done. A fine example of such reconstruction is what was done to the Tomb of the Sufi saint Yassawi in Kazakhstan. Sometimes new monumental architecture can be created by the ruler in the image of an ancient monument to forge an identity, as in the case of the Ram Mandir proposal in India.

In the modern period which, let us say, began in the nineteenth century, active conservation, reconstruction and architecture became an important part of the colonisation process. The colonial powers came to rule in Asia, Central Asia, Africa and Latin America, freshly inspired by the new solutions proposed in their search for knowledge by the so-called Enlightenment period. The natural resources and manpower in the colonised areas could only be tapped by actively ruling these areas. Europe expanded into Asia between 1800 and 1947. The Russian Empire expanded south all across Central Asia to touch the borders of Iran, Afghanistan, India and China. The big powers agreed to keep Afghanistan and Thailand as independent buffer zones to prevent border clashes amongst themselves through two accords in 1907 and 1904. At the height of the Cold War, the Soviet Union broke the Anglo-Russian Accord of 1907 and marched into Afghanistan.

The consolidation of both the Russian and later Soviet rule in Central Asia was evidenced in architecture. Of course, evidence of imperial rule is apparent in multiple aspects that include language, culture, economic activity, etc. but I am here concerned with architecture. The first wave of buildings was European in style. Just as the Russian court had hankered for Russia to be regarded as a part of Europe by adopting the European style in its own court architecture, so it sought to express its European-inspired superiority over Central Asia by building European colonial buildings across present-day Tadjikistan, Uzbekistan, Kazakhstan and the other republics. The National Museum in Dushanbe, Tadjikistan is one such example.

The architecture of the Soviet presence was different from the architecture of the Czarist Court. The Czars controlled their Central Asian colonies with their armed forces. The local government offices and rich traders were housed in European-styled colonial buildings. The Soviets on the other hand were engaged in a complex social engineering activity in Central Asia and the architecture of this activity was a reflection of the first wave of modern architecture that the Soviet government had pioneered in Moscow. In the early period of socialist rule in Russia, the re-engineering of Man into the Ideal Social Human Being was linked to a revolution in the arts which included new styles of living in new internationally styled modern architecture.

Towards the end of the last century, by the time the Soviet presence seemed well consolidated, a whole new generation of Central Asian architects had been trained in the traditions of modernism. As Soviet rule drew to a close, a comfortable solution had been found to give regional flavour to the minimal modern aesthetics of the cold north, a sort of synchronistic style of the Central Asian Modern.

This is a simplified version of the historical context within which I would like to take up some broader issues related to the question of defining a modern identity through architecture.

Architecture and Identity

The built environment and the identity of those who live in it are two parts of a whole. The shape, size and form of architecture influence the identity of a people; conversely, the identity of a people affects the form of architecture of a region.

Monumental architecture in Central Asia was sponsored by Amir Timur in the fourteenth century at an enormous scale. Through his military objectives and campaigns, he collected not only plunder of immense value but also brought together some of the most talented craftsmen and builders in the entire region. We are talking about a vast territory that included India, Afghanistan, Iran, Armenia, Georgia, Iraq, Syria and Turkey. His enormous restless energy and charisma had great impact on the regions that he conquered not only militarily but also culturally. Indeed the cultural impact on the region influenced the region long after his death. Under his rule, Samarkand became a prosperous metropolis with entire *mohallas* occupied by craftsmen who had been brought from Iran, Syria, India and other places. It was in Samarkand that the distinctive style of monumental architecture was first established that became known as Timurid architecture. The Poi-Kalayan Ensemble (twelfth to nineteenth centuries) in Bukhara remains one of the outstanding examples of Timurid architecture.

The urban centres and monuments sponsored by Timur had a deep and almost everlasting impact on the Central Asian sense of identity. The large number of soldiers rewarded generously with booty, the length and breadth of the empire, the extraordinary architecture built by foreign craftsmen, the immense economic activities, the safety of trade routes, and the accumulation of urban prosperity, all combined to define the

Timurid period as a golden period in the mind of the Central Asians.

It was this deep-rooted faith in Amir Timur as the guardian of their cultural values and the pillar of their sense of identity that the Russian and then Soviet rulers tried to replace with modern aspirations. This replacement required the rulers to break the link between the built heritage and the history that produced it. When the Czarist forces invaded the various parts of Central Asia, they destroyed with cannons much of the monumental heritage of the region. It was destroyed for military reasons because these monuments were inevitably surrounded by residential *mohallas*. It was in these *mohallas* that resistance was the fiercest against the Russian soldiers. The monuments were symbols of the culture of the inhabitants and therefore, to rule effectively, the colonial rulers needed to impose new loyalties by plucking away the monuments from the everyday life of the colonised Central Asians, making them into museums and re-housing the citizens. The monuments were therefore encapsulated into a 'heritage'— an open-air museum.

Like most new governments or dynasties, the Russians and later the Soviets consolidated their power and control of the resources by initiating a burst of building activities that introduced the new architectural styles of European civilisation. The indigenous architecture of Timurid society had to be destroyed or separated into heritage and de-linked from history. History could be re-written as indeed it was, but existing monumental architecture cannot be re-invented and this is particularly so for the monuments which have a deep place in the collective memory of the citizens. The only way to deal with the monuments of Timurid society was to re-classify them as heritage whose preservation was made the responsibility of the state.

All monuments that get captured by the government as 'heritage' are plucked from the lives of the inhabitants because new rules get formed by the government about how one is to use these monuments. Once a monument becomes part of heritage, its use in the daily lives of the people is limited because usage is regarded as damaging to the fabric of the monuments.

Following the conquest of the Central Asians' world by the Russian troops, the Orientalists and scholars of Moscow and St Petersburg rushed to the devastated sites to begin the restoration of the monuments. V.V. Bartold, Masson, Zasypkin, Bretanitski, Remple, Shishkin, Pugachenkova were amongst the more well known of these Orientalists who began objectifying the role of the monument in the new lives of the conquered Central Asians. The Russian army had in many of the cases levelled out the surrounding mohalla fabric that had given a historic context to the monument. A similar action of demolishing the urban fabric surrounding the Jama Masjid in Delhi was carried out by British troops after the 1857 rebellion: the isolated monument was surrounded by barriers to prevent access and preservation activities were undertaken by 'experts'.

Just as the architectural monuments became preserved museum pieces, so the objects of everyday cultural practices became parts of museum collections, labelled as 'old' or 'popular', but certainly on the margins of the mainstream culture which was a prerogative of the rulers and which naturally had its source in Northern Europe. As I have commented earlier, the separation of heritage from history was done by both the Czarists as well as the Soviets. These activities that were necessary to rule more effectively had a polarising impact on the local societies by precipitating two cultural worlds — the macro cultural world and the meso cultural world.

Macro and Meso

The meso cultural world is the intermediate world between the macro world of the modern state and the micro world of the household. The word 'meso' is derived from the Greek word *Mesos*, meaning middle. The meso cultural world is a world of temporary stability, a world whose spaces and cultural expressions mediate between the pressures exerted by the modern state and the delicate world of the individual family. The macro world is ruled by the state and is planned by experts and professionals and specialists. Its rules and regulations are evident in written laws of the state. The meso world on the other hand, is an autonomous, oral, self-adjusting world that ebbs and flows in its usage and functions. The meso world is the realm in which community relationships and public life interact with the private worlds of the community members. It is the repository of the deeper oral culture of the community. It acts and lives in its space but does not try to know it objectively. It talks about life but does not try to direct it; it is a world inhabited by people of diverse cultural origins who have been brought together into a synergetic relationship that depends on mutual integration without simplification or classifications. In the culture of the meso world, the distinction between the traditional and the modern are difficult to make out.

The introduction of the modern agenda into the culture of the Central Asian world precipitated this distinction that was rooted in the duality of the epistemology that the colonial rulers introduced into the colonies. We are familiar with this duality in the questionable division between the modern and traditional. The modern macro agenda advocated simplicity and planned uniformity as the necessary instruments of predictability while the meso world of tradition comprising ruled subjects preferred unpredictability, complexity and diversity as the necessary expressions of a creative and opportunistic freedom that was not shackled by a planning process.

The metropolitan rule from Moscow that began with the Czarists in the middle of the nineteenth century took almost a century to consolidate. Borders were changed, republics were invented, populations were moved, oral and spontaneous cultural expressions were planned and redefined, Russian was made compulsory, and a whole host of new Soviet cities was constructed around industrial centres. The replanning of Tashkent and many of the new Soviet cities for Central Asia is evidence of the obliteration of the traditional fabric and the imposition of a 'modern crust'.

The macro world controlled by the rulers from the metropolis formed the modern crust of architecture in Central Asia. Under this crust the meso world continued to exist, continuously imbibing from the modern crust but remaining essentially meso in its identity and activities. The macro crust redefined the identity of the Central Asians through architecture. A new authenticity was formulated for modern Asians. The entire restoration effort in Uzbekistan, for instance, was carried out as part of this re-invention of authenticity. While entire parts of the historic cities were bulldozed to make way for modern buildings, certain museum areas were identified in Bukhara, Samarkand, Khiva and Khokand and reconstructed as open museums to the past.

The remnants of the past were stripped away and replaced with new parts. Ancient Timurid bricks were intermixed with contemporary bricks. Ceramic tiles were re-made and used to cover areas where there was no trace of original Timurid tiling. The Bibi Khanum Mosque in Samarkand, built almost entirely out of mud bricks by Timur in 1398, had large portions of it reconstructed. In the nineteenth century when the Czarist forces invaded Samarkand, the mosque had been blasted by cannon fire. Today the whole structure is being re-built with concrete reinforcement in the minarets and arches, as an authentic symbol of macro Uzbek architecture.

The reconstruction of Timurid monuments was an important activity for the new states after Independence because a new authentic identity had to be given to the new Republics. Extensive brick-manufacturing facilities dedicated their production to supply the materials for reconstructing the monuments. Bricks, ceramics and wood carving resources were developed to feed the reconstruction process.

Contemporary modern Uzbek architecture, on the other hand, was built primarily out of pre-cast concrete panels in a continuum of modernising initiatives. These modern buildings were the face of the modern crust that overlaid the Uzbek identity. It was a thin crust. Hardly had Uzbekistan woken up to its new-found independence in 1991, than bricks began to be diverted to the construction of modern buildings, of which the Humza Theatre is a good example.

The new rulers of an independent Uzbekistan began to distance themselves from the earlier Soviet Republic identity.

The pre-cast concrete panel buildings were, in some cases, covered over with the bricks which had been made for monument re-construction. Ironically, in some ways, the identity of the reconstructed Timurid monuments was adopted by the independent Uzbek rulers as the preferred style for their own modern architecture. Thus Soviet built modern buildings in the international style were re-clad in bricks and given pointed arches.

The reaction to Soviet rule and to the crust of Soviet modernism was to re-invent yet another new Uzbek identity with an architecture which has imagined links with the monumental past of their Golden Age in history symbolised by the reconstructed monuments.

Traditionally, vernacular Uzbek buildings in the pre-Soviet eras were built out of mud and timber. Brick was confined as a cladding material for important mosques, *madrasas* and *khanqahs*. A return to historic authenticity was out of the question because mud and timber could hardly be regarded as the ideal building materials in an independent country wishing to promote a new architecture which was to be considered closer to the national aspirations. Soviet inspired mural images began to be replaced with printed images of the glorious past of the Uzbek people.

Russian graphics on a pro-revolutionary poster with Russian script and the Uzbek language. The industrial theme, the modern graphics and the ever present red colour seek to convey the uniting message of internationalism and the need to abandon national identity based on any form of tradition.

Post-independence Uzbek mural in Kokhand Auditorium painted by a contemporary Uzbek painter re-asserts Uzbek identity through national costumes and graphic decoration. A clear message that informs about the irrelevance of the themes illustrated in the previous image on pg. 25.

Interior of Kokhand auditorium showing the extensive use of brick cladding in the interior. In the post-independence period, concrete was associated with Soviet aesthetics in architecture whereas brick was used to express solidarity with national Uzbek identity.

Bridal wear with clearly Russian influence for an Uzbek bride illustrated in Soviet books to portray a newly emergent modern Uzbekistan Republic within the Soviet family of republics.

Re-assertion of Uzbek national dress in the post-independence period.

A contemporary building in Samarkand designed by a Russian architect prior to Uzbek independence is being clad in brick to try and re-claim it as part of a traditional Uzbek inheritance. International modernism gets re-surfaced as non-modernism with a distinct national identity.

2

Sufi Remains. A Kazakh Story of Today

Kalpana Sahni

In 2001 I spent some time in Turkestan. Preparations were on to celebrate this seemingly insignificant town's 1,500 years of existence. The Kazakh government had brought out a brochure of the new building projects it hoped to construct by raising millions of dollars. I was there in connection with a monument that has been variously described as a memorial complex, a shrine, a mausoleum, a *khanqah*. Built over the grave of Ahmed Yasawi, who also has been variously described as a saint, a philosopher, a healer, a poet and even as the father of the Turks, his name and grave evoke different perceptions in the minds of different peoples on the one hand, and the state on the other.

My paper explores the fate of the Sufi saint's shrine and the vicissitudes it has faced at the hands of successive governments, each of whom imposed their notions of identity on it. Sometimes the nation-state chooses to manipulate history to create a new identity for itself — sacrificing facts, individuals and communities. I was witness to this process.

The Yasawi Memorial Complex occupies a pride of place in Kazakhstan, a national symbol that appears on every Kazakh currency note. There is a university and an award named after Yasawi. The award was recently conferred on the Kazakh President, Nursultan Nazarbaev. Every important visiting dignitary is taken to Yasawi. In 2001, a Turkish construction company was nominated for the prestigious Aga Khan Award for the restoration of Yasawi's tomb.

This is an account of how Yasawi, the monument named after him, and the history of its restoration is linked to the broader sweep of Central Asian history.

Central Asia or Turkestan or Turan or Maverannakhr, depending on which period one is referring to, had a dynamic culture, which had interacted vigorously with the world. It was not a primitive, isolated one. Neither was it a culture that 'progressed' from folk epics to Socialist Realism — something we have come to accept because of our dependence on Russian and European sources, which generally denigrated the life and culture of the Central Asians. Now for North Indians — Central Asia, Samarkand, and Bukhara evoke different reactions. Collective memories in North India recall the close ties with the great intellectual and cultural centres of Central Asia.[1] We have shared moments of a common history, of boundaries, literature and folklore. Our dress, food, language, architecture and racial intermixing were all strongly influenced by these contacts. Our oral and written traditions are replete with heroes and places transcending the geographical boundaries between India and Central Asia.

Turkestan in present-day southern Kazakhstan was once a Sufi centre. Its beliefs were shared and linked to Buddhist Tantric traditions coexisting with Shamanism, nature worship and Zoroastrianism. It is located in the vicinity of the river Syr Darya, Fergana Valley and Pamir Mountains. Consequently, at the time of the Arab conquest it was the Sufi aspect of Islam that caught the imagination of the local population. The Sufi doctrine adapted itself to all local beliefs and, importantly, defended the interests of ordinary people. Some of the most renowned Sufi Brotherhoods, including the *Naqshbandi* order, originated in these areas. Its founder, Bahauddin Naqshbandi, was born in 1318 in the village of Kasr-e-Hinduan (the Fort of the Indians) near Bukhara. The *Kubrawiya* and *Yasawiya* Brotherhoods were also founded in the twelfth century in this region. The most active and significant centres of Sufism were and continue to be located in Fergana Valley and the Osh region.[2]

Khwaja Ahmed Yasawi

Little is known about the life of Khwaja Ahmed Yasawi, the founder of the *Yasawiya Tariqat*. Sheikh Arslan Baba and Sheikh Khwaja Yusuf Hamadani, amongst Central Asia's greatest Sufi saints, taught him. Yasawi seems to have been a remarkable man who preached compassion, asceticism and the need for each individual to seek his or her path to enlightenment. His verse, composed in Turkic, is included in his *Diwan-i-Hikmat*. He spent the last sixty odd years of his life preaching from an underground cave in Yassi (renamed Turkestan in the sixteenth century). He died in 1166 or 1167 and a modest structure for the Sufi *zikr* was built next to his grave to commemorate him, which soon turned into a place of pilgrimage. The cult of the shrine is very ancient in this region. Cemeteries in Central Asia are often located in the vicinity of the grave of a saint and this was so for Yasawi's grave.[3] A saint is said to help people in this life and the next.[4] Two centuries after Yasawi's death, Amir Timur built a huge complex over his grave — an ironic political statement by an implacable conqueror — a gesture intended to claim Yasawi, to legitimise him and to simultaneously valorise Timur. The grand architectural complex with eight big congregational halls and twenty-three rooms under one roof seeks to merge pre-Islamic, Islamic and Sufi practices.[5] Timur is known to have personally drawn up the plans and measurements of the mausoleum. Although construction began in 1391, it remained incomplete. Some 200 years later in 1591, a portal was added, that was also not completed.

The influence of the *Yasawiya Tariqat* spread beyond Turkestan to Afghanistan, India and Persia, moving westwards to Turkey and the Balkans. The *Yasawiyas* preached asceticism, love and brotherhood and believed in the unity of all that exists, and the need for personal spiritual experience in the path to realisation. However, in times of war, the brotherhood, like the *Naqshbandis* of Central Asia and the Caucasus, took to arms to protect their territories and way of life. With an exceptionally effective organisational network, a strong spirit of dedication and willingness to sacrifice, many Sufi brotherhoods were and remain the most successful mobilising force in Dagestan,

Chechnya and Central Asia for over two centuries.[6]

These Sufi brotherhoods were often opposed to the Islamic clergy which was co-opted by the ruling elite. There is a fundamental difference between the Sufi-led resistance movements and the term 'Islamic fundamentalists' and 'terrorists'. Too often the term 'Islamic fundamentalism' is used as an excuse for governments to crack down on their political opponents.

In the six hundred years following Yasawi's death, Turkestan became an important pilgrimage centre for rulers and commoners alike. For instance, important state decisions by the ruling Khans were taken at Yasawi's shrine, including decisions on succession. At the time of the Russian colonial conquest of Central Asia, this town, then a part of the Khanate of Kokhand (in Fergana), put up stiff resistance.

In 1864, the advancing Czarist armies targeted the Yasawi Mausoleum, and bombarded it from all sides resulting in eleven huge craters in its outer façade. The army occupied it and converted it into a military barrack. Dwellings and mausoleums in the vicinity of Yasawi were demolished and the rubble from the demolished site was used to construct the Russian army barracks. However, as with every colonial power, destruction was followed by an attempt to save the monument, a move spearheaded, ironically by a Russian, A.N. Veselovsky, the renowned folklorist.

Vicissitudes of History

After the October Revolution, Kokhand declared itself as an Independent Republic, a move that was initially accepted by the Bolshevik government. Once Bolshevik rule was consolidated in Central Asia, the Red Army moved into Kokhand. A bloody massacre followed and the Independent State ceased to exist. Regions, which offered most resistance to the October Revolution, were dismembered at the time of creation of the Central Asian Republics. The convoluted frontiers between the various territories in the southern parts of Central Asia seemingly defy logic, apart from the successful divide and rule policies of earlier years. The Fergana valley was divided between the three republics of Uzbekistan, Tadjikistan and Kirghizia.[7] Turkestan and the Yasawi monument ceded to Kazakhstan. Fearing that Uzbekistan would lay claims to Yasawi, the Kazakh government demolished the wall enclosing the Mausoleum because the Khan of Kokhand had built it!

Despite systematic destruction of the environs surrounding Yasawi during the Czarist (1864, 1885) and Soviet period (1920s, 1930s), the town still existed in 1950 when the Soviet authorities destroyed the remaining structures, walls and houses located in the outer enclosures of Yasawi.

In 1975, archaeologists working in the precincts of Yasawi discovered a necropolis and a citadel.[8] This confirmed the existence of an ancient urban centre. However, the official Soviet historiography and propaganda had reiterated that Central Asians were primarily a nomadic people. Citing Hegelian dialectics, they often glossed over the existence of an urban culture in the region and evaded arguments in favour of a level of culture which incorporated both urban and nomadic components. Going by such a line of reasoning, how could the officials explain the existence of this sophisticated citadel? It contradicted everything the Central Government was propagating about the rise to civilisation being linked solely to the Central Asians' ostensible 'merger' with Russia. It was easier to change reality and fit it into the textbook description. Bulldozers levelled the entire archaeological site. The Mausoleum of Yasawi remained standing, a lonely forlorn structure in the middle of nowhere, shorn of its historical and cultural context and surrounded by the rubble of the vernacular buildings and necropolis structures that were once an integral part of the complex. The destruction of places of worship ran parallel to restoration of certain monuments as showcases of history and Yasawi was one of them.

Between 1905 and 1945, the Mausoleum was accurately measured, photographed and partially repaired. The significant period of restoration began in 1951. For the next five decades, a succession of remarkable women archaeologists and conservation architects took charge of this monument and devoted extraordinary efforts to recover this ruin and establish it as the most important symbol of present-day Kazakhstan's built heritage. It is due primarily to their efforts that Yasawi is one of the rare Timurid monuments where local material for restoration was used till the Turkish efforts began.

The history of its restorers is inextricably woven into the larger history of the Soviet Union as well as with the personal lives of these women.

Women Restorers

Tina Karumidze came to the site in 1951 after the Kazakh authorities discovered that she was an architect restorer and sought the KGB's permission to send her to Yasawi. One can ask: What did the KGB have to do with restoration and that too in Kazakhstan? Tina Karumidze was one of the innumerable deportees at the time because she was the 'wife of the enemy'. Her husband, who headed the Ideological Committee of the Communist Party of Georgia, was shot dead by Stalin. Their children were sent to an orphanage. Despite the enormous personal tragedy in her life, Karumidze devoted herself to understanding the monument of Yasawi. She began to analyse and document the construction techniques and cladding details of the entire Yasawi structure, after which she began the Herculean task of restoration work on the portions damaged by the Czarist bombardment. Restoration of Yasawi in effect commences with Karumidze whose work was remarkable for its meticulous attention to details of documentation as well as restoration. Although she worked on the site for only four years continuously over long hours, she left behind a wealth of documented material: notes and guidelines in the form of diaries, which formed the basis for all subsequent restoration work during the next five decades. Her sudden departure for Georgia in 1954 was prompted by the death of Stalin and her subsequent release. She hurried back to search for her children.

Karumidze was succeeded by Lyudmila Mankovskaya, who continued the documentation and the restoration work her predecessor had initiated. Mankovskaya's work unravelled the keys to the understanding of Timurid architecture. Using the original 1397 text of the *Zafar Nameh*, which recorded

Timur's visit to the site, she discovered the proportional system that Timur's builders had used to dimension the architecture. The Central Hall, the *Jamaat Khane*, for instance, was recorded in the text as being 30 *gaz* on each side. Subsequently, this proportional system was used by researchers for analysing other Timurid monuments. The Yasawi Mausoleum Complex is a virtual catalogue of Timurid construction practices and Mankovskaya's work and recordings have been seminal in the deeper understanding of this important period of architecture in the history of Central Asia.

Mankovskaya was succeeded by Sofia Tukebaeva who focused her research on the ceramic glazes. Her experiments and production of glazed tiles was undertaken in the workshop and kilns where she often spent over 33 hours at a stretch. Unfortunately, these long hours near the furnaces led to her untimely death in 1992.

Bayan Tuyakbaeva and her husband, Alexei Proskurin began work on Yasawi in 1968 and spent the next thirty years of their lives committed to its conservation. They also combined research work with restoration. Bayan's research was on the epigraphy. What seemed initially to be carpet-like geometric patterns on the façade were a form of Kufic calligraphy.[9] Once deciphered, it became easier to replace missing and damaged words. Much of the restoration work of the monument was completed by 1980. Seepage was the only worry. Funds were scarce and work on Yasawi slowed down. But not for long!

The Turkish Connection

In 1991, the Turkish government offered the newly established state of Kazakhstan 17 million dollars for Yasawi's restoration. The Turkish construction company worked in tandem with Tuyakbaeva and Proskurin, who had the responsibility of approving the strategy and techniques for restoration. Frequent changes in the Turkish team and a lack of sensitivity to the peculiarities of Yasawi led to tensions between the Turks and the Kazakhs. Moreover, the large amounts of money being spent on the project attracted sharks on both sides. Suddenly, there were many people interested in the restoration project, not least among them the local mafia. When Tuyakbaeva realised that the funds meant for restoration were being misused, she wrote off letters of protest to the President and to Parliament. An inquiry commission was set up. Those implicated included the Minister of Culture, Talgat Mamashev and his Deputy, Vladimir Kutavoi. But Tuyakbaeva's actions were not appreciated and there were reprisals. One day, her briefcase with all the documents was stolen, next an attempt was made to set fire to her home. Undeterred, Bayan Tuyakbaeva continued with her work on the Yasawi shrine. But the mafia was not going to let her off. The turning point came when Bayan's seventeen-year-old daughter was kidnapped. That day Bayan finally threw her office keys down, quit work, recovered her daughter and sent her out of the country. Proskurin continued to work with the Turkish team for another two years but a heart attack put an end to his engagement with the project.

The Turkish construction company worked on Yasawi till 2000. Much of its work was based on the five boxes of drawings that had been taken out from the Kazakh archives and shipped to Turkey. They contained the project documentation, which had been prepared for twenty years by Bayan and Proskurin at the Kazakh Institute of Restoration, founded and headed by Bayan Tuyakbaeva. These archival documents are remarkable for their detailed and meticulous attention to every aspect of the monument. Copies were made from the originals and submitted as part of the Turkish research on Yasawi when they were nominated for an award. There was no mention of Tuyakbaeva, Proskurin, Karumidze, and Mankovskaya—neither in the nomination papers, nor by Kazakh officials.

Their fate is symptomatic of the times. Both in Russia and the new states, the old mafia of Soviet times seems to control the reins of power. Kazakhstan, like the other new states, is busy reinventing a past. The ambitious building projects in the vicinity of Yasawi are not to resurrect the spirit of Yasawi but to immortalise the new rulers. Sufi *zikrs* have been organized by the state for visiting UNESCO dignitaries in the main hall of Yasawi. It seems that the state is intent on glorifying the Sufi

Saint but paying no attention to his wisdom and teachings.

Perhaps Yasawi had a premonition that such things would happen to his grave, for he wrote a thousand years ago, "Those accustomed to power are saddled with the festering burden of wealth".

NOTES AND REFERENCES

1. Trade and cultural links with India go back to over two thousand years. Ties were established through the numerous passes located in Ladakh, Gilgit and Afghanistan. These regions were also part of the Kushan Empire. Remains of Buddhist sculptures, monasteries and sites are scattered throughout the region, including present-day Tajikistan, Uzbekistan and further east.
2. The *Yasawi* brotherhood, which had been replaced by the *Naqshbandis* and *Qadiriyas* in popularity in the nineteenth century, got reactivated in the twentieth century. Abumutalib Satybaldyev, a Yasawi murshid, formed the clandestine group of the *Hairy Ishans* in Fergana. Its centre soon became the Osh region in the eastern part of the Fergana valley. Osh, one of the main Sufi centres, has always been considered the second Mecca by the peoples of Central Asia. Incidentally, Khwaja Moin ud Din Hasan Chishti of Ajmer in his writings mentions his frequent visits to Samarkand, Bokhara and Osh where he met the Sufi Darveshes in early twelfth century.
3. The graves of important Khans and ministers, including that of Rabia Sultan Begum, Timur's granddaughter, were buried in the area surrounding Yasawi. In fact, restorers discovered the skeletal remains of commoners also buried along the outer walls of the mausoleum.
4. The graves of the legendary resistance leaders, Shamil and Haji Murad are considered sacred Sufi shrines in Dagestan.
5. Б. Туякбаева, А. Проскурин. *Мировоззренческие основы функционально-планировочной структуры ханаки Ахмеда Ясави*. В книге: *Памятники истории и культуры Казахстана*. Сборник Центрального совета Казахского общества охраны памятников истории и культуры, Выпуск 4. (Казахстан), Алма-Ата, 1989, стр. 106-116.
6. The Sufis spearheaded the resistance movement against the Kalmyk invasion in the seventeenth and eighteenth centuries; in the nineteenth century at the time of the Czarist conquest and on numerous occasions in the twentieth century. There were many Sufis who took part in the resistance movement against the Soviet

rule but also others, like the *Laachi*, who initially fought alongside the Red Guards.

7. More details are in: Kalpana Sahni, *Crucifying the Orient: Russian Orientalism and the Colonization of Caucasus and Central Asia,* The Institute for Comparative Research in Human Culture, Oslo, White Orchid Press, Bangkok, 1997, pp. 109–175.
8. As a Timurid structure, the Yasawi Mausoleum was originally located within the Yasi citadel, a roughly pentagonal, 2.6 hectare site that contained a necropolis and dwellings. To the west and south of the citadel area are the remains of the shahristan, a quadrangle area of about 2.3 hectares which was once the site of a settlement; on the north and west can be seen the remains of the original wall and towers of the citadel.
9. Б.Т. Туякбаева. Эпиграфический декор архитектурного комплекса Ахмеда Ясави. «Өнер», Алма-Ата, 1989.

A 1907 Photograph of Yasawi and the inner wall of the Citadel

Bayan Tuyakbaeva and Alexei Proskurin

Deciphering the text on Yasawi's facade

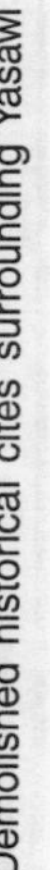

Demolished historical cites surrounding Yasawi

Detail of Yasawi with Tuyakbaeva in the foreground

Kazakh Currency notes with the image of Yasawi

Lyudmila Mankovskaya and M.E. Masson, the archaeologist

The Yasawi Complex

Tina Karumidze at Bayan Tuyakbaeva's PhD viva voce exam

3

Synthesis in the Sky

K.T. Ravindran

I had the privilege of working in Iran for three years from 1975 to 1978 and that opened my eyes to a lot of things because I had the leisure and the lucre to wander through the deserts and photograph many things. I visited many Sufi shrines and collected Sufi memorabilia. It is a long-sustained interest of mine and when I came back to India, I regularly visited many Sufi shrines. I have sustained that interest and have been an avid reader of what can loosely be called Islamic myth, about the beginnings of the religion and how certain concepts of religion were embedded in architecture.

I have called my presentation 'Synthesis in the Sky' because it is also a synthesis of the last thirty years of my having looked at Islamic architecture, not merely from a structuralist, or an architectural, or a technical point of view, but of looking at architecture as a representational art. I think that buildings have many layers of representation in them. Of course, the most obvious and the most often discussed is the utilitarian or the functional aspect of a building. Then there is the style, colour and form. A building also has inherent meanings and these meanings generally reinforce the myths of our community. When it reinforces the myths of a community, it tends to attain an iconic form. An icon has the natural habit of being cloned and it begins to appear in different locations at different times. This is one of the primary conditions of an icon: it becomes iconic by repetition and it forms the anchor point for traditions in buildings.

Reaching out to the Sky

I cannot possibly cover the entire gamut of the development of the Mughal idiom in building in one presentation, so I have isolated the dome as my subject. The dome is often a metaphor for the sky. The reinforcement of the position of the sky in Islamic myth occurs through the construction of domes. The dome is the sky itself: very often domes are painted blue from the interior like a sky; precious stones are embedded into the mud so that it looks like a stellar constellation. Often its interior was the sky itself and in the exterior it was reaching out to the sky. So it was a simultaneous presence of the self as represented in the sky and the non-self that is represented by the form of the outer shell of the dome. The interior represents the self and the exterior represents the form that reaches out to the sky. So there is a creation of a kind of what in our architectural parlance is known as the field and object configuration, where the dome becomes the object and the sky becomes the field. Inversely, if you look at it metaphorically, the ideation of a myth becomes the field, and the representational form of architecture becomes its object. Thus there is a mutually supportive relationship between the object and the field, and it is this relationship which in fact helps anchor the myth and contributes to the importance of a specific building as an icon.

It is the travel of this icon through Central Asia, through Iran to the Indian subcontinent that is the topic of my presentation. I am not looking at it from a very broad perspective. I am not talking about Charbagh, I am not talking about architectonics, I am not talking about construction systems. I am merely looking at the dome as a representational form which affirms the mythical base in Islam as a religion. The basic myth that I am pinning my whole discussion on today is the myth where the Prophet split the moon into two bits as a way of demonstrating the power of the new religion. It is interesting to see that this event, which is described in many places, including the Koran, had ramifications all over the world and the symbol of Islam itself gets anchored in the moon, in which is nesting a star. This is then reflected in the manner in which architecture expresses itself and represents that myth. It is said that when the moon was split into two by the Prophet, by the power of His new knowledge, it was seen all over the world. On that day in the sky there were two moons. According to the myth that exists in Kerala, there are supposed to be seven steps to Heaven, seven layers to heaven. Seven layers of the earth and all that is therein glorify Him. In other words, there is once again a reference to heaven and in fact, this is the interior of a dome. I want to discuss the expressions of Islam in India, according to the myth that exists among the Muslims in Kerala, especially in the Malabar region. The split moon was observed in Kerala by the then king at Kudimaloor. He called his astrologers and asked them what this phenomenon was. The astrologer cast his cowries and said that a new religion has just been founded and there is a great man who is propounding this religion in Arabia. The Arabs were already in trade with the Kerala coast at that time. This king was so interested that he began to talk to various travellers who were invited to his court. He converted to Islam and the story in Kerala among Muslims is that he travelled to Mecca and spent seventeen days with the Prophet. On his way back, he was accompanied by two people, but he died of an illness. The two people who accompanied him travelled back to Kerala, met the family of the king, converted the family and set up the first mosques. This is about thirty-five years after the splitting of the moon.

The Dome as Icon

In the mosque in Gulbarga, by the sixteenth century, the dome had begun to make its presence felt as an icon. The most interesting thing about Gulbarga is that Gesu Deraz (Banda Nawaz) who introduced music as a form of worship into the Sufi tradition, lived and died there. He was a *shishya* (disciple) of Chirag Dilli and he moved with the Tughlaqs and the Bahmanis. He engaged himself with the Sufi tradition through the worship of nature and he adopted many forms which were locally prevalent, including prostration. The mosque in Gaur in West Bengal has a dome that is totally different from other domes. The Lodi tomb, the Ibrahim Roza tomb in Bijapur, which has a very characteristic style, and the Imambara in Lucknow, all represent the iconic importance of the dome in this architecture.

The point I want to make through this image is that the whole cultural region which covered Central Asia, Afghanistan, Iran and what was at that time called Hindustan, in fact became the crucible for the Sufi tradition. A lot of literature, music, building, and art flourished in this cultural region. Rumi says, 'I am Laila and Laila is myself, myself and my beloved are one, there is one soul living in two bodies'. And this is the aspiration which every dome tried to fulfill vis-a-vis the sky. My analogy here is that the dome is the flower, the sky with the moon is the beloved, and the longing of the dome to reach towards the sky is what invested it with a spiritual beauty that only a dome is able to evoke. This tradition flourished in textiles, in paintings, in architecture, in music. The music, particularly Iranian music, transports you. It is really a self-exploratory kind of music and the silences in that music are really very moving.

There were great, fabled cities of this cultural region. The city of Isfahan, which was built in the twenty-sixth century, is one such fabled city. The most crucial thing about Isfahan is that Humayun spent time here in exile, because the Safavid kings were friends of his father. They had a joint enemy in Akbar's cousin who was killed by the king of Ismail in Isfahan. Subsequently, when Humayun was in trouble with Sher Shah Suri, he was given refuge in Isfahan. This proved to be critical to the development of Mughal architecture and the development of the dome in India in subsequent years. It was not just in architecture that the influence was felt, but also in art, literature, music, in the development of thought, the development of warfare, in food and culinary arts, in clothes.... The vehicle through which the influences travelled was the Persian language. It is the power of the Persian language which actually created this plethora of expressions within various art forms, because language is fundamental to culture. Language is the only form which actually can touch the inner rhythm of the life of a people. It was the transfer of Persian language into this whole cultural region, along with Chagatai Turkish, and the mixture of these two languages which led to the flowering of culture in this region. Babar's Central Asian origin and Central Asian architecture and its influence on Afghanistan and Iran remained the single most important influence in the Mughal psyche till the end of the dynasty. Till the very end they were still learning Chagatai Turkish and the Mughals spoke and wrote in Chagatai Turkish even though their love for Persian dominated the cultural life of their empire.

Crucible of Culture

Each culture mediated the form of the dome, using its own materials. Every material has a certain behaviour; that behaviour yields a construction system and that construction system yields an architecture; that architecture is then embellished and celebrated by the local culture which becomes an affirmation of the local version of the myth. Isfahan's architecture was so crucial that it was quintessentially the basis of all domes. Humayun's tomb was commissioned by his wife Hamida Begum, who spoke Persian. The plan is Persian, with the use of the Charbagh. The important thing here is that the dome uses white marble in conjunction with red sandstone, which is a departure from glazed tiles because these glazed tiles originally came from Kashan in northern Iran. It is said that four thousand years ago there was the use of these glazed tiles and in Turkish the blue glazed tile is called Kashi. So Kashan was the original source of the glazed tile, but when it moved into India the local material began to dominate and we have Ghiyasuddin Tughlaq's tomb which uses the red sandstone and the white stone in a very intelligent way. An Armenian church in Isfahan is very similar to the Khan-e-Khanan's tomb in Nizamuddin in Delhi. They both have the same construction system and exactly the same form. The interesting part is that it was Armenian Christian skilled labour who were taken prisoners of war by Shah Baz, who helped build a part of Isfahan. And it was this skilled labour which actually created the whole idiom and transferred it from Central Asia into Central Iran. It is a known fact that every conqueror, when he waged war and dominated a place, took with him the artisans of that area and used them. We know that Timur, for instance, used Indian artisans in building monuments in Central Asia and that Humayun brought with him a whole group of writers, painters and builders who began to influence the building styles in Humayun's time.

The dome of the Taj Mahal expresses the intense love of the dome for the sky. The design of the dome evokes the longing of the lover for the beloved, metaphorically, and is the highest expression of this Sufi quest. There is a section of the Taj Mahal dome which is a double dome. This idea travelled from Central Asia into India. The first double dome building was the Sabz Burj, which is now stranded in the middle of traffic in Nizamuddin, in New Delhi. The double dome helps to define the interior of the building in a certain form and helps to define the exterior that reaches out into the sky in a different form. The same purpose is served with the minarets. They not only define a centralised space where the dome can be sanctified but also reach out to the sky. The Taj Mahal and the dome of the Masjid in Isfahan are such close cousins that they are almost twins although there is over a hundred-year difference between the two of them. It means the idea and the beauty of the dome that affirms the movement of the eye towards the sky, is reaffirmed in a very fine form in the dome in Isfahan. This has actually travelled from Central Asia to Isfahan and then moved to India to be celebrated in the dome of the Taj Mahal.

The dynamic movement of history is actually not located in an object but in the way that object is read by people. When you read an object, when you read architecture, your mind is actively engaging with the idea of what it represents. As long as your mind engages with an idea of representation, that icon, that form remains alive and remains modern. Even if there is a difference of hundred years, you can still create the most modern and perhaps the most beautiful thing in the same form. You can re-invent a completely new layer and have a completely new form. It is in the active engagement of the mind in which the movement of history is located. Otherwise history is static.

Music

4

The Fate of the *Shashmaqom* in Uzbekistan in the XX Century

Dilorom Karomat

Shashmaqom[1] (canonized musical system, cyclic in form, includes *maqoms*[2] – *Buzruk, Rost, Navo, Dugoh, Segoh* and *Iroq*) represents a unique form of the traditional classical music[3] of Central Asia (Uzbekistan and Tadjikistan). *Maqom* existed under different names that changed from time to time under different cultural influences on Central Asia. We know that it was called *'Khusrawani'* (in connection with the musician of the VII century of the Sasanid Empire - Borbad – who was originally from Merv). From the IX till the XIII century it was called *pardah*; from the XIII to the XVII / XVIII centuries it was called *maqam* and had a system named *Adwar* (twelve *maqams*), that was universal for the ex-Arabic Khalifat's regions. At present, the maqam phenomenon is widely prevalent in a vast area that includes the countries of North Africa (*maqam, nuba*), the Near East (in Turkey it is called *makam*, in Azerbaijan – *mugam*, in Iran – *dastgah*) and Central Asia (in Uzbekistan and Tadjikistan it is called *maqom*, in Western China – *mukam*, in Kashmir – *maqam* or *Sufiana Kalam*).

It is well-known that till 1917 a part of Central Asia was divided into the Khiva and Kokhand Khanates and the Emirate of Bukhara[4]. Each of them had their local cultural specificities that were manifested in their traditional cultures. As a result, three local styles of the performance of *maqoms* have come down to us – the Bukharan *Shashmaqom*, the Khorezm *Maqoms* and the Fergano-Tashkent variant of the *maqoms*[5]. The term *Shashmaqom* can be found in *Kulliyot* and *Bayoz*, XVIII and XIX century manuscripts, written in the territory of modern Tadjikistan and Uzbekistan.

Shashmaqom was performed mainly in the cities of Bukhara and Samarkand (or in nearby places), using Persian and Chagatayan[6] classical poetry. It is usually thought that Khorezm *maqoms*[7] and the Fergano-Tashkent variants of the *maqoms* were constituted under the influence of the Bukharan *Shashmaqom* by local musicians after they visited Bukhara.[8]

In all the countries of the East, traditional professional music, although it is performed in a democratic milieu, was nevertheless an 'elite' music, which was heard in the courts of the rulers, by connoisseurs of music and rich people. Thus in the Bukharan Emirate the best musicians lived in the Court of the Emir. A master was chosen among them who led the performances of the musicians before the Khan and his guests and took care of the instruction of young performers.[9] Their performances beyond the walls of the court were strictly regimented. Only on days of big festivals, especially during the Navroz celebrations, did musicians receive the permission to perform on the crowded square, where people listened to them with great eagerness.

After the October Revolution in 1917, in the newly constituted country of the Soviets, many contradictory and complex processes of the adoption and re-evaluation of the cultural values of the past took place.[10] The drawing of national boundaries between the peoples of Turkestan in 1924 helped the Bolshevik government to put into practice the idea of national politics. During the period of the existence of the Soviet Government this politics went through three stages: of divergence, of coming together and then of merging together all peoples into one, unitary Soviet people. The idea and aim of a national politics were realized in life through all the spheres of Culture and Enlightenment, including that of music.

The preservation and performance of the *Shashmaqom* in the Soviet period was, whether directly or invisibly, dependent on the ideology and politics of the government, and on the general tendencies in the region's musical culture. From 1917 to 1932 the foundations for a Soviet musical culture were laid. This was the period when the fundamentals of the further development of this culture were defined. It was possible to operate on the basis of folk art to educate Soviet national cadres. In this three aspects were of great significance, aspects that remained important through the entire period of existence of the USSR:

- the democratization of art[11];
- musical-ethnographic activity[12];
- the introduction to the system of European polyvoiced genres (from monophony[13] to polyphony[14]).[15]

The peoples of Soviet Turkestan had the opportunity to imbibe the experience of world musical culture, and to get closer to the system of European polyphonic genres. But this turned out to be a 'coin' with two faces. On the one hand, the process or the need to be introduced to new forms of spiritual activity, the desire to make use of the European musical culture was observed in the second half of the XIX century, not only in Russian Turkestan, but also in other countries of the East (for example, Rabindranath Tagore's work on music in India). However, the *stimulus* to this process of the turning of the monophonic music (in particular, Asian) towards the polyphonic (European and Russian) music, under the Soviets was a socio-political act. This marked a turning point in the social and cultural life of the people in general and their entry into the sphere of wider international interests, in the first instance the creation of the Soviet Man (who was spiritually developed) and of Soviet culture. However, we must also pay attention to the other side of the 'coin': the turning towards 'progressive' European and Russian classical music led to the formation of 'elites', who stopped responding to their traditional music (considering it to be 'backward') and listened to European music in ecstasy. Although this process can be observed in non-socialist countries as well, in the Soviet Union one of the reasons for this, it seems, was the politics of 'convergence', which facilitated the loss of national roots.

The process of the movement of a given creative work cannot be always limited by dates. However, taking into consideration some of the facts of the existence of the *Shashmaqom*, its history in the Soviet period can be divided into three periods:

- from 1917 (1920) to 1947;
- from 1948 to 1970;
- from 1971 to 1991.

The First Phase

In the First Phase (1917/1920 – 1947) the traditional *'monodiicheskaya'* music (single line of melody which is played by one musician or more in a horizontal direction) was the basis of the national culture of the region. Performers of the *Shashmaqom* and other types of professional music in the very first years of Soviet power had the opportunity to perform in front of uninitiated audiences, in huge numbers in 'red *chaikhanas*', the premises of clubs, at concerts and meetings, etc.

Domla Halim Ibodov,[16] the representative of the Bukharan school of performing the *Shashmaqom*, with Mulla Tuichi Tashmukhamedov[17] and other musicians took part in the concert service of the All Russian Agricultural Exhibition in Moscow (1923). Domla Halim Ibodov's vocal mastery was highly appreciated even by exacting listeners and specialists of Russian vocal music. The performers of traditional music also participated in the display of national art at the annual All Union Radio Festivals (beginning from 1936), the exhibitions of the best collectives in Moscow and especially at the ten-day celebrations of the Republics (1937, 1943 in Moscow, 1944 in Tashkent). The popularization of the *Shashmaqom* beyond the borders of Uzbekistan was facilitated by the joint concerts of Domla Halim with Hodzhi Abdulaziz Rasulev[18] from Samarkand, as well as other performers.

With the appearance in Uzbekistan of radio transmission, many eminent performers of the *maqoms* shifted to Tashkent where they worked in the Committee for Radio Broadcasting as soloist-singers. The famous musician Yunus Radzhaby[19] reminisces:

"The radio station in Tashkent started its work in 1927. Here I gave a concert everyday for half an hour. Later, an ensemble of twelve people was set up. This ensemble grew steadily. In the beginning, eminent performers like Shorahim Shoumarov[20] (vocalist and performer on the tanbur[21]), Mulla Tuichi Tashmukhamedov (vocalist), Domla Halim Ibodov (vocalist, doirist[22]), Imomjon Ikromov (instrumentalist), Hoji Abdurahmon Umarov, Safo Mughanni, Matyusuf Kharratov (chakaryi, Khorezm changist[23]), Anwar Radzhaby, Nazira Ahmedova (vocalist) and Maryam Alishaeva were part of this ensemble. By 1935 it consisted of forty people and I was their direct leader...".[24]

Some of the performers of the *Shashmaqom* ensemble of the Uzbekistan radio division as well as from the philharmonic ensemble in the 1940s shifted to Tadjikistan, where they continued their work in the Tadjik radio division, and carried on with their pedagogic, concert and research work. Among these performers three stand out: Shonazar Sohibov[25], Fazlidin Shahobov[26], and Boboqul Faizulloev[27], who recorded and published the Bukharan *Shashmaqom* as collaborative work.

Many eminent performers of the *Shashmaqom* combined their work as performers with pedagogic and research activity. This was part of the framework of the government politics being followed at that time. As early as 1918 in the Tashkent people's conservatory that had been set up, 'eastern classes' were started, where young people learnt their national music as well as European music culture. In the second half of the 1920s and till the end of the 1940s, in the music schools and colleges that were set up, *Shashmaqom* was part of the programme for the education of the youth. For example, Domulla Halim Ibodov taught in the 1920s in the music school in Bukhara, and Shonazar Sohibov – in the Bukharan music college, even as Fazliddin Shahobov studied at this college. Apart from this, talented musicians also learnt privately from old masters. Yunus Radzhaby remembers that in 1924 he met the great Hafiz specialists, Ota Jalol Nosir, Ota Abdughani (the tanbur player) and Ustad Shodi Aziz, who knew the whole cycle of the *Shashmaqom*. He learnt the rules of the performance of the *Shashmaqom* from them. Towards the end of the twenties he spent nearly four years learning the variations of melody and rhythm from Hodzhi Abdulaziz Rasulev.

Students of schools and music colleges formed unisonic orchestras, where they performed the instrumental parts of the *maqoms* on traditional instruments. For example, my grandfather, an inhabitant of Bukhara, often remembered with satisfaction how Abdurauf Fitrat, responsible for the Enlightenment of the Bukharan Republic, conducted orchestras in such a way that his long hair flew in all four directions. It should be noted that the large number of members in the orchestra and the conducting of the orchestra were not a part of the traditional art of the peoples of Central Asia. These were the 'new trends of the times'.

Abdurauf Fitrat was one of the members of the music-ethnographic commission[28] set up in 1919 in Tashkent. From the very beginning one of the tasks of this commission was the performance of traditional and folkloric music along with their notational 'fixing' and publication, as well as their creative use in composition (the reworking of musical material).[29] The work on the study of the national music heritage was also included in educational establishments (this function was fulfilled only in the thirties).

From 1928 the Samarkand[30] Institute of Music and Choreography[31] becomes the centre for work on folklore and ethnographic work. The Institute not only engaged with the recording of examples of Uzbek and Tadjik traditional art on the phonograph, but also with the publication of notational material and the training of corresponding specialists. Special classes were started where talented youth had the opportunity to study the *Shashmaqom* and to perfect their playing of musical instruments. For this purpose knowledgeable performers such as Domla Halim Ibodov, Hodzhi Abdulaziz Rasulev were coaxed to join the Institute and Yunus Radzhaby, Shonazar Sohibov, and composers who became famous later on such as M. Burkhanov, T. Sadikov, M. Ashrafi and others became their students. The role of the Institute widened even more after it was shifted to the new capital of Tashkent in 1932.

One of the members of this Institute was V. Uspensky.[32] It was he who rendered the service of recording for the first time the whole cycle of the Bukharan *Shashmaqom*, in its instrumental, tanburan version (when he was one of the members of the afore-mentioned music-ethnographic commission - 1922 – 1924). The European notational fixing (done in those days on the basis of hearing, without the aid of recording apparatus) of the *Shashmaqom* in the interpretation of the oldest masters – Hafiz Ota Jalol Nosirov and the tanburist Ota Ghiyos Abdughani make these recordings really unique. In his article 'A Leading Researcher of Folk Musical Culture' musicologist V. M. Belyaev notes: "The work on the recording of the *Shashmaqom* was conducted in a very responsible way by Viktor Alexandrovich, with great dedication, after checking several times and monitoring it himself. The significance of this work must never be undervalued given its exceptional importance in the musical-historical sense, as well as its relation to the study of the national music of Uzbekistan".[33]

The *Shashmaqom*, notated by V. Uspensky, was published in Moscow with the direct help of the Minister of Education of the Bukharan Republic, Abdurauf Fitrat, in a somewhat shortened version and without the poetic text. The question of why the poetic text of the vocal portions of the *Shashmaqom* was excluded from the recording of the musical text inevitably arises. Two answers are possible: 1) the fixing of the poetic text to the notation of the melody in the Arabic print (in use at that time), was very difficult; no one had attempted it so far and it was, therefore, not simple (although not impossible, it would have demanded a lot of time); 2) in 1924, censorship did not allow the publication of the poetic text of the *maqoms*.

In 1925 V. Uspensky recorded separate portions of the Fergano-Tashkent variant of the *maqoms* by Shorahim Shoumarov (*Chorgoh, Nasrulloi, Shahnoz-i- Gulyor, Bayot*). In his article 'Classical Music of the Uzbeks'[34], V. Uspensky writes of the intransient value of *maqoms* and the necessity of studying this particular heritage, the general history of this form, and expresses his opinion about the deep links the traditional form of classical music has with the unique forms of traditional architecture. In these very years one of the leading people in the arts, Ghulom Zafari wrote: "...It is very important for us to preserve the musical wealth of the Uzbek people, to study it exhaustively and to perfection, and to also imbibe the musical theory and methods of Europe, and apply them, to create new Uzbek music".[35]

Thus it was that new forms of performance and the use of traditional music appeared. With the help of those who had knowledge of the Fergano-Tashkent *maqoms*, Gh. Zafari and S. Khurshid gave musical form to the musical dramas they had written: *'Halima'*[36] (Gh. Zafari), *'Farhad and Shirin'* (Khurshid, 1919, 1922)[37], and *'Leila and Majnun'* (Khurshid, 1922).[38] Later on these dramas got a new lease of life when they were formally composed, in which the original melodies of the *maqoms* were preserved. However, the use of *maqoms* in the composer's polyphonic art demanded a caring attitude to harmonization. Such a highly respectful attitude to the heritage of the Uzbek people was felt in the compositional works of V. Uspensky.

Towards the end of the '30s the method of 'quotation' in compositions gives way to composing *in the spirit* of folk melodies. Composers created work taking into consideration the typical structures of traditional music. Citations from *maqoms* were used sometimes with the aim of attributing an emotional aspect to the music, as a creative means. Thus in A. Kozlovsky's opera 'Ulughbek' (1st edition: 1942) the *'Sarakhbori Navo'* is widely used for the communication of Ulughbek's character as well as to create the image of the inhabitants of Samarkand. Some of the quotations from *maqoms* are found in the chamber and symphonic works of Russian composers evacuated to Tashkent at the time of war.[39]

Recordings of *Shashmaqom*[40] performed by Domla Halim Ibodov, Levi Bobokhonov, K. A. Rasulev were especially popular not only in Uzbekistan and Tadjikistan, but also all over the Soviet Union. The titles conferred on the performers can be considered a sign of respect for this national tradition of music in this period.[41]

The Second Phase

The Second Period (1948 – 1971) can be evocatively called 'the black-white period' in the history of *maqoms*. The victory of the

USSR in World War II, which had led to ties with western democracies, awakened in the intelligentsia of the country a hope in some sort of democratisation and weakening of party-ideological control. These hopes, however, were very quickly belied with new Party resolutions (1946 – 1948), by a wave of repression of writers and cultural activists, and by the struggle against 'cosmopolitanism'. In the republics this campaign took on a slightly different aspect – the struggle with 'nationalism' (that is the preservation of national traditions), 'the admiration' for one's historical past and 'remnants of feudalism'. That is why in music, *Shashmaqoms*, Khorezm *maqoms* and the Fergano-Tashkent variant of *maqoms* were singled out as not being in tune with the spirit of Soviet ideology. Concert organisations and music theatres were criticised for the propaganda of 'old archaic music and the sad models of the *maqoms*[42] that tore at your souls'. The theory, that the culture of every people should be 'national in form and socialist in content', was widely propagated.

Yunus Radzhaby reminiscences: "In 1945[43] ...I was once again appointed the Head of the Ensemble for the Radio... 1948 was a year when there were serious ideological difficulties in the sphere of music. In particular, the *Shashmaqom*, the Fergano-Tashkent variant and the Khorezm *maqom*, that had been preserved for centuries and nourished by national culture, were given the designation of 'court music'; their performances were closely watched and investigated. .... And in 1953 an 'orchestra of folk instruments' of the Radio Committee was constituted. The programme of broadcasts of the music division of Uzbek radio for nearly five years followed the resolution of the Central Committee of the Communist Party of Uzbekistan. ....The ensemble of maqom musicians resumed their activity only in 1958 under my leadership".[44]

During these very same years, F. Karomatli (Karamatov)[45] was a research student at the Moscow Conservatory. "It was precisely from 1951 to 1955 that I was ....in the Moscow Conservatory. The topic of my dissertation, confirmed by the scientific-research committee of the Moscow Conservatory was 'The Shashmaqom'. (At the time of this campaign) I did not want to change the theme. The assistant to the Principal (the Principal of the Conservatory then was the well-known choir master, Sveshnikov) very categorically asked me to change the topic of my dissertation. I was forced to obey him...."[46]

We will for a moment shift our focus to India to the time of Mughal rule. Aurangzeb forbade the performance of music in the court and did not take kindly to its performance elsewhere. It was during these years of Mughal rule, in particular, that several treatises were written on music in India. We observe a similar phenomenon in the 'dark' years of the history of the *Shashmaqom*. Yes, the performance of the *Shashmaqom* was forbidden, it was not heard in *official* government institutions, it was not taught in schools and institutes. However, no power could stop the musicians from performing this music in private houses at the time of festivals and marriages and from teaching this music to those who wanted to learn privately. It is possible that it was during those very years that musicians realized the importance of the preservation of national traditional music and the necessity to undertake the notational 'fixing' of the *Shashmaqom*.

At the end of the 1940s, V.M. Belyaev along with A. Mirzoev, E. Bertels, performers of the *Shashmaqom* – Shonazar Sohibov, Fazliddin Shahobov and Boboqul Faizullaev – worked on notational recordings and on the publication of the 'Tadjik Shashmaqom'. This five-volume edition is one of the most complete publications on the Bukharan *maqom*. I have already mentioned that the foundation for this publication were the notations by V. Uspensky. Here it is important to note three moments that are inextricably linked to the politico-ideological orientation of the government:

- in the Foreword (written by V.M. Belyaev and E. Bertels), *Shashmaqom* was called the heritage (only!) of the Tadjik people;
- in the sections dealing with vocal music, Tadjik-Persian poetry (in Cyrillic) was used throughout;
- the first volume of *Shashmaqom* was published in Moscow in 1950 (1951 can be considered the climax of the 'campaign' against the *Shashmaqom*). To a certain

> extent this edition emphasizes the fact that in the Republics, local apparatchiks carried out (or were forced to carry out) these campaigns in a far more severe manner than in the centres.

F. Karomatli remembers that having arrived in Tashkent from Moscow with the first volume of *Shashmaqom* in hand, he set out to complain against the 'campaign' to the leader of the Department of Culture of the Central Committee of Uzbekistan, Bahrom Rahmonov. The latter was an intelligent man, a dramatist, who understood and listened to the *Shashmaqom* with pleasure. But what was his reaction? "I (to this day) remember his face distorted by hatred, his eyes flashing and his hysterical, irritated voice as he referred to the price of the volume on the Tadjik *Shashmaqom* that I had brought: 'Not just sixty five roubles, this is not even worth sixty five kopeks!' I understood this 'artistic performance' of his was firstly, aimed, at saving me from investigations and punishment, and secondly, that he was forced to act thus because he was a leader in the framework dictated by the Party's ideological orientation. ... Happily, such ideological positionings were short-lived".

The edition of the first volume of the *Shashmaqom* by musicians who had migrated from Bukhara in Uzbekistan, gave rise to work on the theoretical study and publication of notational material in Uzbekistan as well. Yunus Radzhaby, the director of the *maqom* ensemble, set himself the task of publishing the *Shashmaqom*. He recorded the instrumental section of the *maqom* from a very old musician, the tanburist Marufzhon Tashpulatov[47]. The vocal portions were recorded by the well-known Bukharan Jews[48]–B. Zakiriev, M. Mullakandov, M. Tolmasov, Y. Davydov. The recorded material was further supplemented by Yunus Radzhaby's own vast fund of knowledge.[49]

The first edition of the *Shashmaqom*, collected and recorded by Yunus Radzhaby appeared in 1959 (Vol. 5, *Bukharan Maqoms*, in the many-volume 'People's Music of Uzbekistan'[50]). The poetic texts and recordings of the compositions of the *Shashmaqom*, in the main, were preserved in the six-volume 'Uzbek Shashmaqom' published later (Tashkent 1966, 1975).

Between the first and second editions of the *Shashmaqom* by Yunus Radzhaby, there is a break of a few years. This time had been used to resurrect those portions of the *maqoms* that had been forgotten, with the help of performers. The shortcomings of the first edition were thus set right, mistakes corrected and more musical material published. This six-volume publication can be considered to be the more complete and reliable one. However, in connection with the text it is necessary to note that in the vocal sections, Turkic classical poetry was used.

The work on the history of the *maqoms*, the study of the manuscripts that have come down to us in Eastern languages, began in the first stage itself. Thus, the music section of the Uzbek Scientific-Research Institute of the Arts[51] prepared a series of manuscript material which was of interest to all the Central Asian Republics. A. Semenov put together a catalogue of manuscripts on issues of the music of the Central Asian people; V.M. Belyaev compiled a dictionary of music terms, used by Uzbek and Tadjik musicians. Although during the years of the 'campaign' the access to manuscripts was limited, specialists such as V.M. Belyaev, A.N. Bolgyrev and I. Radzhabov continued to work on the history of the *maqom*. Their work, however, saw the light of day only in the 1960s.[52]

After the death of Stalin, the attitude to the spiritual heritage of the Central Asian peoples started to change (although there was no reprieve from ideological control). Priority was now given more to the study and performance of music from the Soviet period. Researchers were 'advised' not to confine themselves only to the framework of traditional music, but more importantly, to show its relation to contemporary music.

The 'rehabilitation' of the *Shashmaqom*, Khorezm *maqoms* and the Fergano-Tashkent variant of the *maqom*, did not happen by itself. It happened as a result of the hard and fastidious work that people like M. Burkhanov (President of the Union of Composers), F. Karomatov, and the Maqom Ensemble, under the leadership of Y Radzhaby, put in. In actuality the campaign did not last long (about five years). These few years, however, left a trace on the hearts and minds of the researchers of traditional music. This is the reason why in the years that followed, these researchers *specially* emphasised the fact that the *Shashmaqom* was not a feudal legacy, that it was not born in the courts of khans and emirs who only used it for their pleasure. On the contrary, the *Shashmaqom* was the spiritual heritage of the Uzbek and Tadjik peoples and was intonationally tied to folk music.

It is interesting that in the first phase, when it was necessary to educate national cadres of composers and performers, the *Shashmaqom* was needed – it was propagated and taught. But when these national cadres were 'educated', they repressed the *Shashmaqom*. From 1951 – 1971 orchestras of '*reconstructed*'[53] folk instruments performed (in the main) European music and only two or three pieces based on Uzbek and Tadjik folklore. This 'surrogate' people's music not only occupied the position it did, but also influenced the development of the performance of traditional music (in the accuracy and clarity of construction).[54] 'Europeanisation' penetrated even the manner of performance of *maqoms*: musicians now played the *maqoms* sitting on chairs and not in the traditional eastern pose; in the ensemble maqomists started using choir, that too, with male and female voices mixed; the instruments used to accompany the vocalists as well as those fulfilling the instrumental sections also grew in number.

The Third Phase

The Third Phase (1971 – 1991) in the history of the *maqoms* may be called 'The Golden Phase'. It was in these years that the theoretic study, performance and popularization of *Shashmaqom* all over the world found a culmination. One of the activists who influenced this process was Prof. F. Karomatli (Karamatov). Even when he was director of the Institute of Arts and Head of the Department of Music in the early 1960s, he addressed the problem of the necessity of educating specialists in Eastern Studies. It was necessary to have musicologists with knowledge of eastern languages who could work on manuscripts[55] and on the history and theory of eastern music.

In 1971 Prof F. Karomatli requested Vice-Chancellor

M. Ashrafi to open a special 'Eastern Studies' section in the Conservatory. The Vice-Chancellor and the Ministry supported this idea. In connection with the opening of this faculty, F. Karomatli was given the responsibility of getting acquainted with the activity of teaching departments. Having studied the programme of courses that taught 'reconstructed' folk instruments (where European music dominated without a single example of traditional music) and having conducted a lot of discussions with A. Petrosyants, F. Karomatli came to the following conclusion: the objective of the Faculty of Eastern Studies was not just to prepare musicologists, but to also study traditional music, in which *maqoms* were included. In the 1970s, four or five of the older musicians were still alive, who were masters of the *maqoms*. And so, in a short time, student-musicians were made to learn from these masters invaluable knowledge in order to continue their work. This was possible only due to the enthusiasm of the teachers as well as of the students. As a child I was witness to this enthusiasm that flowered under my father, F. Karomatli's leadership at the Faculty of Eastern Music.[56] I saw the desire to accomplish the impossible in the eyes of the students and teachers who often came to our house with the aim of discussing some issue that had come up. This was the only Faculty of its kind not only in Central Asia but in the entire Soviet Union. That is why musicologists from all over the world[57] came here on field trips to study music. The musician-performers from Tadjikistan were a special draw. This enthusiasm bore fruit: Thanks to them the *Shashmaqom* was popularized in the 1980s and '90s. The performances of the *Shashmaqom* were of a high professional order; a many-faceted study of the form also continued alongside. This was reflected, above all, in the pan-Soviet and international conferences on the issue of traditional creative works and in the competitions of the maqomists.

Text and notes translated from the original Russian by Rashmi Doraiswamy.

NOTES

1. The term consists of two words: 'shash' (six) from Persian, and maqom (in local pronunciation).
2. The term 'maqom' (from Arabic 'maqam': place, staying) means

a musical mode, musical tone, the position of a tone on a musical instrument, or a musical composition.

3. The functions of the maqoms can be compared to the raga in Indian music; they both have a two thousand year history and similar problems of practice in modern times.
4. The Bukharan Emirate lasted till 1920. When the Red Army occupied the Palace and the Emir of Bukhara, Saeed Alimkhan was forced to flee to Afghanistan. In the first years of the '20s the Bukharan Republic was formed on this territory, whose leaders in the main, were the Jadidists.
5. In the beginning of the 20s the masters of the Shashmaqom from Bukhara were very well-known: the singer, Ota Jalol Nosirov, the instrumentalist Ota Ghiyos Abdughani, the singers Domla Halim Ibodov, Hodzhi Abdulaziz Rasulev (Abdurasulov), Mulla Tuichi Tashmukhamedov (from Tashkent), Sadirkhan Hofiz (from Khojent), Madumar Hofiz, Shorahim Shoumarov, Mamatbuva Hofiz, Abduqodir Naichi (from Fergana), Mat'yokub Kharratov, Mat'yusuf Kharratov, Matpano Khudoiberganov, Madrahim Yokubov (from Khorezm) and others.
6. Chagataisky – The name given to Turkish language in this region in the past. It is also called Old Uzbek.
7. Although a few years ago Uzbek musicologists of Khorezm origin proposed a new theory that its origin lies in the Khorezm maqoms and not in the Bukharan Shashmaqom.
8. The musical analysis of the maqoms that have come down to us show that the beauty and completeness of the Shashmaqom is missing in the Khorezm and Fergano-Tashkent maqoms.

   Khorezm maqoms in their intonational melody correspond in many ways to the Bukharan maqoms, but at the same time they contain original melodies. Differences in structure, too, can be observed. They also use Uzbek poetic texts (in the local dialect) in the vocal sections. The Fergano-Tashkent maqoms are the local variants of different parts of the Shashmaqom. The absence of the complete maqom (in structure and cycle), according to traditional rules, does not allow it to be considered as an independent cycle. That is why the local style of the maqoms was called the Fergano-Tashkent *variant* of the maqoms. In the 30s, the leading performer of the FTM, Shorahim Shoumarov (from whom V Uspensky recorded these maqoms in 1925), called them 'Chormaqom' (four maqoms). However, at the end of the 40s, based on the research that was carried out, F.M. Karomatli renamed it the Fergana-

Tashkent variant of the maqoms. S. Shoumarov agreed with this new term.

9. One such master at the court of the Bukharan Emir was Ota Jalol Nosirov and among his students were Fazluddin Shahobov, Shonazar Sahibov, Boboqul Faizullaev. All these musicians contributed a great deal to the publishing of notational material of the Shashmaqom in the Soviet period.
10. One way or the other, the ethical values of religions (Christianity, Buddhism, Shamanism), national traditions and rituals constituted the heart of the spirituality of the multinational government. Along with this, the citizens were at differing levels of social development. Taking into account all these specificities, the Bolsheviks worked out their political activities for the construction of the new Soviet society.
11. The process of the democratization of art, the enlightenment of the masses with regard to music was secured through different ways, the main ones being:
    a) Concerts for the people imparting professional and artistic knowledge (national, Russian, European, and even further, the music of the world);
    b) Attracting the masses to musical self-development: first, choirs for revolutionary songs were set up; later, amateur ensembles and collectives. This also facilitated the development of professional-performative arts.
    c) The opening of music schools. In 1918 the first music schools were opened in Bukhara, Samarkand and Ferghana. These conservatories for the people were transformed in the '20s to musical institutes /colleges with their own musical schools for children. In 1936 the Tashkent Conservatory was opened, the first in the region. The second in Kazakhstan became functional in 1944 where musical education such as the European notational system was imparted and the performance of music and the world history of music was taught.

    If in the first years of this process of democratisation, there was a pull towards the Enlightenment project, after the '30s it was transformed into a professionalism in different spheres of music in societal life.
12. The musical-ethnographic activity in the region had already begun in the second half of the XIX century thanks to the efforts of A. Eikhgorn and V. Leicik who were serving in the Turkestan region. A. Eikhgorn collected not only material on Uzbek and

Kazakh music, but also wrote several research papers on Uzbek music. V. Leicik presented two hundred types of folkloric recordings in 1880 at the World Exhibition in Paris. He also reworked the material on music he had collected. One of his best compositions, based on vocal and instrumental folk melodies, was the 'Asian Potpourri for the Orchestra' which was successfully performed in many European countries. After 1917 systematic work was undertaken to collect, study and publish the folklore and arts of the Central Asian peoples.

13. *Monodiya, monodiynaya muzika*: Single line of melody which is played by one musician or more in a horizontal direction.
14. *Mnogogolosiye, mnogogolosnaya muzika*: When four notes are played together at the same time in vertical direction.
15. National composers and performers appeared (the more talented of them studied at conservatories in Moscow and Leningrad), as did national operas, ballets and symphonies. In the present time, works of Uzbek composers are valued and performed in Europe and America. Uzbek pianists and violinists hold successful concerts and work in Germany, Spain, Turkey, America, etc.
16. Domla Halim Ibodov (1878 – 1943) was a representative of the Bukharan performative tradition. Started singing folk songs when he was ten years old accompanying himself on the *doira* (percussion instrument). He had a beautiful timbre of voice. His huge performative and pedagogical contributions were valued by the government.
17. Mulla Tuichi Tashmukhamedov (1868 – 1943) was a well-known Uzbek hafiz (Tuichi hafiz) and representative of the vocal performative art of the Ferghana Valley and of Tashkent.
18. Hodzhi Abdulaziz Rasulev (1852 – 1936) was an exceptional singer, *dutarist* and master of the Shashmaqom. Talented youngsters came to him to learn. He passed on his musical heritage to them. Rasulaev's repertoire included varied vocal and instrumental pieces. He performed also as a soloist-improviser on the *dutar* (a two-stringed traditional musical instrument).
19. Academician Yunus Radzhaby (1897 – 1976) was a well-known musician of Tashkent, who conducted a traditional ensemble for nearly half a century (from the end of 1950s, he conducted an ensemble of maqomists) under the Radio Committee of Uzbekistan. He had learnt the Shashmaqom from some of the oldest performance-masters.
20. Shorahim Shoumarov: a representative of the Fergano-Tashkent variant of the maqoms.

21. *Tanbur*: Traditional stringed instrument which is played with the nails. One of the main (and most popular) instruments for the performance of the traditional professional music of the maqoms.
22. *Doira*: percussion musical instrument. The only percussive instrument which is used for *'usul''*, as accompaniment for the maqoms.
23. *Chang*: Stringed-percussive musical instrument (somewhat similar to the *Santoor*).
24. *O'zbekiston bastakorlari va musiqashunoslari to'plami* (Anthology of Uzbek *bastakors* and musicologists), Tashkent, 2004, p. 294. (Translated from Uzbek).
25. Shonazar Sohibov (1903-1972) from Bukhara. Learnt the Shashmaqom first from masters at the court of the Emir of Bukhara, and later from other institutes in Uzbekistan. From 1935 onwards, to the 1940s he studied at the Moscow Conservatory. From 1942 to 1946 he was soloist-singer on Uzbek Radio. In 1946 he became music-artistic Head of Tadjik Radio. From 1950 till his death he was a member of the Cabinet for Music at the Republic's House for Folk Art.
26. Fazluddin Sohibov from Bukhara. Learnt Shashmaqom from court musicians. From 1936 – 1941 was a student of Uzbek studio of the Moscow Conservatory. In the second half of the '40s he moved to Tadjikistan and became the artistic head of the radio. He performed as a tanburist and hafiz, fulfilling the instrumental and vocal sections of the Shashmaqom.
27. Boboqul Faizullaev (1897 – 1964) from Kishlak, Bukharan Region, learnt the Shashmaqom from court musicians from 1914 onwards. Served in the Red Army. From 1930 concentrated fully on music. In 1934, he moved to Tadjikistan.
28. Ethnographers were part of the Commission: V. Uspensky and N. Mironov, the Latin composer and music-folklorist E. Melngailis (working in Tashkent from mid-1900 to the 1920s), representatives of the literary section of *'Chagatai churunchi'* (1919 – 1925), the Jadids A. Fitrat and Gh. Zafari. In 1927 in Samarkand A. Fitrat published his book *'O'zbek klassik musiqasi va uning tarixi'* (Uzbek Classical Music and its History).
29. 'Ethnographic concerts' (also called 'Evenings of Eastern Music') were very popular among the people. These concerts of folk music from Turkestan, reworked by V. Uspensky, N. Mironov, and other Russian and European composers were played to full halls.
30. Samarkand in those years was the capital of Uzbekistan.

31. At the present time it is called the Scientific-Research Institute of the Arts under the Academy of Creative Arts of the Republic of Uzbekistan.
32. V. A. Uspensky (1879 – 1949) was born in the city of Kaluga. His childhood years were spent in Osh. After serving in the army during the War, he studied at the St Petersburg Conservatory. In November 1917 he worked in the Republic of Turkestan as part of the creative advisory committee of the Petrograd Conservatory, collecting and studying folklore. Ethnographer-Collector, researcher, composer, pedagogue, social activist – he dedicated more than 30 years of his life to work on folklore in Central Asia. His real victory, for which he deserves deep respect, in undertaking dangerous journeys (in those times) through aiils and deserts, was that he preserved for the people of Central Asia their invaluable cultural heritage. He was one of the organizers of the people's conservatory in Tashkent in 1918 and gave special attention to the 'Eastern Classes', in which Uzbek youth, along with the study of national music, was also educated about music. Uspensky worked on and laid the foundation for the practicals of the course on 'The History of Uzbek Music' (1936).
33. V. Belyaev was an important researcher of folk musical culture – Soviet Music, 1937, No. 4, p. 62.
34. Anthology: Soviet Uzbekistan, Tashkent, 1927.
35. Gh. Zafari: 'On Uzbek Music' (article in Uzbek Language), in the journal '*Alanga*', Tashkent, 1930, No. 1, p. 7.
36. The image of the heroine, Halima, in Zafari's drama was built up through the melody '*Qashgharchai Ushshoq*' from the cycle '*Shahnozi Gulyor*'.
37. V. Uspensky wrote the music, based on a libretto by Khurshid (on a poem by Navoi) in the 1930s. The premiere was held on 26.02.1936). Uspensky preserved the maqom sections used by Khurshid '*Chorgoh* – I' and also brought in new elements.
38. In 1933 a musical drama was written based on this libretto by T. Sodiqov (melody) and N. Mironov (harmonization). The authors have preserved the Ferghano-Tashkent sections of the maqoms. ('Chorgoh', 'Girya', 'Bayot III', 'Feruz' and others), which had been incorporated in the 1920s. Along with this they brought in new elements and also composed original melodies. Towards the end of the 1930s, T. Sodiqov and R. Glier wrote an opera variant of this drama. In the opera, too, melodic materials were provided by the maqoms. Apart from this, keeping in mind the typical rules of traditional music T. Sodiqov also composed

original melodies.

39. M. Krivoruchko reworked separate maqoms into instrumental quartets; this was begun during the years of War, but completed after the War – 'Symphony Fragment' (based on a maqom theme, 'Y. Tulin's 'Uzbek Suite', etc.
40. Recordings on records were made even before the Revolution. For example, in 1909 the company 'Gramofon' specific parts of the maqoms– 'Iroq' – were performed by Rasulev for recording. Specialists from Moscow in 1905, recorded more than twenty famous examples of folk music in the rendition of Mulla Tuichi Tashmukhamedov. 'Zolotoi Amur', records maqoms by Domla Halim Ibodov and by Levi Bobokhonov.
41. Mulla Tuichi Tashmukhamedov in 1927 was given the title of Hero of Labour and People's Singer of the of the Republic; Domla Halim Ibodov was conferred with the title of Renowned Artiste of Uzbekistan and People's Singer of the Republic; Hodzhi Abdulaziz Rasulev was given the title of People's Artiste of the Republic.
42. Following the orders of the Centre, party organs of the Republic acted even more harshly against artistes and writers. The creators of musical dramas and operas such as 'Laila and Majnun' and 'Farhad and Shirin' and others, were accused of propagating 'harmful' ideas. The X Plenum of the Communist Party of Uzbekistan (21 – 22 February 1952) was the culmination of this campaign to expose 'nationalists', 'Pan-Turkic' elements and 'Cosmopolitans', in which the question of 'The Condition of Ideological Work in the Republic and Measures Oriented Towards its Improvement' was discussed. According to A. Nizamov's book the situation was different in Tadjikistan, where in the beginning of the 1950s in the Radio Committee of Tadjikistan the first ensemble of maqomists was set up (p. 315).
43. At the end of the 1930s Yunus Radzhaby was sent to study at the Moscow Conservatory. At the beginning of the War, he was sent to the Front where he fought for his country.
44. *O'zbekiston bastakorlari va musiqashunoslari to'plami*, Tashkent, 2004, p. 297 (trans. from Uzbek).
45. F. M. Karomatli (Karomatov; b. 1925 in Bukhara) – is one of the leading musicologists of Uzbekistan. He is author of several works of folklore and traditional music of Uzbekistan and Tadjikistan. He is the editor of the 6 volume 'Shashmaqom', published in Uzbekistan. From 1957 – 1964: Director of the Institute of Arts; from 1955 – 1992: Head of the Music Department

of this Institute; simultaneously from 1971 – 1980 and 1992 – 1997 was Head of the Department of Eastern Music at the Tashkent Conservatory.

46. Reminiscences of Prof F. Karomatli (manuscript).
47. He was also the student of Ota Ghiyas, Ota Jalal, Yunus Radzhaby.
48. This gave the foundation to European and American researchers to conclude that even Bukharan Jews were creators of the Shashmaqom. Émigré American Bukharan Jews often laughingly said: "What ties you to Bukhara? – The food and the music!"
49. The ghazals and rubai of Atai, Sakkaki, Lutfi, Navoi, Fuzuli, Babur, Mashrab, Nishoti, Amiri, Nadira, Uvaisi, Muazzam, Munis, Ogahi, Furqat, Komil, Saryomi, Abbas Otar, Nisbat and other oral heritage of the Uzbek and Tadjik people served as the poetic texts.
50. *'Uzbek Halq Musiqasi'*, Vol. 5: *'Bukhoro Maqomlari'*, edited by I. Akbarov, Tashkent, 1959.
51. Earlier the Samarkand Institute of Music and Choreography, it was renamed after being shifted to Tashkent. It was closed for two years during the War. Restarted work in 1943.
52. Abdurrahman Jami, 'Treatise on Music' (translated from Persian to Russian, has a chapter on '12 Maqoms') translated by A.N. Boldirev, edited with comments by V.M. Belyaev, Tashkent, 1960; I. Radzhabov *'Maqomlar Masalasiga Doir'* (On the Question of Maqoms), Tashkent, 1963.
53. At the end of 1937, N. Mironov chose 24 young musicians from the unisonic ensemble of traditional folk instruments of the Uzbek State Philharmony and began to teach them simple polyphonic works. The melody was taught on their folk instruments and to create the harmonic basis of the orchestra (for the notational parts), the fortepiano, trumpet and trombone were included. The task of this orchestra was to draw the Central Asian listener to European music, by getting him used to it through the timbre of their folk instruments. A.I. Petrosyants, who becomes the head of the orchestra from 1938, continues the work of the propaganda for many-voiced music, but on a *principally new basis*. Using V. Andreev's experience in the reconstruction of the Russian balalaika and the creation of the Russian folk orchestra, A. Petrosyants, along with a group of masters of music, reconstructs folk instruments from Central Asia. This is how the transfer from instruments with di-tonic untempered sound series to a chromatic one occurs, reconstructed on the basis of a 12-stepped, equal tempered scale. The possibilities of the instruments

widened, as did their diapason (range). The orchestra of reconstructed folk instruments began to perform the prologue to P. Tchaikovsky's ballet 'Swan Lake', to G. Bizet's opera 'Carmen', etc (notwithstanding the fact that in the Republic, right from the start there had existed an orchestra of European musical instruments). In the second half of the XX century there appeared works which had been specially created for this orchestra.

54. Like Indian music (*ragas*), Central Asian maqoms had microtones (Indian *shruti*) which were used by performers. However, the 'Europeanisation' of the music culture of the Central Asian peoples led to significant changes in the reception of traditional music (and to the significant limiting of the use of these microtones). Traditional modes of performance were perceived as 'false' and performers were expected to adhere to European notions of precision and purity of form.
55. In the Department of History of Music at the Institute of Arts treatises were studied only by I. Radzhabov and D. Rashidova. It is necessary to be a musician to study manuscripts on music; otherwise many of the theoretical explanations may seem to be a mere play of words, meaning almost nothing to researchers who are only philologists.
56. The system in the Soviet Union was different from other countries: there was no Bachelor's or Master's degree. There was a 4 – 7 year course depending on the institute and specialization; the students received a Diploma on completion and could then take admission in the university for research. In the Conservatory, students studied for 5 years depending on their specialization, one of which was music criticism. From a group of 20-25 students, 2 - 3, having the talent and desire would be chosen for research on 'Eastern Music'. In the second year, in addition to the main course, they learnt Eastern languages (10 – 12 hours per week) and special subjects (art criticism, seminar on the history of the Eastern peoples, and specialization which included individual studies with a supervisor. On completion of their courses in the fifth year, they defended their thesis.
57. Among the first were: students – A. Malkeeva (Kazakhstan), A. Nizamov, F. Azizova (Tadjikistan); researchers – S. Agaeva (Azerbaijan), S. Gulliev (Turkmenistan), Slavomira Zheranska (Poland), Angelika Jung (Germany), Salahuddin M. Hassan (Sudan), Ted Levin (USA), and researchers from the Czech Republic, Poland, etc.

VISUAL ARTS

5

The Syncretic Nature of Early Central Asian Art

Radha Banerjee

Central Asia occupies a strategic geopolitical position and its history and art are of great interest to a student of Asiatic studies.

Central Asia is a vast stretch of land extending from the western frontiers of China to the eastern shores of the Caspian Sea. This region is broadly divided into two zones: (*i*) Western Central Asia, comprising the newly emergent states of (*a*) Uzbekistan, (*b*) Tadjikistan, (*c*) Turkmenistan, (*d*) Kyrgyzstan, and (*e*) Kazakhstan; and (*ii*) Chinese Turkestan, now called the Xinjiang Uighur Republic of China.

The older scholars described the region of Chinese Turkestan as 'Seres' as it lies between the Seres of the Greeks and India. In general parlance, it is called the Tarim Basin. The Tarim basin is a depression bounded on all sides by mountain ranges. On the north is the *Tienshan,* the 'Celestial Mountain', and on the south is the *Kunlun*, on the east is the *Nanshan* which is a continuation of the *Kunlun* and on the west is the mountain mass of the *Pamirs.*

The Silk Route

For most part, the Tarim basin was arid and inhospitable. Notwithstanding this, it became an important centre of religious and commercial activities during the early centuries of the Christian era, mainly because of the Silk Route trade which became popular with explorations of Central Asia by

Zhang Qian at the behest of the Han Emperor Wu Di (second century B.C.). It should be stated here that until the exploration of Zhang Qian, China had very little knowledge of her Western neighbours.

The main Silk Route which started from Chang'an (Xian) and connected China with the western world passed inevitably through the oasis towns of Chinese Turkestan, namely Miran, Niya, Khotan, Yarkand on the south of Tarim basin and Turfan, Karashar, Kucha, Kizil, Kumtura and Simsen on its north. Both these routes converged at Kashgar and from there the Silk Route proceeded to Fergana, Samarkand, Bukhara and from there on to the Parthian and Mediterranean world. This trade brought many nationalities — Indians, Iranians, Sogdians, Chinese and several others — to the Tarim basin and the Hexi corridor, situated on the western frontier of the mainland of China. Further, the introduction of Buddhism in Central Asia around the first century B.C. and then of Zoroastrianism, Manichaeism and Nestorian Christianity also added to its importance as a centre of culture. Situated at a strategic position, it served as a channel for interchange of the old civilisations, such as those of India, Iran, Sogdiana and China.

Eastern Turkestan was a melting pot and there flourished here a variety of art styles inspired by several streams of religious thoughts. Of all these religions, Buddhism played a dominant role in the cultural growth of the region. The intermingling of the peoples inhabiting the country produced a cosmopolitan or composite form of art combining various art traditions brought to this region by monks and pilgrims and traders and itinerant artists. This kind of fusion of the people and their ideas is not a new phenomenon in art history. It owes its origin to certain political events that overtook Iran and the neighbouring region. Iran had a glorious history under the Achaemenid rule which, however, succumbed to Alexander's invasion. Alexander's conquests of the east, especially Persia, Bactria and Sogdiana were of great consequence in the cultural history of these lands. It brought with it Hellenism and Hellenistic art forms and it will not be an exaggeration to say that the history of these regions was dominated by Hellenistic culture for over a century. Though the people of the region opposed Greek political expansion, the advanced Hellenistic ideas and art traditions found a ready acceptance in Iran and the neighbouring lands.

Alexander, who had a vision of a world kingdom, knew that mere conquests were useless until they were followed by reconciliation between the conquerors and the conquered and their ideas and ideals. This spirit of integration was emulated also by his successor, Seleukos. As a result of all this, there occurred a fusion of the Greek and Oriental arts under the broad policies of Alexander and Seleukos, giving rise to an integrated art form which can be described as Graeco-Iranian art from which the Parthian and Kushan art presumably derived.

Both the Parthian and Kushan kingdoms were suitable venues for the development of a synthetic art as they were vast in extent with various nations and cultural ideas. Regarding the Parthian kingdom, Pliny records: "If a person should carefully enumerate the Ethiopians, Egyptians, Arabians, Indians, Scythians, Bactrians and Sarmatians and all eastern nations comprehended in the vast empire of the Parthians, he would find that quite one half of the human race throughout the whole world live in dominions which have been subjugated by the arrow..." Similarly, the Kushan kingdom also was a vast territory with ethnic and cultural diversities in the context of peaceful co-existence and stability.

The question of the origins of Gandharan art too seems to be inter-related to the art movement which started in Iran after the infiltration of Hellenism. This new trend of art soon spread and gained in popularity in Western Central Asia, Afghanistan and a large part of northern India. All the schools of art which arose in these regions show the intermingling of several cultural ethos. We have positive evidence of the intermingling of various religious ideas and art forms. For example, there is an inscription below a painting from Kara-Tepe — a Kushan site in the Bactria excavated by Professor Stavisky and other Russian scholars which mentions a deity called Buddha Mazda — a product of the synthesis of Buddhist and Zoroastrian deities. There are other examples also of syncretic deities as represented in Kushan art. A gold coin of Huvishka in the British Museum collection shows an interesting type of Siva figure on its reverse. The deity has *trisula, chakra* and *vajra* and perhaps a goat as its attributes. The figure is three-headed and is clearly a Hari-Hara figure going back to Kushan times. Furthermore, the Gandhara Trimurti is also the same type of composite deity. A striking example of this is provided by a seal which contains a four-armed deity with an inscription. The inscription in Tocharian language and script as read by Professor Grishman contains the names of three deities, Mithra (the Iranian form of the Sun god), Vishnu and Siva. This is a clear instance of the amalgamation of Iranian and Indian religious cults: Iranian Mithraism and Indian Vaishnavism and Saivism. The seal in question belongs to the Hepthalite period.

The Kushans

Reverting to the Kushans, they had no distinctive culture of their own. They adopted or patronized various social customs and religions, such as Buddhism, Hinduism and Zoroastrianism and several sects leading to the fusion of many ideas or deities and growth of synthetic art styles. This process of the amalgamation of various ideas can however be traced to the earlier traditions as mentioned above and the Kushans might have been inspired by this approach. It is well known how lively the interaction between the Hellenistic and Parthian arts was and how wide was its influence and application: the Graeco-Iranian, Graeco-Roman, Graeco-Bactrian, and Romano-Buddhist art styles all owe their inspiration to this fusion. This process of integration of ideas and styles continued for a long time in different regions of Central Asia.

The Kushans showed a rare ingenuity in bringing various sects together by means of adopting various motifs, gods and goddesses on their coins: Hellenistic or Roman gods and Indian and Iranian deities. The Kushan dynastic pantheons include Graeco-Roman gods like Herakles, Helios, Salene, Serapes and a few others. The Indian gods on Kushan coins include Buddha, Oesho (Siva), Mahasena, Skanda-Kumara, and Visakha. The

Iranian deities on Kushan coins comprise Ardoxsho, Athsho, Loraspo, Manobago, Mazda, Mithra, Nana, Oado, Oanindo, Oaxsho, Oriagno, Pharro, Rishno, Sharevar, etc. The assemblage of these deities on Kushan coins was not only for commercial interest but also to encourage interaction between various communities belonging to the Kushan kingdom.

The amalgamation of various deities was an important feature also of the Sogdian pantheon. The Sogdians adopted the cult of five gods: Brahma, Indra, Mahadeva, Narayana and Vaisravana. But these Indian deities were identified by the Sogdians with the members of their pantheon. They identified Brahma with Zurvan, Indra with Adbag, Mahadeva with Veshparkar. After these a new list appeared: Zurvan, Adbag, Veshparkar, Narayana and Vaisravana.

Like the Gandharan, Bactrian and Sogdian arts, the art idioms of Eastern Turkestan are also marked by a syncretic character. This is quite natural as all these regions were politically and culturally interlinked, but it is interesting to note that the art of Chinese Turkestan, much more than any other art mentioned above, is very close to Indian Vedic and Brahmanical traditions as adopted by the Buddhists. This phenomenon need not surprise us as Vedic studies existed side by side with Buddhist studies in Kashgar. We know that Kashgar was a very important centre of Vedic learning. Kumarajiva, while returning home from Kashmir, halted on the way at Kashgar for some time to study the *Vedas*. The Vedic tradition is evident in the figure of the double-headed Buddha from Turfan, which is an aspect of Agni. The Indra and Agni myth had tremendous influence not only on Brahmanical culture but also on Buddhist art and thought. When we compare the characteristics of Agni in the *Rigveda* and those of Buddha in Buddhist texts, we find a lot of similarities between the two.

Composite Art

Again, the Mahesvara figure with three heads from Khotan is modelled on the Brahmanic Mahesvara as represented by the Mahesmurti in the rock-cut shrine from the Elephanta. Nilakantha Avalokitesvara from Khotan seems to be a virtual imitation of the Chaturmukha Vishnu from Kashmir. Indra from Balawaste is equally inspired by the Brahamanic epic conception of Indra, who is the lord of the gods. This kind of composite style is quite natural in Chinese Turkestan with diverse communities and art traditions. If the Central Asian art is important for any reason, it is mostly for the conscious efforts on the part of the Central Asian artists to bring various communities together by evolving a composite style. The subtlety of Central Asian art is discernible to one who is not only proficient in Buddhist and other traditions but also in Vedic and Brahmanic lores.

6

Travelling Cultures

Gulammohammed Sheikh

We have had three very interesting and different presentations in the seminar today. My friend Romi Khosla, talking about meso-culture, emphasised how architecture is a lived entity. Another friend, K.T. Ravindran, talked about the significance of sky in the formulation of the domed spaces. He eloquently referred to the Sufi idea of the *darvesh* dance: how the whirling *darvesh* puts one hand up and one down to invoke sky and earth alternately. There was something very beautiful in that. I felt hungry for more. Perhaps I am voicing the views of many others who also felt like that. And Ratnabali Chatterjee, in a way, brought us down on earth to confront what may be seen as the obverse of beauty, the sense of violence. One of the slides she showed portrayed the terrible plight of hapless victims, condemned to death, who were tied up inside the hollowed skin of a freshly killed animal. It pronounced an aspect we generally do not speak about: that of violence.

Melting Pot

What struck me most in this gathering is the emphasis on visual culture. Talking through visuals as serious source material, we seemed to have stepped out of the exclusivity of the verbal domain most conferences seem concerned about. We verbalise the world in word; where people imagine things, but they don't see, ignoring the immense wealth of visual material for illuminating our arguments. Belonging to a tradition of predominantly verbal culture, our academic discourses tend to minimise or marginalise alternative sources offered by other disciplines or practices. But there is some kind of break here and I think we are entering into a realm where our discussions can be far more illuminating in every sense of the word. I am not just talking about architecture or painting: Mr. Abduvali said so many things through music. And in that sense, our dialogue on history or culture does not remain a dry-eyed document. It may come to life, relate to life, relate to us in our times today. So the pre-modern and modern need not remain two separate categories, but come forth as interconnected. We have had in this gathering, a non-verbal dialogue of sorts, which focused on what rests outside the realm of words. There is something to ponder about here.

To reflect upon Central Asian cultures, I have some brief observations. Historians have often compared it to a melting pot from which many cultures sprang. What I find fascinating is the coexistence of a multiplicity of diverse cultures surviving for a long period of time. Take, for instance, the faith systems that existed there. You had the Buddhist system, the Pagans, the Christians and the Islamic components in addition to the cult of the Mithras, the Manicheans, the Zoroastrians, etc., all in the same region. It would be worthwhile to investigate what sustained these parallel and diverse cultures. In the context of today's multiculturalism, the example of a pre-modern time might provide food for thought in the divisive world we live in.

Motifs in Transit

When I visited Uzbekistan in 1975, I was struck by some of the examples of visual culture I saw in the Tashkent museum and elsewhere. Looking at the large embroidery on display in the museum I was immediately transported to my hometown in Kathiawad. The similarities of colour, motif and mode of structural patterning with Kachchhi and Kathiawadi embroideries were so striking, one suddenly felt at home in a faraway land. The difference was more particularly in the scale of most often alternating flower and fruit forms which were much larger than I remembered in the Kachchhi/Kathiawadi embroidery. I was reminded of comments of Babur about how he missed the fruits of the Oxus valley in the dusty lands of India and wished he had tried our mangoes! However, in terms of the scents or aromas, both exotic and familiar, the associations of colour conveyed a close bond between the two traditions. So, rather than being just in one or the other place, one felt in transit within multiple cultures through which these visual ideas traversed back and forth, changing yet retaining something of their origin.

The copies of the fragments of murals found at Afrasiyab near Samarkand on display in the museum revealed other links in different ways. Afrasiyab was one of the signposts on a trade route through which the traders, pilgrims, wayfarers and armies traversed. If I am not mistaken, it was on this route that Alexander travelled on his Indian expedition. The paintings were figurative with a clearly Buddhist content but interspersed with the portrayal of daily life. In one, there are what seem to be portraits of traders, their racial origin represented by different colours of their skin. Both the mode of representation as well diverse imagery are most interesting. There are clearly elements of rendition that one could associate with Ajanta. So there is an aspect of Ajanta travelling northwards and changing in interaction with multiple local traditions; changing yet retaining some essences of its journeys as well as origins. The figures of leaping wild animals, like leopards, lent an unusual dimension to the familiar idiom of Ajanta.

This tradition seems to have travelled further to Pjindikent through Turfan up to the great murals of the Mogao grottoes at Dun Huang in China in the Gobi desert. It is known that an early phase in the long tradition of Dun Huang murals is known as 'Indian'. It has been suggested that Timur took a contingent of Indian craftsmen and artists along with his spoils. So it would not be difficult to trace elements of certain craftsmanship visible in the architectural patterns of Tashkent and Samarkand. Interestingly, the passage is never one-way, it is always two-way, or even multiple-way. The return passage can be seen in the example of the new idiom that was developed at the Mughal court with the basic components of book illumination that flourished in the workshops of Herat, Tabriz, Shiraz and other centres of the Persian-speaking world, mostly of Central Asia.

There are many texts which represent the world of pre-Islam. The *Shahnama,* for instance, deals with stories prior to the birth of Islam, yet it is part of Islamic lore. So the definition of Islamic culture need not be narrow, because it carried aspects of cultures that precede the birth of the religion. Moreover, the faith system in each region evolved new forms based upon the people and customs of the region. The greatness of the faith coalesced with the greatness of the region to create its own culture, overlapping yet distinctive. The architecture or paintings all sprang from the life of people and in that sense everything was born or grew locally.

If we were to move a little further from here, the example of Mani, the legendary inventor of painting who established the Manichean faith, makes a fascinating case. I understand reference to his name also appears in some Islamic texts as artist par excellence. Interestingly, this tradition is also conveyed through to Mughal painting. In a painting by Sur Gujarati, Mani is shown painting a dead dog on a built platform. The extremely realistic portrayal of the carcass of the canine was meant to warn thirsty travellers from a misleading depiction of water. Can we reiterate here that Islamic culture has produced one of the greatest traditions of painting or that it ranks among the greatest visual traditions of the world? No matter what injunctions or restrictions we are told about, the great paintings that history has left behind is what people in the Islamic world made. Were those who made these paintings any less Islamic?

The question about the repetitiveness of traditional painting can be tackled by the example of music. It is like playing the same raga or the same *bandish*. You may listen to Bade Ghulam Ali Khan singing the same raga ten times but not find it repetitive; or listen to the same raga sung by another musician 'repeating' the same *bandish*. If you listen carefully, you would find subtle twists or changes in each 'repetition'. Surely, one could savour the 'repetitions' of a 'miniature' as one would relish a raga.

Literature

7

Ramayana and *Alpomysh*: Two Epics, Two Heroes

Qamar Rais

There are reasons to believe that the concept of an epic in the West has been different from that of the heroic narratives of the East. However, keeping in view some basic and famous texts of the West and East, one may conclude that epics narrate the story of legendary heroes. These heroes go through hardships and face evil forces in pursuit of their noble motives. They travel into unknown, dark and mysterious areas, which provide abundant opportunities to test their valour, wisdom and moral virtues. Sometimes they themselves are endowed with divine qualities. The gods are kind to them. They help them in crisis and calamity. The text of these heroic narratives have very often originated from oral traditions. They have digressions and many side stories. Sometimes their narratives have beautiful poetic images and symbolism. Ultimately the heroes of the epic succeed in their missions, conquer their enemies and live life happily ever after. In the long narrative of the conflicts, adventures and victories of the hero, many historic events and cultural facets of the period are also described in a subtle manner. The life of the people, their customs and traditions and social milieu are also reflected in the narrative.

Heroic Characters

We find many common features in the rich narratives of two epics, the *Ramayana* and *Alpomysh*. The narratives of the two epics revolve around the love of the heroes for two beautiful and virtuous women. Rama is in love with Sita, who happens to be his devoted wife and who is abducted by a wicked demon, Ravana. In *Alpomysh*, Barchin, the fiancé of the hero, is kidnapped by the Kalmuks. Both the heroes take an oath to rescue their beloveds from the clutches of their enemies. On one occasion, Alpomysh says with determination, "I will bring my beloved back from the land of Kalmuks. I will look for Barchin till the end of my life". Rescuing their beloveds is the main motive of their long struggle against hostile and evil forces. Another common feature of the epics is exile: Rama is banished from his land for fourteen years, while Alpomysh is imprisoned for seven years. They pass this period of separation from their beloveds and family in grief and pain. Ultimately both the warrior heroes succeed in rescuing their beloveds from the captivity of their enemies.

Rama and Alpomysh were born warriors. They demonstrate their skill in archery in their childhood. Rama at the age of sixteen killed two demons, Subahu and Maricha, through the mastery of archery. Similarly, Alpomysh at the age of seven pulled the strings of the heavy bow of his grandfather Alpen-biy and shot precisely at the peak of the Asqar Mountain. Both heroes are courageous, compassionate, worldly-wise and physically strong. Rama and Alpomysh are crown princes of two small kingdoms: Ayodhya and Boisin respectively. The parents of both heroes were initially childless. They were born only after fervent prayers to holy men and gods.

The narratives share another characteristic feature of the epics of the East: both heroes succeed in getting married to Sita and Barchin only after passing a difficult test with their exemplary valour, which was a precondition for the marriage. Many brave men attempt to fulfill the condition but fail. Rama fulfills the condition of bending and stringing an exceptionally heavy bow, while Alpomysh fulfills four conditions of winning the hand of Barchin, including one to shoot accurately at a small coin, from a distance of one thousand steps. An important motif of both the epics is to establish the virtue of sincere friendship and loyalty. Rama has two devoted friends, Hanuman and Sugriva, who assist him in all his trials and tribulations to rescue

Sita. Alpomysh has also two devoted and loyal friends in the characters of Kaiqabad and Karajan. They are prepared even to sacrifice their lives while participating in wars against the enemies of Alpomysh.

Social Context

These are some apparent similarities of the characters of Rama and Alpomysh. But when one does an in-depth analysis of their characters, subtle variations are found. These differing facets of their characters owe their origin to the social environment of the ages to which their stories are attributed.

Although the story of *Ramayana* is said to be prevalent in oral tradition even before 800 B.C., the first written text, Valmiki's *Ramayana*, was written—according to scholars—between 800 and 600 B.C. At this period of time, society was in an advanced stage of agricultural development. There were settlements of large populations with small kingdoms. These kingdoms were quite stable, with good civil governance and a strong army. According to the scriptures of this period, communication and conflict between human beings and supernatural forces or deities was taken to be a reality. A type of paganism was in practice, which gave birth to rich mythology. Dharma or a code of religious or spiritual values was respected and practised, at least in the upper strata of society. On the other hand, in *Alpomysh*, a tribal society was depicted. This society consisted, in the main, of a nomad population. Influential tribes had their own lifestyles and traditions. There were frequent tribal wars and intrigues to get domination over the other tribes. Harsh living conditions had made the people sturdy and strong. Even women were courageous and physically strong, if we go by the depiction of Barchin. Islam as belief in one true God was becoming popular among the masses. But the religion was not as deep-rooted as Hinduism, as reflected in the epics *Ramayana* and *Mahabharata*.

Thus despite many common characteristics between the heroes of the two epics, the differing social contexts have made the characters of Rama and Alpomysh distinct from each other in many respects. Many basic elements of Vedic and Puranic philosophy are epitomised in the character of Rama. In the epic poem, on one occasion when Rama asks Brahma: Who am I? Brahma replies:

> You are Narayana
> Armed with the Chakra
> You are truth that begins,
> Truth that grows,
> And truth that ends.
> You are the Dharma
> That rules the Worlds.
> You are origin and end
> You are Vishnu
> The lotus navelled lord
> I am your heart
> Devi Sarasvati your tongue
> The cosmos is your body
> The earth your seat.[1]

In serving Dharma and also in defending it, he sometimes performs acts which are supposed to be ungodly and unheroic. For instance, he believes in the rigid caste system. On one occasion, on the advice of Narada (a deity) and his Brahmin advisers, he kills a *shudra* (a person of low caste) named Shambuk by his sword as punishment for the crime of his practising *tapasya* or asceticism. (This was forbidden for *shudras*, according to the Holy Scriptures). Such acts are never committed by Alpomysh, who seems to be more human and rational in this respect, with a faith in the equality of mankind.

Rama is the *avatar* (incarnation) of Lord Vishnu. Thus he himself possesses godlike, divine and superhuman qualities. On many occasions during his wars with evil forces and especially with Ravana, he makes use of his godly powers. He is also characterised as an ideal symbol of the virtues of Hindu religion. On the other hand, the character of Alpomysh is depicted in a secular, human context. Here the emphasis is on his personal human qualities; his physical strength, his valour, his moral values, his will and determination to defeat the enemies without seeking any help from supernatural powers. No doubt, some situations in the epic are exaggerated enough to be seen as fantasy, but the human element always remains alive. Professor Shaislam Shamohamedov has rightly said, "In this *epos* there are elements of fantasy, but the happenings are so effectively described that they seem to be events of real life."[2]

Another important aspect of his character, which can be compared with that of Rama, is his unwavering faith in the loyalty and chastity of his beloved Barchin. Although Barchin was a captive of Kalmuks and she lived in their captivity for a long time, Alpomysh never suspected her chastity. On the other hand, Rama doubts the chastity and honour of his devoted wife Sita (after she was rescued from the captivity of Ravana), and orders her first to go through the test of fire and then, when she is found pregnant, she is banished to the forest. This act of Rama has been questioned even by some devoted Hindu scholars. They called it not only ungodly but against the common code of humanity. It is important to note that Alpomysh, although a believer in Islam who fights against Kalmuk infidels, never claims his fight to be a *jehad*. His motives in waging war are not given a religious tint. His noble character represents the moral virtues of his family and tribe. At the most, one may say that Alpomysh and his family members were inspired by the spiritual and moral teachings of a Qalandar or saint. The inculcation of secular and human values in the delineation of Alpomysh's character is significant. It brings out the folk sources of his character. This is emphasised when, after his victory over Taicha, the Khan of Kalmuk region, he makes Kaiqabad, a poor shepherd, the ruler of this Khanate.

Apart from certain variations, in the best tradition of heroic tales of the East, the main motifs of the two epics, out of which flow the noble deeds of two heroes, are almost the same. They delineate ideal, righteous men, who may be taken as models for human behaviour and family relationships. They fight against and gain victory over evil forces. They are noble and courageous men, who unite the community and create an atmosphere for happy and harmonious living. They finally establish a peaceful, just and humane society by defeating forces which try to perpetrate discord, conflict, and acts of tyranny among the people. After achieving victory over their enemies and after returning to their homeland, Rama and Alpomysh are both credited with establishing an ideal society in the lands that they were destined to rule.

NOTES

1. The *Ramayana*, Tr. by P. Lal, Vikas, New Delhi, 1993, p. 157.
2. *Epos*, S. Shamuhamedov, Tashkent, 1987.

REFERENCES

1. *The Ramayana* by Valmiki, Tr. by A. Sattar, Viking, Delhi, 1996.
2. *The Ramayana*, Tr. by P. Lal, Vikas, New Delhi, 1993.
3. *Asian Variations in Ramayana*, K.R. Ayengar, Sahitya Akademi, Delhi, 1983.
4. *Alpomysh* (Russian), T. Mirzaeva, Sharq, 1998.
5. *Alpomysh* (Uzbek), T. Mirzaeva, Sharq, 1998.
6. *Epos*, S. Shamuhamedov, Tashkent, 1987.

8

MANAS: The Socio-Cultural Heritage of the Kyrgyz People

Neelima Singh

Manas is the thousand year-old epic reflecting the traditions and culture of Kyrgyz society. In the world of epic literature, it is considered to be one of the largest[1] as it contains more than half a million lines. This epic has been kept alive in Turkish verbal literature for many centuries. The oral version was encoded in written form in many versions. One of the first versions in writing is by Chokhan Valikhanov, who wrote it in the mid-nineteenth century. It was compiled in Russian with commentary and explanations, which enriches the reader's knowledge of the Kyrgyz people and their nation. *Manas*, like any other epic, has been analysed by researchers from all disciplines. The question of its authenticity and historical importance is a point of contention. Though many researchers argue that *Manas* is merely a literary work and purely a product of people's dreams, imaginations and their artistic capabilities, others have proved that the content of *Manas* has its roots in the historical past. It has the characteristics of an epic: a long narrative with elevated language, complex sequence of adventures and actions with cosmic significance, supernatural forces, elaborate metaphors, etc. The epic is based on closely interwoven legendary and real events.

Manas has lived in the memory of the Kyrgyz for so long that it has become a key to their socio-cultural and historical identity. It is a valuable oral and written source for documenting the social lives of Kyrgyz people, ethnic groups and inter-society relations. *Manas* represents the unification of Kyrgyz people under a just leadership. It is a saga about patriotism, brotherhood, friendship, heroism, and justice for the people. Manas, the legendary (or the real) hero is not only the defender of his people, but also the force for unity among people, and a force for social equality.

Manas is a great warrior who united scattered Kyrgyz tribes and brought them home to the Altai region after the Mongols (Kalmaks) had driven them out. The epic reflects not only historic events, but also acquaints us with many facets of social, economic, political life, the people's struggle and achievements, customs and rituals. The epic has three sections: Manas, Semetei, and Seitek. In these three segments, the epic deals with the life of three generations in poetic form. The later two segments are about the life and times of Manas's son and grandson respectively. The first part of the epic deals with the life and heroic deeds of Manas — the founder of Kyrgyz national identity. The next part 'Semetei' is the story of Manas's son, who continued Manas's incomplete efforts for getting their independence. The third part is about Manas's grandson 'Seitek', who brought the efforts of his father and grandfather to fruition. The story of Manas, Semetei, and Seitek has travelled orally through generations. It is a saga of Kyrgyz heroes who, after defeating the Uigurs, Kitais, and Mongols united the forty disparate Kyrgyz tribes and led them to Altai where they are found today.[2]

Manas is an epic that has adapted itself to different spaces and times. Manaschis[3] have over the years developed and enriched its content. It has constantly been redefined in the course of history. For example, there is a mention of usage of some of the more modern weapons and artillery (guns, cartridges, gun powder, etc.) which were inducted, in all likelihood, much later through the fertile imagination of Manaschis.

The epic is interesting as it unites multiple themes, plots, and sub-plots. The hero is portrayed as having superhuman strength and qualities and deals with human emotions in a specific social context. The child Manas is born after his aged father Jakib prays to Allah. The story begins with Jakib (Manas's father) wailing that he is getting old and still without a son. Jakib wants to be blessed with a son — a son who can look after his wealth and his people. The main plot begins with the birth of Manas who, by God's grace, is born to his elderly wife Chiyirdi. The epic has used metaphorical language to describe many events and to unfold their hidden meaning.

The birth of Manas is also used as a symbol. Researchers have argued that it symbolises the birth of the first man. (The twelve women who delivered Chiyirdi's child Manas actually represent the twelve constellations of the zodiac, and the labour, which lasted for 6-7 days, actually reveals how God created a man on the seventh day).[4] Manas grows up to be a great warrior and vows to protect his homeland and unite his people. The plot is woven with battles, miracles, preaching, legends and mythologies.

The epic recounts actions, adventures and heroic episodes through narrative poems. The hero is larger than life and he is the victor. He is superhuman but also a national hero. Manas is also one such, who has been a Kyrgyz national figure. He is the protector and savior of the Kyrgyz people. He unites forty youngsters (used again to symbolise forty tribes), and with their help seeks freedom of the Kyrgyz people. His actions are portrayed without bias and reveal both his vices and virtues. Since he was born to ageing parents he was initially pampered, which made him arrogant and fiercely independent. Many a time he would not listen to his parents or elders. This became a concern for Jakib, who says:

> He, as I see it, does not learn well.
> Good-for-nothing, with riches drunk,
> Unbeliever, a self willed skunk;
> Let's make him listen to sense, dear wife,
> Understand the real values in life.
> To an old shepherd, the best of men,
> Give for six months, as assistant then!
> We shall not spoil him any more —
> Let him learn..."[5]

Manas's whimsical behaviour in childhood was due to his independent personality traits and also due to the fact that he not aware of the responsibility that lay on his shoulders, being the son of Jakib. It was only when a Kalmak actually attacked one of their horse herd chiefs 'Iyman', that Manas asks his father why Kalmaks are beating him up. His father Jakib, who by then was very old and pained, as Manas was of no help to him, tells him that a weak leader cannot protect his land and people. This was the first lesson in Manas's life. Old Jakib gave him the age-old advice that only the "fittest survive". This was the turning point in Manas's life: he begins his journey to protect his land and people.

The epic *Manas* deals with everything under the sun: history, philosophy, geography, genealogy, customs, rituals, beliefs and ethics. That is perhaps one reason why Chokhan Valikhanov called it an encyclopaedia. Each event, each line, every word is a document in itself.

War in *Manas*

Manas is full of description of battles and wars of all kinds: for the sake of revenge, for protection, for assertion of one's might, etc. The battles in *Manas* are often fought for safeguarding the people from enemies: Kalmaks, Kitais (Chinese), and Mongols. These battles also reveal characteristics of the democratic set-up of the military. There are equal rights among warriors when distributing the military loot, appointment of their chiefs, and in the joint resolution of important questions. There is evidence that events in the epic have parallel with historical events. Barring a few cases, the mention of more than 6,000 places and water reservoirs where the events of *Manas* take place are spread over present-day China, Altai, the lower regions of Kazakhstan and regions of Central Asia.

Manas's father, who is cursed and beaten by a bunch of Kalmaks, tells him that "herds without a protector get lost". That is when Manas understands the real meaning of his life. The plot here unfolds in a symbolic dream, which is actually vision of his life: forty Chiltens come and tell him that these will be able warriors who will help him in achieving his dreams and goals. This was a premonition about how he could actually unite tribes and protect his people. From this point onwards Manas, though still very young, takes up the challenge of protecting his people and wealth.

In Kyrgyz society, which was primarily nomadic, it was the herd (horned cattle, camels, sheep and goats, and horses) which was counted as wealth, and not the piece of land owned. The herds were considered a real treasure among migratory tribes and it was according to them that the status of the person (Khan or Bey) was decided. Manas's endeavours were primarily to protect his people from enemies. Many a tribe subjugated itself and handed its properties to him, thus enhancing his empire. Battles take place in order to capitalise on the wealth of the enemy. In these battles horses, camels and sheep along with human beings are won. These battles also take place within a defined system of warfare, where certain rules and regulations are followed. In order to get protection, tribes could pay the price with their horses, sheep and camels and even by pledging human beings. In the case of Khan Shooruk, he had to surrender in front of Manas. He chose to offer his daughter (Akilai) so as to have a peace accord with Manas for the sake of his people.

Wars were won purely on the basis of strength. The descriptions of battle weaponry included clubs, axe, spears, armours, guns, pistols, cannon, arrows, etc. Post-war everything belonging to the side which lost the war became part of the empire of the winner. Sometimes to put enemies to shame and demoralise them completely, the winning side ruthlessly mutilated everything and outraged the modesty of women. Another facet of such a war is also described where many times, the chief or people subjugated themselves willingly to the opponent. They had to offer everything they owned, including their women. There is also a mention about the fact that wars were fought with equal strength. Once Manas had a battle where his opponent who, on foreseeing his defeat, stabbed himself. This was the time when Manas did not pick anything as his booty as it was considered cowardly. In fact, he asks their people to elect a true leader (Khan)[6] for themselves.

The leader had to have certain qualities so as to be elected.

Leadership was not always a family affair. Normally in an open gathering the leader was elected according to the following criteria:

> He who is valorous, move up here,
> He who is just, and shows no fear,
> He who is ready to take the rein,
> He who in tourneys shows his might,
> He who is fearless in any fight,
> He who is sharp of speech and sight,
> He who knows what is power used right,
> He who is elder, or younger he,
> He who is ready our khan to be![7]

There was thus a clear-cut description of desirable attributes in the candidate contesting for the chief position of the Khan. There is no clear-cut mention that the sons or the heirs automatically become leaders. To be a leader one had to be valorous, just, bold, fearless, sharp, strong and skilful. At several points in the narrative there is a mention of electing the most suitable candidate in an open gathering. The able ones even had the right to come forward and give their own name for leadership.

The Women of *Manas*

The epic depicts a male-dominated society. The women represented are creators and preservers. Though there are events dominated by men, the women of *Manas* do not have a quiet presence. Jakib prays for a son but even he mentions that he is a poor man as he has no child: "Not just a son, even daughter I've none..." Though this is a minor indication, it is proof enough to say that even a girl child had a place in the family. The birth and marriage of a daughter called for elaborate celebrations and special feasts were organised for them as well.

There are different categories of women depicted in *Manas*. There is a mention of women as caretakers and mothers (Chiyirdi, Bakdeelet, Kanimdzhan, Alikai), who looked after the family and reared babies. These women were known and recognised by the name of their fathers or their husbands.

However, the description of Chiyirdi gives us some insight into the world of widows. In the commentary of Part I, there is also a description of the fate of a widow. In patriarchal times, among the Kyrgyz tribes, a widow could marry some close relative of her deceased husband, thus maintaining the genealogical line of the tribe. When Shakal, a widow, married Jakib, she received the name Chiyirdi, which reflected the name of her previous husband Chiyira. This was another means of keeping in mind the names of predecessors.[8]

The women retained their right in domestic affairs, especially when it related to children and their upbringing. But at the same time, the children normally grew up under the watchful eyes of the father also. It was Jakib who decided to send Manas to a chief herdsman Oshpur, because he thought that his son was spoilt. Kyrgyz people lived in *yurtas* (a round tent). In this society polygamy was prevalent, but each wife got her own *yurta*. So the rights of each were defined.

Sometimes even the women were good warriors (Saikal and Kanikei). Saikal almost managed to wound the great warrior Manas, (though Manas could not show his full strength as he was really charmed by the beauty of Saikal). When nobody dared to accept Saikal's challenge, it was Manas who came forward, saying that since it was only a woman why should he fear a fight. Women warriors did exist but their strength was not considered to be something to be afraid of.

Worldly Knowledge in *Manas*

The epic offers guidance to people to live their lives. At almost every event, a moral is elaborated. A few excerpts are worth quoting from *Manas*. When young warrior Manas sets out to bash his enemy, Jakib makes him understand that he cannot fight alone and he should wait and watch for the right time:

> My dearest son!" he said, "Look here!
> More observant you should be found—
> Here are none of your kin around!"
> Not in good time valour you show,
> Want with kalmaks to get even, so.
> On equal terms you still can't speak,

While your heart muscles as yet are weak.
Time has not come yet for warriors deeds,
While your body manliness needs.
Time to rush into battle is not here.[9]

The men of *Manas* preferred to die instead of being disgraced. Even the women, on finding themselves defeated used to take out their knives and daggers to protect themselves from the wrath of the enemy. They were courageous enough to fight till the last breath. Once Manas is instructed by his father to retreat from the enemy. Still a young lad, he is unwilling to retreat and he says he would prefer death to such a disgrace: "Dead, not dishonoured, I'd rather be found."

Jakib describes how and why they are no more as powerful as the grandfather. Nogoi was a strong ruler who had not only suppressed Kitai, but had also taken over Kashgar right upto the boundaries of Kara Shaar (a town in Sinkiang region). He also began the subjection of Sara-kol and made Orol (a mountain range, most likely, the Urals) his headquarters. And on the foothill of Dang Doong (a mountain where the Chinese and Kalmaks live) most of his people were settled.[10] As the years passed by, they started living carelessly and then came a time when the enemies became stronger. Jakib states self-critically: "We have been thoughtless, so we fell".

The spiritual values referred to in the epic are of great importance. They give continuity to human activity, which is reflected in culture. The values influence the course of events at given stages in the development of society. The epic is long and beautiful, each word and line is a revelation of the thoughts, aspirations and actions of the people of those times. A great deal of knowledge is required to unfold the real meanings of the epic. Historians, ethnographers, geographers, linguists, and scholars from other disciplines have made their valuable contribution to unravel this encyclopaedia of the Kyrgyz people.

NOTES

1. Some versions of the epic are 20 times the size of *Iliad* and *Odyssey* combined and 2.5 times larger than the ancient Indian *Mahabharata*.

2. Iraj Bashiri, 'Kyrgyz National Identity', http://www.angelfire.com/rnb/bashiri/Kyrgid/Kyrgyd.html
3. Manaschis are those who recite this epic. There is a belief that the Manaschi are special people who get consent from God to recite *Manas*. Manaschis while reciting *Manas* fall into a spiritual trance. They lose their self-control and adapt themselves to the events in the epic.
4. N.V. Atamamedov et al., 'The Semantic Meaning of Character Names, Events and Titles in the Manas Epos', Askarov Tendik et al. (Compilers), *"Manas" Epos and the World's Epic Heritage,* (Bishkek: Myrac, 1995) pp. 8-10.
5. Sagymbai Orozbakov, *Manas,* Two volumes, trl. Walter May (Bishkek: Door and Kirghiz Branch of International Centre 'Traditional Cultures and Environments', 1995), vol. I, pp. 80-81.
6. Khan—a leader of a tribal union, chosen by the people as their chief and war commander. A figure always held in deep respect.
7. Sagymbai Orozbakov, *Manas,* Two volumes, trl. Walter May (Bishkek: Door and Kirghiz Branch of International Centre 'Traditional Cultures and Environments', 1995), vol. I, p. 250.
8. Ibid., vol. II, p. 474.
9. Ibid., vol. I, p. 104.
10. Ibid., vol. II, p. 107.

REFERENCES

Sagymbai Orozbakov, *Manas,* Two volumes, trl. Walter May (Bishkek: Door and Kirghiz Branch of International Centre 'Traditional Cultures and Environments', 1995.)

Askarov Tendik et al. (Compilers), *'Manas' Epos and the World's Epic Heritage,* (Bishkek: Myrac, 1995).

Iraj Bashiri, 'Kyrgyz National Identity' http://www.angelfire.com/rnb/bashiri/Kyrgid/Kyrgyd.html

Iraj Bashiri, 'Manas: The Kyrgyz Epic' http://www.angelfire.com/rnb/bashiri/Kyrgid/Kyrgyd.html

Padideh Tosti, 'Identity in Kyrgyzstan: The Epic Manas and Chingiz Aitmatov', http://www.spgi.org/articles/tosti_identity.shtml http://open-site .org/Regional/Asia/Kyrgyzstan/Society_and _Culture/

9

Literature in the Khanate of Bukhara in the Nineteenth Century

Saifullah Saifi

Before the Russian conquest of Central Asia, the languages that were being spoken in the region included Persian and Turkish. Most of the inhabitants were bilingual. These languages were the offshoots of two main lingual families: (*i*) the Ural Altai family and (*ii*) the Iranian language of the Indo-European family. The Chagatai language prevalent in Transoxiana was a dialect of Turkish, which flourished in the region from the fifteenth to the seventienth century. It was one of the dominant languages along with Persian in the region until the XX century. During the Czar's Government, the attitude towards the language and its use was said to be one of indifference. The Russians used to carry on their official work in their own language and they were not supposed to study or learn the vernacular language. Like all 'imperialist nations', some of them were generous enough to study the language for their own purposes.

The art and literature that developed in Central Asia during this period serves as an index of the mindset of the people. The development of literature may be classified into two distinct categories: the oral traditional literature of the nomadic people, and the written literature of the sedentary people. The Central Asian region, even before this period, had produced great thinkers in the fields of medicine, philosophy, logic, literature mathematics, historiography, astronomy, exact sciences, botany, zoology, chemistry and physiognomy. It is significant to note that in Bukhara, philosophers and men of learning, historians and poets were highly valued and their acknowledgement clearly indicated the interest the people of Central Asia had in philosophy and literature.

The development of literature during the first half of the nineteenth century in Central Asia continued the classical literary tradition. This period was marked by infighting among the Khanates and characterised by prolonged disturbances and great political upheavals. The growth and development of literature, however, did not suffer in any way in comparison to earlier periods. Apart from rich treasures of historical works, poetry and oral literature continued to flourish with ritual songs associated with weddings and funerals and long epic poems. The literary history of Bukhara was altogether transformed during the second half of the nineteenth century till the establishment of the Soviet regime in the early twentieth century. It is presumed that after the establishment of Czarist Russian hegemony over Central Asia, indigenous literature ceased to exist. However, works produced in Persian and Turkish languages during the second half of the nineteenth century prove that the literature in Bukhara continued to develop. A closer look at the literary works shows that there were two distinct ideological orientations. In the first phase of growth and development, the influence of Russian culture was strongly felt on Persian language and literature during the nineteenth century. The other orientation, a little later, was gloomy and despondent because of the prevailing socio-political conditions, which included the failure of the Jadid Movement for reform.

There were several novels written during this period. It would be wrong to presume that in Central Asia before and after Russian conquest, only poetry was written. The development of poetry at this juncture was quantitatively (though not qualitatively) far more and reflected the political tensions of the age. The poems of this period are full of pathos and disgust against corrupt officials and degenerating social norms. In order to get a better understanding about the literature of the times, it is indispensable to go through

Sadriddin Aini's *Namuna-i-Adabiat-i-Tajik* and Wazeh's *Tohfat-ul-Ahbab fi Tazkirat-ul-Ashab*.

In the long list of poets in Bukhara, we have Mirza Mohammad Sadiq, who was a court poet of Emir Haider (1800–1826) and was considered to be a follower of tradition of the Bedil School. The *masnavi, Dakhma-i-Shahan* (1785), is considered to be his masterpiece. Though this book does not cover the period of our study, it is essential to name it as it throws light on the state of affairs of Bukharan Emirs of the time. The famous *Rah-i-Firuza*, published in Khiva, was well-known for being a collection of the works of thirty court poets under Khan Muhammad Rahim II. Ahmad Tabib (pen name Tabibi), a follower of Navoi, also earned a great name for himself for his excellent poetry. Two poets of this period, Fazly and Musharaf, contributed two separate volumes with the title *Majmua-i-Shuara*. In Khokand in the beginning of the nineteenth century, the talented democratic poet Makhmur openly criticised the feudal system and the exploitation being perpetrated by feudal lords and nobles. His poems express sympathy with the suffering of the people. *Khapalak*, in his famous *Mukhammas*, is considered to be one of the best works of classical Uzbek literature. Another democratic poet of Fergana was Gulkhani, who had caricatured people of different classes, like the Sultan, royal officials, Sufis and Saiyids. In the first half of the nineteenth century, the poet Makhdum Haziq migrated from Herat to Bukhara. *Dastan-i-Yusuf-o-Zulaikha* is the only work that remains of his larger body of writings.

Enlightenment in Bukhara

The era of enlightenment that overtook Central Asia in the middle of the nineteenth century produced many significant poets and writers in Bukhara. Ahmad Makhdum Danish (born in Bukhara in 1827), a man of many talents, was one of them. Apart from being a poet and musician, he also served as court astrologer. Although he was not much patronised and was not held in high esteem by fundamentalists on account of his moderate ideas, he was supposed to be an asset to the empire which he served. Danish was sent to St. Petersburg thrice as ambassador of the Bukharan Emir because of his political understanding, scholarship and vast knowledge, despite opposition from a group of theologians. His visit to St. Petersburg revealed to him a very different world that was highly developed. He realised that Central Asian society was reeling under poverty and backwardness. It is said that the journey to St. Petersburg played an instrumental role in shaping his reformist ideas and he pledged to work for the betterment of his people. He got together a group of intellectuals who, inspired by reformist ideas, came into conflict with the government. Danish was of the view that the Emir was supposed to be a servant of people and therefore, must make all possible efforts to ensure the well-being of his subjects. He believed that the suppression of the people had contributed to the underdevelopment of the region. He was of the view that everyone had the right to a modern education and that Russian language should be the medium of instruction. He was firm in his belief that for a civilised society it was essential that everyone should be equal before the eyes of law irrespective of social status and political privilege. His impact among his compatriots, however, was limited.

Among the various literary works by Danish, *Nawadir-ul-Waqae* is considered to be a summation of all his ideological theories. This work was written between 1875 and 1882. In *Nawadir-ul-Waqae,* he describes in detail the day-to-day problems and miseries of the people. Danish suggests to Emir Muzaffar that a canal should be dug in Bukhara to overcome the problems of water faced by the people. He was not only impressed by Russian language and culture, but also by Russia's advances in science and technology. His *Tarjumni-i-Emirani-i-Bukhara-i-Sharif* is next to *Nawadir-ul-Waqae* in importance, from the point of view of the ideas it expounds. In this treatise Danish has condemned and criticised the Emirs of Bukhara and their systems of governance. During his last span of life, Danish wrote two more books, which were religious in nature: *Namus-ul-Azam* and *Mirat-ul-Din*. Danish strongly advocated the idea that any literature written in simple form would have a lasting effect on people.

Another important name in the literary history of Bukhara was Abdul Qadir Khoja Sauda. Sauda (born in 1823) was considered a literary genius. Literary sources and annals written in the latter half of the nineteenth century describe Sauda as a promising poet, philosopher, painter and musician. In his works he not only castigated the Emir but also officials who lost touch with ordinary people and their grievances.

Shamsuddin Makhdum Shaheen occupies a special place among the poets of Bukhara. Shaheen (born in 1859), had a formidable reputation as a poet despite his short life. It is said that after 1889 Shaheen developed close contacts with the court. He had left behind invaluable works both in prose and poetry. *Bada-us-Sanae*, written during the last years of his life, is considered the most important. This work consisted of proverbs which not only gave advice on how life was to be lived, but also criticised life. In 1888, Shaheen wrote the *Masnavi Laila Majnu* in which he speaks about the position and condition of women in society. This *masnavi* was dedicated to his beloved wife who predeceased him.

Sadriddin Aini (1878–1945) was considered to be one of the most celebrated poets and thinkers that Bukhara had ever produced. His philosophy of art and literature may be divided into two distinct phases: the first before the Revolution and the second phase, after it. His contribution to literature and poetry was supposed to have bridged the two worlds. Aini spent his early days in Bukhara in extreme poverty. Despite this, Aini got involved in study and in creative work. During his period of struggle in Bukhara, like other students, he too believed that the rule of the Emir was of divine origin. Quite early in his life, however, he witnessed the harsh reality of kings whose actions were contrary to the prescribed faith. Like other poets, Aini too was associated with the Jadid Movement. He strove for the betterment of schools and the system of education. He became member of a secret society called *Talim-i-Tiflan*. The most remarkable achievement of the Jadids was their perception that in order to create a more civilised society it is necessary that talented people use their abilities in the right direction. For them, educating people was a theoretical issue and a political and economic necessity. It was a moral duty. It is said that Aini along with Mirza Abdul Wahid Munzim, under the influence and guidance of the Jadid ideology, had opened a new method school at the latter's house.

Aini was victimised by the Bukharan Emirs for his association with the Jadid Movement and was ordered to leave Bukhara several times. In his book *Truth,* published in 1920, he described the undemocratic attitude of the government. In one of his *marsiahs,* considered to be one of the best literary works in the history of Tadjik literature, he lamented over the system of government in Bukhara and held it responsible for the death of his brother in 1918. Aini was an accomplished poet who was acquainted with the developments in literature not only in his own country, but elsewhere also.

In his *Namuna-i-Adabiat-i-Tajik,* Aini praises the people of Tajikistan for their nature, humble behaviour and sense of culture. Aini is said to have believed that prose in comparison to poetry is a more powerful weapon in describing events and influencing the minds of the people. Apart from being a social and political activist, he produced works that are considered to be masterpieces of Tajik literature. Aini wrote the first novel of Tajik language. His autobiography, a voluminous work, outlines his philosophy and manifests his literary skills. It records for posterity his struggles in shaping his own life through political turmoil and the revolutionary movement.

10

Abai: A Prophet of Renaissance, A Bard of Enlightenment

Abhai Maurya

Abai Kunnanbai is to Kazakhs what Pushkin has been to the Russian people and literature, and what Mahatma Gandhi is to Indians.

Abai was born in 1845 in the family of a cruel and despotic steppe ruler of the Kazakh nomad tribe Trobikty. The Kazakh people in those days had formally adopted Islam, but due to the total lack of scientific education and enlightenment they were still reeling under the scourge of Dark Ages. Cattle breeding—rearing of sheep, camels and horses—was the main occupation of the menfolk and domestic chores those of the women. Society was riven by intrigues and family feuds. Tribal chieftains, drawing their power from Russian tsarist authorities, used to be more often than not, the most wanton tyrants. Abai in one of his exhortations has described the ruthlessness of tribal chieftains quite aptly: "The strong are again having their way with the defenceless. What laws, what customs can justify the tyranny that has been thriving for a whole century? Only the names of the tyrants have changed: one was called Kengirbai, another Kunanbai, and the present one is Azimbai. Also the methods of violence. In the old days they used to stone people to death, and now they starve them to death."[1] Abai's own father was the main fountainhead of the cruelty and tyranny that had been let loose on the Kazakh people of that area.

A Different Education

Abai was lucky to get education at a *madrasa* situated in the nearest town of Semipalatinsk, but he was withdrawn midway by his father who wanted to train him in managing the family affairs, and practising unbridled 'chieftainism' over hapless Kazakh nomads. His father, indeed, wanted Abai to utilise his educational skills for scoring over his enemies in family feuds, litigations and all sorts of scheming plans. But Abai had another calling. He was endowed with a sensitive heart and a sharp intellect. Moreover, he came in contact with Russian exiles, the opponents of tsarist autocracy in Russia in the city of Semipalatinsk, where he had to often go in connection with the litigation in which his father was constantly embroiled. Indeed, "Beginning with the exiled Dostoyevsky and ending with the Marxists exiled in different times, a continuous stream of sick and enfeebled prisoners—victims of the tsarist arbitrariness—came plodding to Kazakhstan form the heart of Russia. They did not speak Kazakh, and the Kazakhs did not know Russian. But the hearts of the ordinary people were open to friendship."[2] Abai met Y.P. Mikhailov, who had been exiled to Kazakhstan for his anti-autocratic stand. He also visited Abai in his village several times. Thanks to Mikhailov, Abai was initiated into Russian culture and literature, and he got to know the magazine *Sovremennik*. Subsequently he developed a deep interest in philosophers and classics of Russian and European literature.

Though Abai had begun writing poetry in his youth, he became a poet when he was forty years old. Earlier he used to scribble love poetry, but he had been keeping it close to his chest, because poetry was not an honoured vocation in his clan. In the novel *Abai* M. Auezov describes Abai's brother Takezhan saying to their mother Ulzhan: "Praise be to Allah that we have brought forth not a single *baksy* or *akyn*."[3] *Baksy* and *akyn* were the wandering bards who used to go singing about form *aul* to *aul* in those days.

Being unable to connive in his father's ruthlessness and injustice against poor Kazakhs, Abai grew into a truth-loving and recalcitrant son. At the age of twenty eight he broke with his father and began charting out his own course in life. In the novel *Abai,* Auezov has given a vivid portrayal of an episode which set Abai on the path to final *bodhisatva*. His father had set his eyes on a small piece of land of a poor Kazakh called Kodar. This was a frail-looking old man who was struck by tragedy caused by the sudden death of his young son. The young wife of the deceased was left high and dry with the hapless Kodar. Both the father and daughter-in-law were in deep grief when Abai's father organised a farce of a trial against Kodar, blaming him of living in sin with his daughter-in-law. Before the gathering of all the people of the area, Kunnanbai passed the sentence on Kodar: 'Hang till death!'. Both Kodar and his daughter-in-law were hanged in full public view. Abai, on seeing this grim sight, felt as though an arrow had pierced his heart. He jumped into the saddle of his horse and galloped off into the steppes. Auezov described Abai's state thus: "Never before had Abai suffered like this. What had he known of human misery? But now he was plunged into its very depths, and his whole being responded with great intensity of emotion. He was overcome with pity for those two guiltless human beings, who had died so fearfully tormented and abused. A great rage and hatred welled up in his breast."[4]

In his youth Abai did come under the influence of the Orient and read most of the Arabic-Persian epic poems and Eastern classics: Firdausi, Nizami, Saadi, Hafiz, Navoi and Fizuli in the original (and partly in translation into Chagatai). Subsequently, folk art became the richest source of his poetry even though he continued to read works like *1001 Nights,* Persian and Turkic folk tales and epic poems. People in the Kazakh steppes came to know and love *Shahnama, Leila and Majnu* and *Kor-Ogly* in Abai's oral rendering.

Later, after coming into contact with Russian progressive democrats like Mikhailov, Abai began reading Pushkin, Lermontov and Krylov. He also read Leo Tolstoy and Saltykov-Shchedrin. He read Goethe, Byron and other West-European classics in Russian translation. He translated some of Goethe's and Byron's poetry into Kazakh from Lermontov's Russian translations, apart from rendering Lermontov's *The Dagger, The Gifts of the Terek, The Sail, I Walk Into the Night Alone* and fragments from *Demon* into Kazakh. The inspired rendering of Pushkin's *Eugene Onegin* became particularly popular with Kazakh *akyns.* He set Tatyana's letter to Onegin to music and the song was on the lips of young Kazakhs. Pushkin's *Dubrovsky* became Abai's most favourite work, maybe because of the closeness of the plot, i.e., Dubrovsky's rebellion against the persecution of his family by a stronger landlord. This was very close to the atrocities committed by his own father on poor Kazakhs or weaker clans. Mikhailov also introduced Abai to Chernyshevsky's world outlook. In the novel *Abai,* Auezov conveys Mikhailov's description of Chernyshevsky's world view to Abai thus: "According to Chernyshevsky, the peasantry, the millions of toiling people, must join the struggle against the autocracy. He told Abai about Chernyshevsky's leaflet to the peasants of Russia. The leaflet was titled: 'To the Peasants of the Landlords with Compliments from Their Well Wishers'. In it the author had called upon the peasants to go to battle, axes in hand, for the people were being kept in slavery. The tsar had simply deceived them with the phantom of liberation in 1861 because he was not a people's tsar, but a landlord's tsar. Mikhailov remembered this leaflet from his university days and repeated it almost word for word to Abai: "He's pulled the wool over your eyes... What is he if not just another landlord? ...You are the serfs of the landlords and they are the serfs of the tsar. He's their landlord... He sides with them, of course!" And then followed the words about freedom: "...that the people should be in charge of everything and that the chiefs should obey the community... and nobody should dare abuse the peasants". Mikhailov said with emotion that deliverance from the tsarist system lay with the axes of people and not with the actions of four or five solitary conspirators. The assassination of a minister or the tsar was futile."[5] Abai at once perceived the correctness of Chernyshevsky's view that it was the people who were the decisive force: "The real duty of the people's well-wishers is to awaken the people's minds and to call them to struggle against the hordes of evil and violence."[6]

Preparations For Struggle

While working among the people of the steppe, Abai realised that the struggle for helping the suffering people would be difficult and protracted and he could not have afforded to take an adventurous plunge fighting the enemies of the people all around. He decided to prepare himself well before launching himself into the action. First, he studied a lot to prepare himself for the decisive battle. Indeed, after his marriage to Aigrim he closed himself in his *aul* and read books in Russian avariciously. Russian books, which he had collected quite diligently in the city, became his inseparable friends. After reading *Dubrovsky* he was elated. This is vividly described in the novel *Abai*: "The book seemed to him like a fellow traveller who had unexpectedly come to be a friend. It was a long time since he had been so elated. His life of seclusion and escape from household cares was at last justified. He had found and crossed the ford he had sought so patiently for years."[7] Indeed, he was so engrossed in reading books, that he did not have time to look after the new house that was being built for him and his family. His brother even mocked at him that he had tied himself to the skirt of his newly-wed wife. But at the end of the day he knew that the Russian democratic ethos had taken root within him and brought forth new fruits of purity and humaneness. He was alone but he was happy that it was not education alone that he had acquired, but a new outlook too.

He then went to the city of Semipalatinsk and tried to deepen his knowledge by continuous reading and discussions with Russian friends like Mikhailov who told him about the struggle that was being waged by the Russian revolutionaries against the tsar. From Mikhailov he learnt about the assassination of the tsar in the 1880s and felt that the throne of the tsar was tottering and that Russian society was heading for a revolution led by its finest people. Abai was eager to know when and how revolutionary thought had come into being in Russia. Mikhailov told him of the origin of the struggle against the autocracy, about Pushkin, Belinsky, Herzen and the new upsurge of the revolutionary movement stimulated by Chernyshevsky. In the novel *Abai*, Auezov describes Abai's state of mind in touching notes: "Abai was greatly impressed. This brave and fearless girl (who had thrown flowers at Chernyshevsky's feet when the sentence had been pronounced upon him by the tsarist court – A.M.) was the sister of his friend! It was most surprising that Mikhailov, who had told him about so many revolutionaries, had never as much as mentioned this. He set it down to his friend's natural modesty. Mikhailov never talked about himself or his activities. Abai could not remember him ever having said, "I acted thus or thus." The heroes of his stories were always others, while he seemed somewhere dissolved among the crowd. All Abai knew was that he had been exiled two years before Chernyshevsky was arrested.[8]

Abai had often shared his concern over the fate of the Kazakh people with Mikhailov and as is described in the novel *Abai,* he came to the conclusion that "the Russians had brought both good and evil to the steppes. The evil was plain for all to see, while the good was difficult to discern. The evil lay in the local authorities and the officials, deaf and blind to anything but promotion and bribes. The good lay in Russian culture, a matter which was still a closed book to the Kazakhs, who could only see brute force in most Russians. Russia possessed a treasure of knowledge respected the world over. She had her thinkers, who had won universal recognition, but the Kazakhs knew little of this — it was all too far removed from them. And yet there were perceptible stirrings among the Kazakh people. Men like Abai were already able to draw on the spiritual treasure-store of Russia. The way lay open for the entire Kazakh people, the way of enlightenment".[9]

Poet's Mission

After having prepared himself sufficiently Abai started writing poems permeated with social concern. He also penned brief philosophical sketches that carried succinct exhortations to readers. The exhortations, termed *'slovo'* in Russian, are forty-five in number, but each of them conveys some complete thought or philosophical idea. However, the most important point of his concern revolves around his Kazakh people—their lot, their strengths, their weakness, their drawbacks and their virtues. While analysing the Kazakh people, Abai deals with them like a doctor called upon to cure an ailing person. That is why, according to Abai, a correct diagnosis of the disease of his people was necessary for treatment and recovery. In his poem *O My Luckless Kazakh...* Abai is most concerned about the lot of his people:

> O my luckless Kazakh, my unfortunate kin,
> An unkempt moustache hides your mouth and chin,
> Blood on your right cheek, fat on your left —
> When will the dawn of your reason begin?

No wonder Abai is most forthright while describing the diseases with which the Kazakhs were afflicted. In *Exhortation No. 5,* for instance, Abai writes, "Kazakhs have no interest in knowledge and science; they are not concerned about justice and peace. They want to earn money, but they do not know how to do this. That is why they indulge in cunning tricks, deception or even in sycophancy so that they could grab the wealth belonging to other people. If they fail to do so they will become your sworn enemies, they will not hesitate to rob their own real father and in doing so they will not think that this was an ignoble act."[10]

Can there be anything more scathing than what Abai said about his own people? But as was mentioned above, he was approaching his people like a doctor who would embark upon curing his patient after correctly diagnosing him. In his exhortations, Abai time and again calls upon the Kazakhs to acquire knowledge, humaneness, discipline and honesty. He persuades the Kazakhs to shun pettiness, obscurantism, and the tendency to indulge in self-praise, greed and selfishness. In *Exhortation No. 17,* while showing a debate taking place between desire, intellect and heart, Abai establishes the paramountcy of heart over the other two faculties. In *Exhortation No. 18,* he condemns the tendency to indulge in superficial showing-off and boasting and calls for modesty and sincerity, demolishing at the same time the evils of arrogance and self-conceit. In *Slovo No. 19,* Abai upholds the trait to learn and acquire first-hand knowledge. While exposing the mentality of imitating the crowd blindly, as well as negative traits such as robbing, cheating, backbiting and jealousy often found in the Kazakhs, Abai calls upon his people to rise above all these petty traits by acquiring knowledge. In *Slovo No. 32,* he indeed enlists six ways of acquiring knowledge. In *Slovo No. 35,* he calls upon the Kazakhs to conduct themselves selflessly while dealing with their fellow beings. In *Slovo No. 36,* Abai underlines the importance of having the sense of shame, shyness, modesty and humility. In his lengthy exhortation *No. 38,* Abai discusses as to what is humaneness and what it is to be a human being. He dwells at length on about eight incarnations of human beings, thereafter Abai discusses notions like sense of justice, truthfulness, sincerity and wisdom. He also establishes the difference between a scholar and a sage. Finally, there was his judgement:

> Among ourselves, Kazakhs, make peace.
> Let none abuse you. None can fleece
> United clans. Your quarrels cease.
> While powers-that-be can lie and steal,
> Misusing trust, with no appeal,
> Your life will be one long ordeal.
> Let honour and your heart awake!
> My warning comes for all to take.

While discussing modern-day mullahs and other priests, Abai writes: "Modern mullahs are enemies of scientific scholars. This is happening either due to the ignorance of priesthood or on account of their greed and distorted way of thinking."[11] Talking about the modern *madrasas,* Abai thinks that contemporary education was obsolete as *madrasas* were teaching young people only to learn by rote and such an education did not create any analytical and critical minds among the students. Indeed, Abai writes: "As regards the mullahs, I want to particularly warn you against these people. Their teachings are dangerous. Majority of them are ignoramuses; they are ignorant about the real laws of *shariat.* They only follow the path of superficial worship. Being themselves quacks, they try to impose on people the load of false teachings. Their teachings for all practical purposes inculcate greed in people and hence are harmful even for the lowest of the low. They find support among stupid people, their words are false, they flaunt their scholarship by counting the beads, by their turban and nothing else."[12] In his poem *His Addled Brain Thinks...* Abai conveys the quintessence of his thought quite pithily:

> The mullah with his mighty turban,
> Who twists our laws in every way,
> While looking wise and very urban,
> Is he not a bird of prey?
> From any soul that is mean and dark
> It's useless to expect much good —
> But very few my words will hark ...
> By fewer they're understood.

In *Exhortation No. 40,* Abai poses a number of questions which have social and political relevance:

1. Why is it that we do not speak ill of the dead, while we do not consider them worthwhile when they are alive?
2. Why do people lie prostrate before distinguished persons from other families but not value their own people who are much higher in worth and ability?
3. Why is it that an impoverished son of a landlord is not shy of stealing, but considers working with another landlord a great insult?
4. Why are people jealous when their friends prosper?
5. Why do some people look for innocuous advisers but shun those who know them through and through?
6. Why are people who are restrained and peace-loving considered cowards, while wicked, boastful and quarrelsome people are considered fearless? ...

Exhortation No. 37 consists of twenty-three wise axioms which could serve as guiding principles or testaments for all human beings. A few of them would suffice to prove the point we are making:

1. Crowd is generally senseless: it poisoned Socrates, burnt philosophers, hanged Christ on the cross and buried the prophets in camel camps. Lead it on the path of truth.
2. Noble thought once pronounced loses its dazzle.
3. If it depended on me I would snap the tongue of the

persons who say that human beings cannot be reformed.

4. Impotent anger, insincere love and a teacher without pupils are meaningless and useless...

His poems also are replete with similar concerns and they were loaded in social message. However, the first and foremost task that Abai wants to undertake is to define clearly the mission of a poet. In his times there were numerous *bakasis* and *akyns,* like Bukhar-jirau, Shartanbai and Dulat, who sang panegyrics for those who paid them and "who embodied the reactionary ideology of the feudal khans". He calls their poetry "patchy" and "full of imperfections and faults".[13] He has no respect for such poets. In his poem written in 1887, one finds the following lines:

> Let's take my predecessors, for example:
> The *biys,* who had a well-known predilection
> For garnishing their speech with proverbs. The *akyns* —
> Those wingless poets who could neither read nor write,
> Who spun their crudely rhymed and worded tales
> And, fingering the strings of their *kobyz* or *dombra,*
> Cried out their lofty-sounding dedication
> And then passed around the hat, collecting coppers.
> ....
> They did not flatter everybody — just the purse-proud *bais.*

Abai defines the mission of a poet in the following lines in the poem written in 1889:

> "To Ali-azret I don't sing a hymn,
> Nor to a beauty with a 'golden chin'.
> I don't preach death nor voice forebodings grim,
> I do not teach the young *jigits* to sin
> Or honour to forget. My love for men is genuine,
> My one ambition is their confidence to win."

In the poem *When the Heart of a Bard...,* Abai is most powerful in defining the mission of a poet:

> "With an eagle's keen eye,
> And, alive to its woes,
> Goes to battle against
> Man's most pitiless foes.

And with faith at his side,
Sits in judgement upon
Brutal tyrants whose role
Brings contentment to none."

In his poetry, Abai dwells on a novel understanding about family, parental duties, upbringing and education of children and, most important, about the role and place of women in the society. Abai reveals the very soul of a woman, her sufferings, her feelings and selflessness. He shows that if she is allowed to choose her own love, she is capable of rising to great heights. For Abai, a woman in all her multifaceted roles as sister, wife, mother, grandmother and so on is the mainstay of the Kazakh family, Kazakh society. But, more often than not, a woman in Kazakh society are not allowed to prove her qualities as there is no scope for her to act freely, to display all the virtues with which she may be endowed. In the novel *Abai*, for example, it is described that Abai's wife Aigrim was a gifted singer, but this great gift of nature had to die a slow death because Abai was often rebuked by his relatives for his wife's singing. Mukhtar Auezov's is correct when he says that Abai "glorifies a woman's readiness for self-sacrifice, her wisdom, her loyalty as a friend, and her generous heart. Passionately denouncing such aspects of the Kazakh marital institution as paying bride-money, polygamy and enslavement, he demands equal rights for women"[14] which is what could be seen in the following powerful lines.

"A maiden languished in the palace of a khan,
He was an elderly, infatuated man.
He gave her slave girls of her wishes to take care,
And dressed her in brocades and satins rare.
The khan was confident that she was his to buy,
And did his best to bring surrender nigh.
The maiden threw herself into the lake instead,
Preferring death to sharing his brocaded bed."

Abai proclaims alternative mores and values in place of the existing obscurantist, fossilised life mode of thinking. In his poem *Old age is here...* he counter-poses virtuous and noble souls to base, treacherous, foolish and stupid people, knaves and fiendish people. In the poem *'Tis laughter we should praise...* with evils like base mercantility, lechery and the despotism of the ruling class, Abai contrasts friendship, sincerity, harmony, generosity as the values that should become the hallmark of Kazakh society. In the poem *You should not vaunt your knowledge while you are still untaught...* Abai calls upon people to shun evil, reject falsehood and not to flaunt titles. In the poem *It pains me now to realise...* Abai sings a powerful hymn to friendship:

> "Yes, friendship is a gift from God, a gift divine.
> You cleanse your conscience when confessing to a friend.
> I tried to form some friendships in my time,
> But they were savaged into shreds by ignorance again.
> My soul craves friendship, seeks it daily,
> My heart is aching for it, and while I
> Have never known a friend who'd not betray me,
> I sing a hymn to friendship for all time!"

Abai is most ruthless in subjecting vices such as flattery, hypocrisy and double-facedness prevalent in Kazakhs to most scathing criticism in the poems, like *Wit is the mother of sorrow* and *My soul, what are you seeking...?*:

> "I am sickened by their words of honey,
> By praise so crude, it's really funny.
> It's like expecting love form whores
> Who sell their hot embrace for money..."

Relentless Fighter

Abai did not want that his words, his exhortations flowing in his poems remain confined to mere words. In a way Abai's fate resembled that of Buddha, with the difference that the latter, being a prince, did not know the miseries under which the people had been reeling. He had to leave the four walls of the palace to get to know life and then seek, after extensive wanderings and soul-searching, while Abai knew what the suffering of people was and sought answers to the vexed questions in books, in science and enlightenment. Moreover, Abai did not want to rest on laurels after attaining his own *bodhisatva*. He wanted that it should serve the more important cause of the reformation of his pre-modern society. He was happy to find support in Chernyshvsky's aesthetics, according to which words of art should be at the service of the people. But in his society, which was languishing under the most reactionary and obscurantist value system and customs, Abai's poetry could have not made any significant dent had it come from an unknown bard. His literary word indeed became his most powerful weapon only when he had become a force to reckon with in his milieu.

Abai's action plan began to unfold when he felt the fit of nausea at the scene of Kodar and his daughter-in-law being hanged. Thereafter he began subjecting the actions of his father to critical scrutiny. He not only refused to participate in the unjust actions of his father, but gradually started building up a protest campaign against the rule of tyranny that had been let loose by his father on his hapless subjects. Abai had openly begun to protest when his father tried to usurp the lands and pastures of poor people on one pretext or the other. He openly advocated resistance to the injustice being perpetrated by his father and his ilk, not caring much for the wrath his despotic father could let loose on him. When the poor people, who had worked all their life as labourers or servants with his father and other clan rulers, were thrown out to die in penury in old age, they came to Abai for help. Abai took up cudgels on their behalf and exhorted them to hold together in their fight against injustice. Abai defied all odds and fought valiantly till justice was not given to the suffering people.

Similarly as and when the lands were snatched by his father and other chieftains from poor Kazakhs on one pretext or the other, Abai would consider it a great tragedy and rise wholeheartedly in the defence of people wronged by the powerful *byis* and *volost'* rulers. Things came to a head at the time of a natural calamity created by an untimely blizzard. Poor people began suffering from an untold misery as their cattle, particularly the sheep, the camel, the horses, started dying in big numbers. Abai allowed them to take shelter in the lands of his father, his brothers and other close relatives. In the novel *Abai,* M. Auezov offers a powerful portrayal of the encounter that Abai had with his father who had accused him of three crimes: (*i*) while helping the suffering people Abai did not hesitate to squander the treasures of his relatives senselessly; (*ii*) in his extreme zeal to help people in distress Abai did not distinguish between friends and foes; (*iii*) Abai leaned too much towards Russians.

To these charges Abai retorted in following words: "I cannot accept a single one of your reproaches, father. I am convinced that I am right. You say that I am a lake with flat shores. Would it be better to be like the waters of a deep well, accessible only to him who has a rope, a pail and strong arms? I prefer to be accessible to the old men and the children, to all whose arms are weak. Secondly, you have spoken of keeping the people in hand and of the sort of men needed for such a task. In my opinion the people were one like a flock of sheep: if the shepherd shouted, 'Ait!' they would all jump up, and if 'Shait!' they would all lie down. Then the people came to be like a drove of camels: if you throw a stone before them and shouted, 'Shok!' they would first look around, think—and only then turn from their path. But now the people, who have overcome their former meekness and boldly opened their eyes, are like a herd of horses obeying only riders who share all their hardships — the frosts and the blizzards — who can forget their own homes for the sake of the herd, who can use a lump of ice for a pillow and a drift of snow for a bed. Thirdly, you spoke of the Russians. The most precious things for the people and for me are knowledge and light. These things are in the hands of the Russians, and if they will give me the treasures I have sought all my life how can they be alien to me? Were I to reject this, I would remain ignorant and I cannot see much honour in that."[15]

Abai indeed became a relentless fighter against the backwardness, corruption and prejudices prevailing in the pre-modern Kazakh society and in particular against the ignorant and ruthless local rulers who were oppressing their own poor people. The Russian officials governing the area were hand-in-glove with the Kazakh ruling tyrants. Abai often intervened on behalf of the oppressed people against the high-handedness of Kazakh and Russian rulers. Once an arrogant Russian district official came to Abai's area for conducting elections of *volost'* chiefs. He came and occupied the tents of poor Kazakhs and converted them into his election office. The poor people were left high and dry in the cold winter, with no shelter on their heads. When people protested, the officer ordered public flogging of those who had ventured to raise their voice. Abai intervened, snatched the whip form gendarme's hand, provoking people to an open revolt. The crowd immediately tore down the election office and the Russian officer had to flee to the city empty-handed. Abai had to suffer a jail term for this action of his.

Abai also often intervened whenever a case of injustice was brought to him by any victim. He received a petition once from a young girl that she was being given in marriage to an old man who already had two wives. Indeed, this episode flared into a major conflict between two clans, that is, between the one representing the girl and the other standing behind the old bridegroom in waiting. The local Kazakh rulers and the city court had failed to resolve the tangle. Ultimately the feuding clans and Russian authorities sought Abai's help in resolving the case because he had acquired a reputation of being a fair man among the entire community. Abai was able to resolve the conflict to the satisfaction of both parties. It was for the first time that in a pre-modern society, a young girl was allowed to marry a man of her own choice. Besides, Abai declared publicly that the old law which held women in bondage should be changed. This was nothing less than blasphemy for the village elders, but in the eyes of the majority of the masses, Abai became a sage, a messiah. They started coming to him, seeking his help in times of hardship and misfortunes, to get their disputes resolved or to seek justice when they were being persecuted by the ruling elite of the village. "Whole clans and tribes from regions far and near sought his advice and begged him to settle their disputes for them, even long-standing land claims and such like cases. Very often he was called in on cases of raids and murder involving different regions, too baffling for the authorities to solve. These cases were tried at specially convened large meetings, called 'extraordinary conventions', where decisions were passed on the payment of damages to the poor peasants who had been victimised, and on the punishment to be meted out to the clan rulers whose endless feuds and intrigues caused the population so much grief and damage."[16]

The ruling class of the village and the clerk class of intellectuals was quick to see a dangerous man in Abai. They unleashed a dirty war against him in which no holds were barred. Indeed, a great divide took place in the society. On the one hand, there were poor people, particularly the youth, among whom Abai's poems, literary works and ideas had become immensely popular. They all rallied around him in big numbers. On the other hand, Abai's enemies consisting of the local ruling elite and those oppressors, who had been slighted by him in the process of handing out justice to people, closed their ranks and began relentlessly hounding him and his friends. They began to viciously slander Abai and even made an attempt on his life in 1897. It was in such moments that Abai wrote:

> "One honest man cannot defeat
> The legion of rogues who bait us and cheat —
> With them our existence is riddled, replete....
> My life's finest years have faded and fled,
> My most precious forces lie shrivelled and dead,
> While hot coals of scorn are heaped on my head."

All this mood of despondency notwithstanding, the fact is that Abai's stature had soared higher among the masses. But the office of the *uyezd* chiefs and tsarist courts were flooded with reports and complaints against him that had been sent by clan elders accusing him of inciting the people against the tsar, mocking at customs and traditions of their fathers and forefathers. The police even came and searched Abai's house with a view to arrest him. The governor of Semipalatinsk tried several times to eliminate Abai, but fearing the wrath of the masses, he could not execute his nefarious designs. Abai could not be isolated from his people.

Indeed, as Abai was acquiring the image of a sage, a messiah being persecuted by the powers that be, young *akyns* and people were talking of him in crowded fairs: "A good man has appeared in the steppes and his name is Abai. He has special words and behests for us. He is a wise man, a protector of the downtrodden and enemy of the tyrants. He was born among the Tobikty, but is truly a son of all the people. We shall heed his words and behest."[17]

No wonder that his poems and melodies gained even wider currency among Kazakh masses. M. Auezov has described this phenomenon beautifully in his novel *Abai*: "The poems and melodies born in Akshoky (Abai's *aul*—A.M.), taken down in writing and learnt by heart, spread far and wide. Every new word sped over the steppes like the gentle but persistent wind of the Sary-Arka. Songs never heard before were carried by the winds over the steppes bringing a long-awaited reply to a desire that had lain dormant through the centuries. The voice of a new tribe, the songs were the harbingers of a new spring. Born in the still lingering winter, they were songs for the summer that was to come, a summer that would see a fresh blossoming of life. They rang for those who were seeing a new life and fresh horizons, who had a keen mind, a responsive heart, for the strong and bold, who were concerned for the people and were ready for battle."[18]

NOTES AND REFERENCES

1. Nurpeisov A., Foreword to Mukhtar Auezov's novel *Abai*, Progress Publishers, Moscow, 1975, p. 10.
2. Ibid, p. 16.
3. Auezov Mukhtar, op. cit., p. 457.
4. Ibid., p. 59.
5. Ibid., p. 393.
6. Ibid.
7. Ibid., p. 296.
8. Ibid., p. 394.
9. Ibid., p.395.
10. Abai, *Kniga slov, poemyi* (*The Book of Exhortations, Poems*), Almaty, 1993, p. 149.
11. Ibid., p. 226.
12. Ibid., p. 228.
13. Auezov Mukhtar, *Abai Kunanbaev (1845 – 1904)*, in the book: *Abai Kunanbaev—Selected Poems*, Progress Publishers, Moscow, 1970, p. 17.
14. Ibid.
15. Mukhtar Auezov, *Abai*, op. cit., p. 259.
16. Ibid., p. 435.
17. Ibid., p. 458.
18. Ibid., p. 455.

Cinema

11

The Encounter of Modernities: Cinematic Adaptations of Two Stories by Aitmatov

Rashmi Doraiswamy

I
MODERN, MODERNITY, MODERNISM

The terms 'Modernity' and 'Modernism' refer to effects of the Modern and cover different aspects of the Modern. The Modern in its everyday usage stands for the contemporary as distinct from the traditional. It also signifies the period in Western history that dates from the Renaissance. The landmarks of the Modern include, among others, the Protestant and Reform Movements that challenged the authority of the Roman Catholic Church, Erasmus' scepticism, Galileo's scientific discourses, the Industrial Revolutions in France and England....

The socio-economic, political and cultural effects of this period are usually classified under the term 'Modernity'. According to Lawrence Cahoone, "'Modernity'... has a relatively fixed reference in contemporary intellectual discussion.... It refers to the new civilization developed in Europe and North America over the last several centuries and fully evident by the early twentieth century. 'Modernity' implies that this civilization is modern in the strong sense that it is unique in human history.... Everyone admits that Europe and North America developed a new, powerful technique for the study of nature, as well as new machine technologies and modes of industrial production that have led to an unprecedented rise in material living standards. It is this form of 'modernity' that is today described as 'modernization' or simply 'development' in the non-Western world. This modern Western civilization is generally characterized as well by other traits, such as capitalism, a largely secular culture, liberal democracy, individualism, rationalism, humanism."[1]

Modernism refers to movements in the arts and philosophy in the Western world, roughly between 1850 and 1950.

The prehistory of the Modern would be the Feudal if the Modern is seen in the context of economic and political systemic change. The prehistory of Modernity would be Tradition if Modernity is defined by the effects of the modern on social, political and cultural life. Modernism's prehistory is Realism in the arts.

The possible relationships amongst these three phenomena are many. The Modern period saw three major movements in the Arts: Romanticism, Realism, Modernism. Modernity engaged with traditional representations through Realism, and then engaged with Realism through Modernism. To quote Cahoone again, "At any rate, one way of understanding the relation of the terms 'modern', 'modernity' and 'modernism' is that aesthetic modernism is a form of art characteristic of high or actualised or late modernity, that is, of that period in which social, economic, and cultural life in the widest sense were revolutionized by modernity. By no means does this imply that modernist art endorses modernization, or simply expresses the aims of modernity. But it does mean that modernist art is scarcely thinkable outside the context of the modernized society of the late nineteenth and twentieth centuries. Social modernity is the home of modernist art, even when that art rebels against it".[2]

This schema, however, is not universally applicable. According to some writers, the Renaissance in Asia occurred much earlier in the eleventh and twelfth centuries.[3] Here the debate with tradition envisaged the new in a premodern/ feudal context. The Asian Renaissance is defined by some of the above, but not all, of the markers of modernity.

In colonial and other contexts, where modernity is brought

in in an escalated manner, many time-frames begin to coexist. In Central Asia, for instance, the transition after the formation of the Soviet Union was one from pre-modern to that which was conceived as post-capitalist, that is, socialist. From a mythic consciousness, these societies engaged not just with Realism, but with Socialist Realism. This paradigm is similar to that of many colonised and post-colonial countries that adopted and adapted Western Realism in the Arts. The 'prehistories' of the modern, modernity and modernism, began to adapt to the new. The new also incorporated the older forms. Realism, for instance, would thus begin to bloom, but with a strong streak of Romanticism. Since the Realism of these societies was not developing as a canon against Romanticism, or prose was not pitting itself against the dominant genre of poetry, hybrid impulses could be felt coursing through the veins of this literature. It is the freshness of this impulse that Konstantin Simonov refers to, when he speaks of Aitmatov's prose: "When I think of the wonderful Kirgiz writer Chingiz Aitmatov then for me it is not only associated with the thought of the appearance in our multi-national literature of yet another happy talent, strong and pure. This phenomenon has a wider significance. Along with Aitmatov, a new strain of a very special, severe, and at the same time, a tender, a firmly grounded romanticism of a very high order has appeared in our literature".[4]

The difference between the processes of colonisation and the processes of socialism initiated in precapitalist societies would be that the latter, by virtue of occurring a few centuries later, had the advantage of the repertoire of knowledge of earlier social formations. The processes were also quick and result-oriented, backed by a political will that was conscious of its own self. The literacy campaign, as part of the Enlightenment project and one of the effects of modernity in the Central Asian states was far more thorough and far-reaching than the complicated and slow processes through which Western education became part of colonised societies. Alex Stringer points out that "Levels of education in Central Asia were very low at the time of the Bolshevik take-over: literacy was as little as 2 per cent among the native population (although it was over

35 per cent among Russians). ... Literacy is one area in which Central Asia appeared to be on the cusp of parity with the more developed parts of the USSR. Soviet census statistics show a leap from 3.6 per cent average literacy amongst the nationalities of Central Asia in 1926, to 52.1 per cent by 1959."[5]

II
THE 'THAW' GENERATION

Chingiz Aitmatov is one of the Soviet literary authors most adapted into cinema, theatre and opera. The works have been adapted by Central Asian artists as well as Russians.[6] This paper focuses on the adaptation of two short stories by Aitmatov into films by Larissa Shepitko and Andrei Mikhalkov-Konchalovsky. *The Camel-like Eye* (*Verblyuzhij Glaz*/1954) and *The First Teacher* (*Pervij Uchitel'*/1955) inspired *Heat* (*Znoi*/1963) by Larissa Shepitko and *The First Teacher* by Andrei Mikhalkov-Konchalovsky (1965). Aitmatov's *Jamilia*, written in 1953, had made him famous in the Soviet Union and abroad.

In the first phase of his career, when Aitmatov was still working with short stories, he was following socialist realism as a guide to writing to the last rule. This was the time of the last period of Stalin's reign, of the opening up after his death[7], a little before the XX Party Congress in which Krushchev denounced the cult of personality.

The Camel-Like Eye takes up the theme of the clash of generations at work where old and new attitudes to labour are explored. *The First Teacher*, set in the early 1920s is a layered story about the sacrifices and commitment of the first generation of communists and Party workers after the Revolution. Both stories have as their lead protagonist an outsider who comes into a Kirgiz village and ruffles feathers with his new ideas. These outsiders are of Kirgiz origin, but are 'outsiders' not only because they have lived elsewhere before they arrive at the village or aiil, but by virtue of their ideas. Their progressive ideas bring them into conflict with their new surroundings.

The changes made during adaptation are not merely due to the filmmakers' predisposition, but reflect the change in the times as well. When the works were adapted, nearly a decade later by the filmmakers, the Soviet Union was well into the period of the Thaw. This influenced the interpretation of the literary works by the filmmakers who were themselves products of the Thaw generation of filmmakers.

The 1960s saw the emergence of a whole range of filmmakers who were questioning previous modes of filmmaking and working out new styles with their diploma or very first films. Among them were Marlen Khutsiev (*I am Twenty*/1964), Andrei Tarkovsky (*Ivan's Childhood*/1962), Sergei Parazhanov (*Shadows of our Forgotten Ancestors*/1964), Georgi Shengalaya (*Pirosmani*/1968), and from Central Asia, Shukrat Abbasov and Ali Khamraev from Uzbekistan (*Tashkent, City of Plenty*/1968), Tolomush Okeev from Kirgizia among others.[8]

Russian film historian Evgeny Margolit points out that although Kirgizia was the last to develop its own cinema among the Central Asian Republics, within ten years of its inception from the 1950s to the 1960s, critics were already talking of the 'Kirgiz miracle'. One of the reasons, according to him, was the lack of standard equipment.

> Another reason for the late development of cinema was that the people of this Republic were at the stage of clans and tribes when the Revolution broke out. The sharp and sudden launch into a new historical phase led to great deal of introspection over what was happening. The generation of the 'Thaw' had the capacity to deal with and theorise about global changes: on the one hand, was the reality of the traditional way of life with its mytho-poetic basis; on the other, word culture, particularly European culture, which it had imbibed. The feeling of existing simultaneously, in a parallel way, in two different worlds, and the suffering caused by having to choose between two close but non-corresponding worlds, was characteristic of all Central Asian cultures but was most acutely felt in Kyrgyzstan. This explains the appearance of a phenomenon like Chingiz Aitmatov, a writer, whose role and authority in Soviet culture in the last decades of the USSR cannot be overrated. His prose in a certain sense provided Soviet culture with definitive narrative parameters....
>
> That is why the 'Kyrgyz miracle' in feature filmmaking begins with the adaptation of stories by Aitmatov: Larisa Shepitko's *Heat* based on *Camel's Eye* and Andrei Mikhalkov-Konchalovsky's *First Teacher*. Both these films... were collaborations with Mosfilm and

> were made by people who had come to Kyrgyzstan for the first time. The views of a talented new 'Thaw' generation, not bound by cinematic stamps, allowed for the cinematographic opening of the landscape of the Republic and defining the imaging of the people and their existence. It is precisely through the debut works of directors, who went on to become famous Russian directors, that the Republic received its first opening into feature filmmaking.[9]

It is possible to delineate the aspiration towards a kind of modernism *within* the parameters of socialist realism. As such this modernism was very different from the outrightly modernist works of the 1920s in the Soviet Union in the arts. The modernism of the 1960s can be defined to a large extent by its debate with the canons of socialist realism. In the cinema it veers towards a new classicism, creating ever new models of depth, saturation and images of the duration of time in the works of Tarkovsky, towards a new primitivism and simplicity in the works of Parazhanov and a questioning of the rhetoric of the 'positive hero' in the works of Shepitko. Where the works of the 'socialist modernists' deviated from socialist realism, was in the construction of narrative, character and image. What they, however, shared with the dominant canon, in distinction from European modernism, was the emphasis on connectivity with the people and with a history. They thus asserted the primacy of the notion of 'totality' and 'wholeness' anathema to European modernism, built on notions of fragmentation and alienation. In fact, the Soviet Avant Garde of the 1920s, too, particularly in the work of artists who either aligned themselves with the Socialist Revolution or were Fellow Travellers, also focused on innovations within their forms rather than on the angst of solitariness in a disintegrated world.

The concept of 'totality' was an important part of the debate on Realism and Modernism in the Western world. Georg Lukacs makes the following distinction between the aesthetics of Modernism and Realism:

> Man, for these writers, is by nature solitary, asocial, unable to enter into relationships with other human beings....
>
> This basic solitariness of man must not be confused with that individual solitariness to be found in the literature of traditional

> realism. In the latter case, we are dealing with a particular situation in which a human being may be placed, due either to his character or to the circumstances of his life.... But it is always merely a fragment, a phase, a climax or anti-climax, in the life of the community as a whole. The fate of such individuals is characteristic of certain human types in specific social or historical circumstances. ... In a word, their solitariness is a specific social fate, not a *condition humaine*.
>
> The latter, of course, is characteristic of the theory and practice of modernism.... Man is 'thrown-into-being'. This implies, not merely that man is constitutionally unable to establish relationships with things or people outside himself; but also that it is impossible to determine theoretically the origin and goal of human existence.[10]

Criticising Lukacs' views on German Expressionism and his notion of 'totality', Ernst Bloch states:

> Lukacs's thought takes for granted a closed and integrated reality that does indeed exclude the subjectivity of idealism, but not the seamless 'totality' which has always thriven best in idealist sytems, including those of German classical philosophy. Whether such a totality in fact constitutes reality, is open to question. ... What if authentic reality is also discontinuity? Since Lukacs operates with a closed , objectivistic conception of reality, when he comes to examine Expressionism he resolutely rejects any attempt on the part of the artists to shatter any image of the world, even that of capitalism. Any art which strives to exploit the *real* fissures in surface inter-relations and to discover the new in their crevices, appears in his eyes merely as a wilful act of destruction. He thereby equates experiment in demolition with a condition of decadence.[11]

This debate about totality was not of relevance to the modernism of the Soviet 1960s. The emphasis was on formal, characterolo-gical and thematic innovations. In fact, both the socialist realists and modernists engaged with the larger social contexts their characters were inscribed in. The breaking of all unities, the fragmenting of the body, of vision and the disintegration of the material world, even if it provided a higher form of realism, was alien to the Soviet ethos. This was probably due to the long tradition, more than a century old of making the *narod* (the people) the centre of philosophical, political and cultural debates. For the new modernists of the Soviet 1960s, the very possibility of speaking of their history and themselves without conforming entirely to the straightjacket of socialist realism was a step forward.

The distinctions between those who tried to innovate within the parameters of Realism and those who crossed its limits, are not often very clear. Elements of Realism and Modernism coexist in several works, creating hybrid forms. In the case of Aitmatov's stories and their adaptations, the fact of filmmakers from the European part of Soviet Union encountering their Asian counterparts unleashes its own dynamics. Is the 'Modern' that is being articulated in the story and film then different, and how 'Modernist' is the articulation?

III
THE ADAPTATIONS

Kirgizia saw rapid modernisation after the creation of national socialist republics in Central Asia in 1924. The new republics saw change at an unprecedented level. Two of the most important markers of modernization in the Soviet period in Kirgizia were the literacy drive and the drive to educate women. According to Robert Lowe, "The 1920s and 1930s were also years of structural change in Kyrgyz society. Soviet schools were opened and the previously negligible level of literacy shot up during the 1930s. Islam, a major element in Central Asian identity, was suppressed, while the *khudzhum* (attack) campaign encouraged women to enter education and the workplace. For the nomadic Kyrgyz, the most significant Soviet scheme was the forced settlement and collectivisation drive. A centuries-old way of life, and much of its accompanying tradition, was brought to an abrupt end as the rural system was transformed."[12] Both the stories by Aitmatov address these two important modernisation drives of literacy, particularly for women and mechanisation of cultivation.

The critique of authoritarianism within and without the Party became an important theme in the post-Stalin times in socialist realist and modernist works. In Aitmatov's works, the critique was built up gradually within the parameters of socialist realism. In his first stories, it is the internal weakness of character of the main protagonist that propels the narrative forward. Later, in works such as *Farewell, Gulsary!* and *White Ship*, it is the conflict between the positive, creative characters and the negative ones that drives the narrative to a climax. Conflict is thus 'socialised'. In Aitmatov's works of the first period, the problem of how to represent conflict in a society that was ostensibly peopled with the new Soviet Man is felt deeply. It is, in fact, one of the themes of *The Camel-Like Eye*. Kemel, the young idealist, who has come to a beautiful and remote aiil with the dream of becoming a tractorist finds himself in conflict with the thirty-year-old Abakir, the man who drives the sole tractor in the area and does not easily allow anyone else to drive his tractor. Unfriendly and hard, he makes Kemel wonder what makes men like Abakir so cruel and unbending. Vladimir Voronov points out:

> Taking up issue with contemporary problems and characters, Chingiz Aitmatov could not ignore the ugly phenomena of life, ignore limited, greedy, evil people. ...
>
> ....
>
> In *The Camel-Like Eye*, this question is sharply raised by the author and the young hero of the novella although the answer to it ... cannot be given by Aitmatov now. Maybe, after five-eight years in *Farewell, Gulsary!* and *White Ship*, the prose writer will be able to expose and research the social reasons for the appearance of such people...
>
> As of now the social core of Abakir's character, and those characters similar to him , is not clear to the author. He is however convinced of one thing — the psychological incompatibility of people such as the young Kemel and Abakir. It manifests itself in everything: in work, in love, in relationships with people, to the past, to spiritual values....
>
> The conflict between Kemel and Abakir is not just a conflict between two characters, but is a conflict of two worldviews, communist and petty-bourgeois...[13]

The Camel-Like Eye contrasts the enthusiasm of youth with hardened age; the ability to work with others with the inability to accommodate others. Even if the older tractorist is a good worker, his inability to get on with his colleagues is represented as a negative trait.

The old statue of the woman with the camel-like eye, standing from time immemorial, watching historical times come and go, which lends the story its title in the literary work, is dispensed with by Shepitko. This is probably one of the reasons she changed the title of the film to *Heat*. There is a 'thinning' of narrative, a 'flattening' in the film that makes its aesthetic intention quite different from that of the short story. The 'baba' on the wayside in the story gives a sense of another time, a distanced one, from which the events that happen are watched. This sense of distance is absent from the film.

The First Teacher contrasts the raw enthusiasm of the first generation of party workers with the post-World War II period where the struggles of the older generation are forgotten, and a superciliousness has crept in, with all the progress and modernity, towards the pioneers, who may not have been very enlightened. Altynai, one of the lead protagonists of the story, a sought-after academician, says of her first teacher, who is now serving as a village postman, "I've seen such things happen before, this case was not unique. And that is why I am asking myself: when did we forget to how to respect an ordinary man the way Lenin respected him? I'm glad at least that we now speak about such things frankly without hypocrisy. It's very good that in this, at least, we have come so much closer to Lenin".[14] The reference is to the period of Thaw, the need to 'go back' to Leninist principles, and to respect 'ordinary people'.

Aitmatov, in fact, raises the problem of representation of these issues within this long story. The story is narrated by an artist who is wondering how to paint this little history that has come her way in the form of a letter from Altynai, who explains why she left the banquet organised in her honour in her native Kirgiz village and returned abruptly to Moscow. The letter is thus also a confession of the complexity of Altynai's feelings towards her first teacher. Altynai's narration is a 'flashback'. The events she speaks of happen in the 1920s. She is an orphan, the oldest student in the school that Diushen, despite the scepticism of the villagers, sets up. This is the first school of the village. Her feelings for him are those of respect and affection for someone who has taken notice of her for the first time in her life and wants to teach the illiterate children the little that he knows. She does not like being away from him and longs for his return when he is away. When she is married off against her will, and subjected to torture, it is Diushen who saves her. Whatever his feelings for her, Diushen realises that her capabilities in the field of academics lie beyond anything he may have to teach and that she deserves a better education. He arranges for her to go to a proper school in another city. At the station he assures her that he will tend to the poplars they have planted: " 'Well, we must say goodbye'. Diushen took me in his arms and kissed me hard on the forehead. 'Good luck, good bye, my dearest'..."[15] Confused by his own feelings, he runs after the train she leaves in, shouting her name.

> There was such urgency in his shout as if he suddenly realised he had not told me something terribly important, but now it was too late, and he knew it. Till this day I can hear that shout, rising from the very heart, the very depths of his soul.
>
> The train dived into a tunnel, came out onto a stretch of straight road and, gathering speed, carried me through the Kazakh plains to my new life...
>
> Good-bye, teacher, good-bye, my first school, my childhood, good-bye, my first love... .[16]

The story ends with the artist debating what images she should paint in her painting. By creating a narration within a narration, Aitmatov is doing much more than creating a sense of time having passed and things having changed for the better and worse. He is, in fact, pointing to the possibility of the 'real' history being missed, not once, but many times over, not just in lived experience, but also in art. The authentic history is not the opening of the new school, but the forgetting of the first school and its teacher and their significance.

> I was so upset, so ashamed of myself, that's why I decided to leave at once. I knew I could not face Diushen, I could not look him straight in the eyes....
>
> I felt embarrassed and ashamed for another reason too: it's not I that all that attention should have been lavished on, it's not I who should have had the place of honour at the school opening ceremony. That should have been the privilege of our first teacher,

> the first Communist in our village, Diushen.... But everything was just the other way about. We were smugly enjoying the banquet, while he, that man of pure gold, had been riding hard to deliver the telegrams of congratulations to us, and after that he hurried off to deliver the rest of the mail.[17]

The adaptation by Mikhalkov-Konchalovsky dispenses with this layering of narrative in flashback. The film begins with Diushen entering the aiil and his idea of setting up a school being met with hostility by the village community. The film, thus, does not unfold from the point of view of the artist or Altynai. The film ends with Altynai leaving for another town and Diushen going back to the aiil. On his return he finds that the school has burnt down. He starts cutting wood to build another school and is joined by the local people. The farewell scene too, at the station, is made more explicit, eliding the ambivalence of feelings and their expression in the novella. The poignancy of the ending in the novella is thus missing. The larger context of the contrast between the post-Revolution times and the post-Stalin times is lost.

K. Bobulov points out, "Chingiz Aitmatov's innovativeness lies in the fact that he notices new aspects in the character of the Kirgiz people, which have appeared in the Soviet period."[18] *The First Teacher*, in fact, encapsulates in the small form of the novella, the sharp contrast between the time of revolutionary zeal and the time when progress and modernisation had blunted the memory of the sacrifices of the post-1917 generations, not just for the Kirgiz people, but for the Soviet Union as a whole. According to Vladimir Voronov,

> The protagonist of Aitmatov's novella became the epitome of representative characteristics of the communist-Leninist in the Soviet prose of the sixties. At that time in criticism there often rose voices putting under suspicion the necessity in literature of the character of the positive hero. The novella was written at a time when in literature fairly complex processes were taking place, when under the flag of the struggle with dogmatism, in the name of self evaluative analysis, there were voices which did not fully appreciate the creative, transformative and educative function of the writer's word.
>
> That is why *The First Teacher* became for the thirty-three year

> old Kirgiz prose writer an examination of his maturity as a citizen, and a specific, original answer to the schematic constructions of modernising critics.[19]

The novella's delicate use of sentiment in the changing relationship between teacher and student also encapsulated social conditions that had changed very fast. The story of Altynai, who became an important academician, far outpacing her humble teacher in the span of two decades, 'corresponds' to the 'reality' of the rapid rise in literacy levels in the Republic. G. Gachev, a specialist in Aitmatov's works, astutely notes that it is not only Altynai who could not meet the eyes of her teacher; Diushen, too, would have found it difficult, had he come face to face with her, to meet her eyes. "And this is why she is afraid in the aiil—because of the fear of one's roots."[20] What the film lacks is the strain of nostalgic romance and romanticism, that runs through Aitmatov's story. There is also the implication that Altynai, in going away from the aiil, moved away from a limited social realm into a world that offered her choices far greater than what even Diushen would have dreamed of for her.

The film thus presents a relatively non-ambivalent reading of the novella. For Konchalovsky, Diushen is the most important character. The revolutionary nature of his commitment, portrayed in the novel, is underplayed, although the fact of his having a completely different point of view on life, different to the point of seeming idiotic, is shown in the film. Gachev, too, notes that Diushen is an 'idiot', but in the Dostoevskian sense: "...Diushen is a completely transparent form.... The forces of attraction go through him, without any barrier, tying people to each other and to the big world. He just fixes them like Prince Myshkin, also an 'idiot' from the world of Don Quixotes. ... He only ... moves with air and spirit. And this soul performs miracles with this weak flesh."[21]

The film deviates from the story in several crucial ways. The film dispenses with the three-layered structure of the novel. One of the script writers of the film is Aitmatov. He is also, therefore implicated in this simplifying of narrative. If Margolit is to be believed, these films actually paved the way for the Kyrgyz cinema to flower. The more difficult passage to different flashbacks may well have been the reluctance to confuse the audience that did not have a well developed cinematic tradition with so many layerings.

Certain scenes are bypassed while others are introduced. The centrality of the motif of the poplars to the story, the mark of 'Diushen's spiritual love for Altynai' is absent in the film. The new school, to inaugurate which Academician Altynai comes to Kukureyu again, and which triggers off a chain of memories and events in which she recalls her passage to youth as a student of Diushen, is also presented in a different way.

The new school is built in the film after Altynai leaves for studies in Tashkent. It is built because the old one is burnt down, when he is away, killing and injuring some of the children inside. The entire village wants him to leave, but Diushen refuses to, cutting down wood to build a new school. The film ends with the titles coming on to the sound of the trees being felled, as one of his few well-wishers joins him in felling the tree. The contrast is interesting: in the story two poplars are sown by Diushen and Altynai, which are called 'Diushen's school' by later post-war generations that do not even know that his rudimentary school had existed there; in the film, the tree is cut down to build a new school.

The simplification of narrative involves the two script writers of the film and the director. (The credits state: 'Authors of the script — Chingiz Aitmatov and Boris Dobroded' with the participation of Mikhalkov-Konchalovsky.) This small network of three would have been inscribed in a bigger system, which would include other smaller systems such as censorship, funding, the nascent stage of the film industry in Kyrgyzstan and the developed cinema of western Soviet Union. What is at work here are two imagined 'others' vis-à-vis modernity that have come into play in the final film text: Mikhalkov-Konchalovsky's vision of literacy being brought to Kyrgyzstan as an 'outside' modernising process of socialism and Aitmatov's conceding to this reading of his own story, and actively contributing to the refashioning of the literary work for the screen. For him, probably, the act was modernist, in accepting the non-inviolability of the 'original', and — for us —

postmodernist in impulse in his participation of the 'pleasure' of creating a variant of his own narrative! This seems to be the reason that details of the plot, that are not very crucial to the unfolding of the film's narrative, have also been changed. Altynai's husband's first wife, for instance, in the story is happy to be free when he is arrested. In the film she is unhappy and starts crying.

The film is about the coming of modernity to a sleepy aiil in Kyrgyzstan. Aitmatov's story was about forgetting the 'real histories' of the struggle to modernise, now that modernity is here!

The biggest casualty of this rewriting of the narrative is the complexity of the emotions of love between Diushen and Altynai. This is a bonding that begins in the manner of a kinship tie, but carries within it the possibility of other relationships. In the book, Altynai only articulates the different facets of the cluster of feelings she has in her heart for Diushen. The film makes it into a more straightforward love story. Diushen is less hesitant in expressing his feelings for her. In the goodbye scene in the railway station in the film he kisses her on the lips, whereas in the story he kisses her on the forehead.

The aesthetic project of the director and writer are not the same. Aitmatov was practising the canon of socialist realism. It is we who can provide a modernist reading of this realist text in the manner of Barthes reading the classic realist author Balzac's *Sarrasine* in a post-structuralist manner in *S/Z*. In our reading, it is the problem of representation that is being foregrounded, not as a crisis of realist representation, as it was in Western modernism, but as part of the realist project itself, as an attempt to capture 'real histories'. Konchalovsky, on the contrary, is on the one hand, taking up the theme of modernisation in Kyrgyzstan, as a one-way process, from the West to the East. On the other, he is inscribing a critique of the rhetoric of socialist realism, a critique that is absent in Aitmatov. We thus see two different articulations of the modernist impulse in the story and film: Aitmatov's modernism integrates itself into socialist realism; Konchalovsky's stands at a distance from the demands of socialist realism. This emerges in certain sequences, where the teacher is teaching the students. In the very first class he takes, he comes across as authoritarian and unable to control his emotions. The sequence begins with his teaching the children a few basics and telling the students about world revolution and Lenin. He then asks the children if they have any questions. The children muster up the courage to speak. On further urging, Altynai asks about death. The children then ask if they will die and the teacher, too will die one day. Diushen answers these questions sportingly enough. However, when one of the children innocently asks whether Lenin, too, will die, he loses control and shakes the child so hard that he starts crying. The other children cower, frightened of this sudden change in mood and know better than to ask questions.

The mise-en-scene of this scene is also interesting, and is part of the Thaw cultural ambience. There are hens in the foreground cackling and running about throughout the scene. This, when lofty issues like 'World Revolution' and 'Lenin' are being discussed. The incongruity of his lecturing to the small kids, on their very first entry into the 'classroom' on these issues, is presented as comic initially, but it turns serious with his change of mood. Konchalovsky also weaves in an obsessive trait in Diushen's character, a facet missing in the story. There is a hint in the film that the teacher's obsession with Lenin could well turn into fanaticism. On one of his visits to the city he learns of Lenin's death. He returns to the aiil late at night and wakes up all the inhabitants, determined not to allow them to sleep in peace. In the next scene, he is seen talking to an old man, who has been sympathetic to him. On the wall is the picture of Lenin he had put up. The picture is now crumpled and there is a cross created by the folds of the paper on Lenin's face. The cross and the crumpled look of the picture call up their own associations. (The picture of Lenin Diushen puts up in his school is shown several times and after the first time, it is crumpled.) The old man says that there cannot be a second sun in the universe. Diushen says that nothing would change and there would be a hundred 'suns'—the lights brought about by the electrification of the Soviet Union. The discussion is once again part of the Thaw milieu where the issue of whether something would change or not in the nature of leadership after the death of Lenin is being referred to. The old man's face is impassive and his expression inscrutable when Diushen talks of there being no change. Konchalovsky is also showing how difficult the realisation of the establishment of socialism in one country is, let alone the world revolution that the teacher keeps talking of. In one scene, the children in the school repeat after the teacher the word 'socialism'; the camera moves out and we see the mountains, eternal and unchanging and a few horses in the distance. This is a sleeping landscape in which it seems nothing will ever change. Yet, he is determined to save Altynai. When the village community attacks him for bringing back Altynai and getting her husband arrested, he tells them that she is the 'first, free woman of the East' and that although she was alone today, there would soon be many like her. The story avoids this series of confrontations between the teacher and the village community and is softer in its delineation of the teacher's ideological commitment.

Conclusion

The analysis of the two adaptations of Aitmatov's works foreground interesting consequences of the encounters between texts from Russia and Central Asia in the larger context of Soviet socialism. While the written works are far more layered in time-frames, the films are more straightforward in their presentation of the narratives. Aitmatov's works, particularly in the early phase are part of a larger modernising impulse, of breaking with those aspects of tradition, or of everyday life that are claustrophobic and limiting of an individual's aspirations. The enlightenment project is best encapsulated in the figure of the 'outsider' in both stories, who is a catalyst of change. Aitmatov firmly positions himself on the side of the Modern with an aspiration to Modernity, critiquing all those feudal and traditional values that hinder progress. There is also an engagement with Modernism within the framework of socialist realism. This modernism is of a socialist realist kind. The differing time-frames posited in both stories, create disjunctions in the linear narrative. (This technique of disjunctive time-frames matured in Aitmatov's later works to include autonomous narratives with legend, myth on one hand, and science fiction on the other.) The differing time-frames of the early works is, in fact, creating a realist discourse under different gazes, thus putting the veracity of a single point of view under question.

The film adaptations of the works, even if they had Aitmatov's active cooperation, were less complex. In going into the interiors to the Asian part of the Soviet Union, these two directors were interpreting their history from their own point of view. For them, this was the exotic. Both films, in fact, simplify the literary texts they are based on. There is a flattening of the narrative. They emphasise the themes of modernising traditional lives in a linear narrative. One may conjecture that there is thus a conjunction of two factors in this drive towards simplification: an Orientalism according to which change is affected only from the outside; and the setting up of a tradition of filmmaking that would be more mass-oriented, thus calling for lesser flashbacks and stories within stories. In their reading, what is important is that first, the modern view comes from the outside. Both filmmakers highlight this and take away any other framings of narrative that point to other references

If these filmmakers are modernist in these two films, it is only because they break the sense of totality provided by the stories. Modernism in fact harks back to Romanticism in its fascination for the other or the exotic, and often in its nostalgia for an imagined simplicity of the Other. It is this imagined conception of the Other that has prompted the specific adaptations of the stories.

The 'encounter of modernities' thus throws up interesting points for consideration. Kyrgyz writer Aitmatov, who honed his talents in the Soviet school of socialist realism, produced works that were more in tune with the larger problematic of socialist aesthetics, while mixing modernist elements into it, creating a quietly hybrid form. These stories were read in a romantic realistic way by the 'western', Russian filmmakers, coming to the 'East'. (Konchalovsky was to later emigrate to the West, to Hollywood. This film, therefore, may well have an attempt to deliberately stay away from the mainstream, since he could not subscribe to Soviet views either ideologically or aesthetically.) While both Shepitko and Mikhalkov-Konchalovsky were to make many more films, and these stories were as much part of their early oeuvre as they were part of Aitmatov's own early literary career, it is Aitmatov who emerges as the more complex artist, even though he is working within the framework of socialist realism! Such is the paradox of aesthetic practice, that the filmmakers who are not only credited with laying the foundation for a modern Kyrgyz cinema, but of also creating works that debated with socialist realism in the western part of the Soviet Union, subscribed to romantic notions of 'the Other' and 'the East' in *Heat* and *The First Teacher*.

NOTES AND REFERENCES

1. Introduction, *From Modernism to Postmodernism*, Lawrence Cahoone (ed.), Blackwell Publishers, Oxford, 1996, p. 11.
2. Ibid, p. 13.
3. Chingiz Aitmatov and Shakhanov, for instance, state: "The West and the East, huge regions of the earth, situated at a significant distance from each other, during the course of several hundreds of years, developed in very different ways. In the XI-XII centuries, the countries of the East were richer, in their culture and economy, science and literature flowered. The Asian Renaissance and Enlightenment began". *Plach Okhotnika Nad Propastiyu: Ispoved' na Iskhode Veka*, Chingiz Aitmatov and Mukhtar Shakhanov, Rayan, Almaty, 1996, p. 284.
4. Konstantin Simonov in *Zemnaya Pravda Romantiki*, in *Pravda* 18.12.1965, quoted in 'Chingiz Aitmatov' by K Bobulov in *Istoriya Kirgizskoii Sovetskoi Literatury*, Nauka, Moskva, 1970, p. 474.
5. 'Soviet Development in Central Asia: The Classic Colonial Syndrome?' by Alex Stringer in *Central Asia: Aspects of Transition*, p. 156.
6. Selected List of Adaptations of Aitmatov's Works:
   Into Film—
   Jamilia by I. Popslavskaya; *Echo Lyubvi* based on *Na Reke Baidamtal*; *Krasnoe Yabloko* by Tolomush Okeev; *Znoi* based on *Verblyuzhij Glaz* by Larissa Shepitko; *Pervij Uchitel* by Andrei Mikhalkov-Konchalovsky; *Beg Inokhodtsa* based on *Proshai Gulsary!* by S. Urusevsky; *Belij Parakhod* by Bolotbek Shamshiev; *Voskhozhdeniye na Fudjiyamu* by Bolotbek Shamsiev and the telefilm *Arman* based on *Cvidaniye s Synom*. There were also reports that *Tavro Kassandry*

would be shot aboard the Mir Space Station.

Into Opera :

Jamilia by Composer Raukhberger; *Krai Tyulpanov*, based on motifs from *Topolek...* by Rudyansky (operetta); *Mat'* based on *Materinskoe Pole* by Composers A. Maldybaev and V. Vlasov.

Into Ballet :

Asel, based on motifs from *Topolek...* by Bolshoi Theatre.

Into Theatre :

Materinskoe Pole, adapted by many theatres; Composition of *Materinskoe Pole* for stage in two parts by V. Lvov Anokhin.

7. Joseph Stalin died on 9 March, 1953.
8. Andrei Tarkovsky is said to have contributed in credited and uncredited ways to many of the films from Central Asia in this period: Zahid Sabitov's *Look Out, Snake!*/1979/Uzbekfilm (script); Shaken Aimanov's *The End of Ataman*/1971/Kazakhfilm (coscriptwriter); Bagrat Oganisian's *The Sharp-Tasting Grapes*/ 1973 (artistic advisor); Tolomush Okeyev's *The Ferovious One*/ 1973/Kirgizfilm, and even to Konchalovsky's *Pervij Uchitel'*.
9. 'Central Asia: Shared History, Many Destinies' by Evgeny Margolit in *Being and Becoming: The Cinemas of Asia*, Aruna Vasudev, Latika Padgaonkar, Rashmi Doraiswamy (eds.), Macmillan, Delhi, 2002, p. 55.
10. *The Meaning of Contemporary Realism*, Georg Lukacs, Merlin Press, London, 1979, pp. 20-21.
11. 'Discussing Expressionism' by Ernst Bloch in *Aesthetics and Politics*, Verso, London, 1980, p. 22.
12. 'Nation Building and Identity in the Kyrgyz Republic' by Robert Lowe in *Central Asia: Aspects of Transition*, Tom Everett-Heath, Routledge Curzon, London, 2003, p. 110.
13. *Chingiz Aitmatov: Ocherk Tvorchestvo*, Vladimir Voronov, Sovetskij Pisatel', Moscow, 1976, pp. 84-85.
14. 'Diushen' (aka 'The First Teacher') in *Piebald Dog Running Along the Shore*, Chingiz Aitmatov, Raduga Publishers, Moscow, 1989, p. 143.
15. Ibid, p. 136.
16. Ibid, 136.
17. Ibid, pp. 142-143.
18. 'Chingiz Aitmatov' by K Bobulov in *Istoriya Kirgizskoii Sovetskoi Literatury*, Nauka, Moscow, 1970, p. 477.
19. *Chingiz Aitmatov: Ocherk Tvorchestvo*, Vladimir Voronov, Sovetskij Pisatel', Moscow, 1976, p. 112.
20. *Chingiz Aitmatov i Mirovaya Literatura*, G. Gachev, Kyrgyzstan, Frunze, 1982, p. 168.
21. Ibid., p. 125.

II. NEW HORIZONS

Thinkers, Travellers, Explorers

12

Remembering Al Farabi

Devendra Kaushik

Al Farabi has an added significance in the current international situation when certain forces have launched a tirade both on the national and global scene against Islam accusing it of fostering intolerance, fanaticism and hatred resulting in acts of terrorism. It is important in this context to project the rational and enlightened face of Islam as represented by Al Farabi, who was born in Central Asia and after a short stay in Bukhara for studies, proceeded to Baghdad for further studies, living there for most of his life during the first half of the tenth century.

Although Al-Farabi was born in a small village on the territory of present-day Kazakhstan, it would be more appropriate to refer to him as a Central Asian or even ancient Eastern scholar. About his early life we do not know much. Before the twelfth century, no full bibliography of his had existed. His fame began to grow as a result of the renown of Avicenna or Abu Ali Ibn-Sina (1980–1037 A.D.), author of several works on medicine and philosophy, whose work, *Canon of Medical Science*, was translated into Latin in the twelfth century. In his writings Ibn-Sina mentioned himself as Farabi's successor in philosophy. Hence when in the twelfth-thirteenth centuries Arab biographers began to write about philosophers in the Islamic world, there was scanty information available. This often resulted in tendentious reconstructions based on legends. Thus while Ebn Abi Ossaybia mentioned that Farabi's father was of Persian descent, Ebn Kallekan was out to prove that he was ethnically Turkish.[1] According to M. Mahadi, "Ultimately pointless as the quest for Farabi's ethnic origins might be, the fact remains that we do not have sufficient evidence to decide the matter".[2] Ebn Kallekan, in line with his pro-Turkish bias claims that Farabi knew no Arabic when he came to Baghdad but only "Turkish and numerous other languages and that he mastered Arabic only afterwards". He also writes that Farabi knew more than seventy languages. It is interesting to note that in his work on logic, Farabi's references and glosses are confined to Persian, Sogdian and Greek, but no Turkish.[3] However, M. Mahadi suggests on the basis of Al Farabi's allegedly particular brand of Platonism, that he studied in Constantinople.[4] That Farabi knew Greek and stayed in Greece for eight years, informs the unpublished *Kabul Manuscript*.[5]

Renaissance of Ideas

In the ninth-tenth centuries, a great upsurge in science and literature occurred in Central Asia. The work of Mohammed Ibn-Musa al Khwarezimi, the founder of Arab mathematics is related to this period. It is from the title of his work *AI Jabr* that the term algebra is derived. He was not only a mathematician but also an astronomer, geographer and historian. His work represents a synthesis of Indian algebra and Greek geometry which forms the basis of modern mathematics, largely influenced by Indian and Greek cultures which had arisen on the basis of such practical needs as irrigation, travel, trade and construction.[6]

It is through his works that the Arabs learnt the science of mathematics. With the establishment of Arab power in Central Asia, there began a process of dialogue between the Buddhist-Hindu, Indian, Greek and Islamic ideas. Several new schools of thought appeared which sought readjustment to new situations. According to a noted Indian scholar of medieval history, K.A. Nizami, "When the Abbasid Caliphs evinced interest in Indian sciences and invited Indian scholars to work in their bureau of translations, a new source for the transmission of Indian ideas to Central Asia came into prominence. Ibn Nadim gives a long list of Indian works which were translated into Arabic at the instance of Barmakids. It was but inevitable for these Indian works to reach the Central Asian scholars."[7] In Nizami's opinion, Baghdad played a prominent role in this transmission of ideas. Indian astronomer Aryabhatta's works and the works of Charaka and Susruta on Indian medicine, which had been translated into Arabic in Baghdad, were well- known to Al Khwarezmi and Ibn-Sina respectively.

The incorporation of the Maverannahr region of Central Asia with its famous cities of Bukhara and Samarkand into the Arab Caliphate resulted not only in the spread of Islam but Arabic language as well. The Arabic language was both the language of the religion and the state. The local aristocracy and the intelligentsia supported it in order to come closer to the Arab rulers. The Arabic language was used as the language of science by scholars of Central Asian origin. Al Farabi along with Al-Khwarezmi, Al Fargani and Al Marvezi belonged to the category of such scholars who wrote their works in Arabic. It is unlikely that Farabi did not know Arabic before coming to Baghdad.

The achievements in science during the Samanid period of Central Asian history when Bukhara was the state capital were no less than the achievements in the field of literature and art. In the countries of the Muslim East, Arabic language played the role of an international scientific language for several centuries. The Arabic language possessed a large scientific terminology which was not the case with the local Iranian and Turkic languages. Moreover, the local scholars tried to write their scientific works in Arabic in order to make them available to the large scientific circles of the countries of the East.

Al-Farabi and Ibn-Sina were two leading philosophers of Central Asia during the ninth-tenth centuries. Both these scholars had to spend most of their time outside the region in Baghdad and Damascus and Hamadan and Isfahan respectively. Both of them played an outstanding role in the sphere of mastering the heritage of Aristotle and other Greek philosophers and its transmission to the peoples of the Near East. In Central Asia, Farabi is known as the 'second teacher' after Aristotle. Farabi wrote a large number of original works on logic, metaphysics, mathematics, political philosophy and music.

The 'Second Teacher'

Born in a small village – Wasij – near Farab on the Syr Daria in A.D. 870, Farabi completed his earlier education at Faqrab and Bukhara. Later on, he moved to Baghdad for higher studies. There he studied and worked for a long time from A.D. 901 to 942 acquiring mastery over several languages and various branches of science and learning. He lived during the regimes of six Abbasid Caliphs. Al Farabi travelled to many distant lands and studied for some time in Damascus and Egypt. According to one source, he even stayed in Greece. He returned after some time to Baghdad to join the court of Saif al-Daula, the Syrian ruler in Aleppo. He became one of the constant companions of this ruler and his fame spread far and wide. During the early years he was a judge but later changed over to the teaching profession. He died a bachelor in Damascus in A.D. 950 at the age of 80.

Farabi made a remarkable contribution to science, philosophy. logic, medicine, mathematics and music. As a philosopher he may be classified as a Neo-Platonist who tried to synthesise Platonism and Aristotelianism with theology. He wrote several commentaries on Aristotle's physics, methodology and logic. He also wrote a book on music titled *Kitab-al Musiqa* and invented several musical instruments, besides contributing to the knowledge of musical notes. It is reported that he could play the lute so well as to make people dance with joy or weep at will. In physics he demonstrated the existence of the void.

Although many of his works have been missing, still 117 manuscripts are known, out of which 43 are on logic, 11 on metaphysics, 7 on ethics, 7 on political science, 17 on music, medicine and sociology, while 11 are commentaries. Some of his best known works include the book *Fusus al Hikam* which remained a textbook of philosophy for several centuries and is still taught at some institutions in the East. The book *Kitab al lhsa al Ulum* deals with classification and fundamental principles of science in a very lucid manner. The book *Ara Ahl al Madina al Fadila,* or 'The Model City' is a significant early contribution to sociology and political science. Farabi exercised great influence on science and philosophy over a period of several centuries. His work aimed at the synthesis of philosophy and religion and paved the way for Ibn Sina's work. In the opinion of Soviet scholar B.G. Gafurov, "Farabi tries to answer some important questions about the origin of state, about the causes of social inequality. His socio-utopian views had a great progressive significance for his times".[8] In the post-Soviet period, there has been a noticeable resurgence of interest in the ideas of Al Farabi, particularly as contained in his work *The Model City*. A. Jalalov, a Uzbek scholar of the Institute of Philosophy in Tashkent, who is also head of the People's Democratic Party's Parliamentary faction, in his article published in the Journal *Contemporary Central Asia* edited by me, discussed at length the ideas of Farabi as expounded in his celebrated work referred to above. Jalalov wrote: "The fact that a fair and happy life cannot be achieved by humanity without philosophy was noted by thinkers long ago. Let us take, for example, the book by Abu Nasr al Farabi, *Treatise on Views* of a *Virtuous Town's Residents* in which he wrote the following "The common things that ought to be known to all residents of a virtuous town are as follows: First, they must know the primary reason and its attributes, then go to things that exist separately from matter along with their attributes as well as the stages that they occupy up to Active Intellect and the activity of each of them; further, they need to know celestial substances and attributes typical for each of them; further, natural bodies that are below the substances and the way they are formed and destroyed as well as the fact that everything that is going on in them is being done in a perfect, complete, careful fair and wise manner and there are not any shortcomings, flaws or any sort of injustice in all this; further, they must know about the origin of a human being, how capabilities of a soul emerge and how active intellect sheds light on it forming the first notions in it along with will and freedom of choice; further, they must know the first master and how revelation is performed; further, those masters who have to replace the first master in his absence at this or that moment in time; further, they must know about the virtuous town, about its residents and the happiness that their souls reach, they must know about towns that are absolutely different from it and what happens to the soul of their residents after death, that some of them will face unhappiness, others non-existence; they must know about virtuous peoples that are opposite to them". Jalalov further comments on this, "Proceeding from this it is not difficult to understand why Islamic religion places knowledge in a more favourable position than prayer, while intellect is valued more than anything else in the world."[9]

It is interesting to note what the *Great Soviet Encyclopedia* has to say about Al Farabi. Besides mentioning the great contribution made by Al Farabi to the theory and aesthetics of music, it highlights his idea about the dependence of soul on the body which, according to it, resulted in his persecution at the hands of the Muslim clergy accusing him of being an atheist and a non-believer in the indestructibility of soul and life after death.[10] While the characterisation by the *Great Soviet Encyclopedia* of Al Farabi as a humanist opposed to religious orthodoxy is valid in general, it undoubtedly seeks to oversimplify Farabi's world view and philosophical outlook.

Al Farabi's Views

In his above-cited book, Al Farabi clearly states that though the rational faculty is the only faculty that has access to the knowledge of divine or spiritual beings, there also exists an imaginative faculty having three functions, namely, acting as a reservoir of sensible impressions after the disappearance of the object of sensation, combining sensible impressions to form a complex sensible image, and producing imitations. Imagination is thus subordinate to the rational faculty and depends on it for the 'originals' that it imitates. The rational faculty is, in Farabi's view, the only faculty that provides access to the knowledge of the divine or spiritual beings and it is this faculty which must exercise strict control so that the copies offered by the imaginative faculty are good or fair imitations. Farabi does not rule out in rare cases the imaginative faculty overwhelming all other faculties proceeding directly to receive or form images of the divine or spiritual beings. This rare case relates to prophecy.

When communication with the active intellect is done through imagination, the person so doing is a prophet while the one communicating with it by means of his rational faculty is 'a wise human being, a philosopher'. Wisdom or philosophy is indispensible for the founding and survival of the virtuous city. Prophecy, on the other hand, is indispensable for founding a virtuous city, but not for its survival.

There are only a few who are philosophers or can be addressed through philosophy and there are many who are not philosophers because they lack necessary natural endowments or have no time for sufficient training. They live by opinion and persuasion and the ruler must initiate them by means of similitude or symbols. Farabi is thus offering a simple formulation of Plato's view on the Philosopher King. In his opinion the coincidence of philosophy and prophecy is extremely rare.

The virtuous city can survive in the absence of a philosopher ruler as successor only if provisions are made for the presence of proper substitutes consisting of the body of laws and customs established by the 'true princes' and the proficiency of the successor in the 'art of jurisprudence', i.e., knowledge of the laws and customs of his predecessors, willingness on his part to follow these laws and customs rather than change them, the capacity to apply them to new conditions by the deduction of new decisions, and the capacity to meet every new situation through understanding the intention of previous legislators rather than the law. The new ruler has thus to be a jurist-legislator rather than a prophet-legislator.

He, however, must possess all other qualities, including wisdom to discern and promote the common good of the regime at a particular period during which he happens to rule. Prophecy can be dispensed with by preserving old laws and the capacity to discover new applications for old laws to promote the common good. It is enough to have wisdom in the person of a philosopher who rules the virtuous city jointly with another human being or a group of human beings who possess, among other things, the capacity to put old laws to new uses. Unlike prophecy, wisdom cannot be dispensed with, for Farabi believes that there is no substitute for living wisdom.

Al Farabi was a dedicated teacher. Education had an important place in his philosophical system. It is through education that the individual is prepared from an early age to become a member of society to achieve his own level of perfection, and thus reach the goal for which he has been created. There are no specific writings of Farabi devoted to education but still one comes across scattered texts throwing light on his views on education which are in harmony with his overall philosophical views. Farabi's system of education unites moral and aesthetic values. The good is beautiful and vice versa. The perfection expected by him from education combines knowledge and virtuous behaviour. It is happiness and goodness at same time. One of the aims of education is the formation of political leadership. Farabi wrote: "Ignorance is more harmful in monarchs than it is in the common people".[11]

Al Farabi considered it a duty of the state to put aside a budget for education, taking a portion from the alms tax (*Zakat)* and land tax (*Khiraj)* as well as other state resources for this purpose. One of the goals of education, according to Farabi, is learning with practical action. Following Plato, Farabi recommends the use of the method of dialogue and debate for imparting education. In the curriculum recommended by Farabi, language and its structure receives the first priority. Mastery of the language is the foundation of all other knowledge. After language comes logic, which is closely connected with language and provides a proper methodology leading to sound reflection, then comes mathematics. The study of optics, astronomy and the natural sciences in general requires mathematics.

Mathematics according to him imparts precision and clarity and trains the intellect. This is followed by natural sciences and then, following the exact sciences, comes theology or metaphysics. Academic theology comes last and is preceded by jurisprudence and human sciences (political science) in particular. Philosophy was described by Farabi as the highest form of learning; it is the knowledge of distant causes by which all beings are governed.

NOTES AND REFERENCES

1. See M. Mahadi's article in *Encyclopedia Iranica,* http://www.muslimphilosophy.com/farabi/default.htm
2. Ibid.
3. R. Walzer, *Al-Farabi on the Perfect State,* Oxford, 1985.
4. M. Mahadi, *Al-Farabi in* C. C. Gillispie (ed.), *Dictionary of Scientific Biography,* Iv, New York, 1971, p. 524a.
5. S.De Laugier de Beaurecuil, *Manuscript d' Afghanistan,* Cairo, 1964, p. 293.
6. See Devendra Kaushik, *Central Asia in Modern Times,* Moscow, 1970, p. 57.
7. K.A. Nizami, "India's Cultural Relations with Central Asia during the Medieval Period" in Amlendu Guha (ed), *Central Asia — Movements of Peoples and Ideas from Times Pre-Historic to Pre-Modern,* ICCR. New Delhi, 1970, pp. 158-159.
8. B.G. Gafurov, *Tajiki* Vol. 2, Delhi, 2005, pp. 124-125 (English translation).
9. A. Jalalov, "The Philosophical Basis of Nation/State Building" *Contemporary Central Asia,* Vol. 111, No. 2, 1999, pp. 33-34.
10. See *Bolshaya Sovetskaya Entsiklopediya,* No. 44, Second Edition, 1956, p. 524.
11. Al Farabi, *Talkhis Nawamis Aflatun* (ed) Abd al Rahman Badawi, in *Aflatan fi L islam fi L Islam, Beirut.* Dar al Anadalus, 1982, p. 54, cited by Ammar al Talbi, Al Farabi, *Prospects: The Comparative Review of Comparative Education,* Paris, UNESCO, International Bureau of Education, Vol. XXIII. No. 1/2, 1993, pp. 353-372.

13

Sir Marc Aurel Stein (1862–1943): The Expeditions and the Collections

Arup Banerjee

Our knowledge of subjects of great and variegated import, like east to west trade between the second and tenth centuries A.D. along the so-called network of silk routes, the diffusion of Buddhism from India to China or social life in regions of northern China around the Taklamakan Desert received a decisive, if not initial impetus, from the exploratory, archaeological and treasure-gathering expeditions launched by men like Sven Hedin, Aurel Stein, Albert Grunwedel, Albert von Le Coq, Paul Pelliot, Baron Otani or Langdon Warner from the 1890s to the 1930s.

Sir Aurel Stein's contributions to our knowledge of ancient Chinese civilisation are, arguably, incomparable among the archaeologist-geographers of his day. They are also diverse. His discovery of the 'library' in Cave 17 of the Tun-huang complex has been likened in momentousness and impact, to the discovery of the Dead Sea Scrolls. He was, in all likelihood, the first to accurately survey the Mustagh Ata Massif and the glaciers in the Nissa Valley that feed the headwaters of the Yurung-kash (White Jade) branch of the Khotan River. As one of the objectives of his first expedition, Stein fixed the position of Khotan for the first time in April 1901. Of greater import, in 1907, he definitively identified the position of the gateway to the Northern Silk Route, as Yu-men-kuan (the 'Jade Gate'). He proved its great age from examining Chinese documents on wood that he found in one of the towers or block-houses built along the wall, bearing dates equivalent to the first century A.D. On his third expedition, as he investigated the desert site of Loulan, he succeeded in tracing the so-called 'Route of the Centre', between Loulan and Tun-huang.

Stein's three major expeditions (1900-01; 1906-08; and 1913-15) lasted seven years and covered some forty thousand kilometres on foot or horse. Stein never learned to read Chinese, spoke it haltingly and always regretted this, but he was, probably, fluent in all the other important languages, living and extinct, of Chinese Turkestan.

Among the most oft-repeated accolades that Stein received were from Sir Leonard Wooley when he retrospectively characterised Stein's expeditions as 'the most daring and adventurous raid upon the ancient world that any archaeologist has attempted,'[1] and from Professor Owen Lattimore, who called Stein "the most prodigious combination of scholar explorer, archaeologist and geographer of his generation". Alternatively, the Chinese regard Ssu-t`an-yin as the most villainous of the 'foreign devils'.

Life and Times

Marc Aurel Stein was born in Central Pest in November 1862. He was christened Marc Aurel after the Roman Emperor Marcus Aurelius, who died near Budapest. He was from a family of baptised Hungarian Jews. His father, Nathan Stein's business had already collapsed when Stein was born and subsequently his wife's family wealth sustained the family. Stein's uncle Ignaz Hirschler (his mother's younger brother) and Stein's own older brother, Ernst, supported Stein's education.[2]

At the age of ten, Stein was sent to the renowned Kreutzschule in Dresden, where he mastered Greek, Latin, French and English. His most noticeable talents during his five years there, from 1872 to 1877, were an exceptional facility in languages and the ability to study harder, longer and better than most of the other students. From the Kreutzschule he went to the Lutheran grammar school in Budapest, which prepared him for university and where he began his Oriental studies. During his two years there, 1877–1879, he became familiar with the Indian, Persian and Central Asian collections in the library of the Hungarian Academy of Sciences and first began to prepare himself for a teaching post in Oriental Studies. It was at the Kreutzschule that one of his teachers gave him a copy of *The Campaigns of Alexander* by Arrian. Alexander became his hero and provided the incentive to become immersed in Greek and Roman histories and later to master the ancient languages of India and Persia.[3]

Two other men found permanent places in his imaginary and inspirational universes when he was a graduate student. One was Hiuen-Tsang (Xuanzang), whom Stein referred to either as his Buddhist Pausanius or his 'patron saint'. The other was Marco Polo. Both had travelled through many of the places that Stein was to visit, and their accounts provided useful referents for the identification or confirmation of sites.[4]

Jeannette Mirsky encapsulates their braided influences on Stein by pointing out that it was from Alexander, Xuanzang and Marco Polo that Stein formed a triangle whose sides connected antiquity with the Middle Ages, East and West, international trade with a universalistic religion, Buddhism. Stein's role was to perceive their interconnections.[5]

Another 'bridge to India' was provided by the Hungarian Csoma de Koros (or Korosi Csoma, 1784 – 1842). He was the first European to acquire a systematic, scholarly knowledge of the Tibetan language; his published grammar and dictionary of Tibetan were acknowledged as standard authorities on the language. He had travelled alone and on foot from Hungary to Leh but died in Darjeeling before he could reach Tibet.[6]

Two men guided his University Oriental studies, giving them depth and focus. They were Rudolf von Roth (1821–95), Professor of Indo-European languages and the history of religions and an authority on the Vedic period, at the University of Tubingen, and J. George Buhler (1837–98), Professor of Indian philology and antiquities at the University of Vienna. Roth was co-author of a monumental Sanskrit-German dictionary and had an authoritative knowledge of Sanskrit manuscript materials. Buhler had been Professor of Oriental Languages in Bombay before he moved to Vienna where Stein studied under him. In fact, Stein's interest in Kalhana's *Rajtarangini* was triggered by a search that took Buhler to Kashmir in 1875 to find the original manuscript.[7]

In 1879, after graduating from the Lutheran *gymnasium* in Pest, Stein began undergraduate studies in Sanskrit and Philology in Vienna. Two years later he moved to Leipzig and attended Buhler's lectures on Indian philology and antiquities. He then moved to Tubingen to attend the lectures of Rudolf von Roth, and it was here that Stein was awarded his doctorate in 1883.[8]

The same year, Stein received a stipend from the Hungarian government to support him for two years of research in Oriental languages and archaeology at the Universities of London, Oxford and Cambridge. His spell in British universities, from 1884 to 1886, was interrupted for a year in 1885, when he completed his compulsory military training. Fortunately, for his later career, this military training was at the Ludovika Academy, the Hungarian Army's map-making school. Its director, Captain Caroly Kuess, an outstanding cartographer, introduced him to the best methods then known to military surveyors. Stein put the techniques he learned here into practice on his Central Asian expeditions, all of which included a two-man team of Indian surveyors, trained by the Indian Survey Department; Stein directed and co-ordinated their exertions, which produced an array of cartographic intelligence that nourished the British end of the Great Game.[9]

Stein published his very first paper, 'Old Persian Religious Literature' in a Budapest periodical in 1885. Much of 1886 was spent studying the coin collections at the British Museum, London and the Ashmolean Museum, Oxford. His first scholarly writing, 'Zoroastrian Deities on Indo-Scythian Coins', was published in the *Oriental and Babylonian Record* in 1887. In the late 1880s in England, he studied Oriental manuscripts and coins in The Ashmolean Museum and the Bodleian Library, Oxford, The British Museum and the India Office Library, London and Persian manuscripts at Trinity College in Cambridge.

As the term for Stein's grant from the Hungarian government was drawing to a close, Sir Henry Rawlinson[10] suggested to the India Council, of which he was Member, that Stein was well qualified to fill the dual vacancy of Registrar of Punjab University and Principal of Oriental College, Lahore. Stein arrived in India in December 1887 to take up both posts and he held them for a decade. Other than his administrative responsibilities, Stein concertedly involved himself with locating and translating Kalhana's *Rajtarangini* into English, a project in which he was to remain immersed until the beginning of the next century. There were problems with the language of the extant manuscript, as well as locating it in its entirety. The copies available were in the *Devanagri* script, which did not actually become common in Kashmir until after the 1820s, when it replaced the *S'arada* script used by Kashmiri scholars. Buhler had only been permitted a glimpse of the original *S'arada* script in Kashmir in 1875, before it had actually been snatched from his grasp. Since Buhler's visit, the manuscript's owner had died and three of his heirs had physically divided the manuscript amongst themselves! Stein kept trying to obtain it and, in 1889, with the help of a Member of the Kashmir State Council, did so. The manuscript dropped into the sea while Stein was crossing the Channel to England but then, curiously enough, dried without a trace of its immersion![11]

Lockwood Kipling (1837–1911) had come to India in the 1860s to serve as architectural sculptor to the Bombay Museum of Art. He later became curator of the Lahore Museum, a place his son Rudyard described in *Kim* as 'The Wonder House'. Under Kipling's tutelage, Stein studied the Lahore collection and became familiar with Graeco-Buddhist Art, knowledge that proved useful in writing the first proposal for leave and funds to undertake the First Expedition in 1900.

Kipling also introduced Stein to Fred Henry Andrews (1866–1957) in 1890 when Andrews became the Vice-Principal of the Mayo School of Art in Lahore. Andrews went on to succeed Kipling as Principal and Curator of the Lahore Museum. In later expeditions, Andrews added his photographic skills to Stein's (and his own lesser) archaeological ones. Andrews was appointed as a Temporary Assistant at the British Museum when Stein arrived with the first expedition collection; his job was to prepare a complete inventory. Andrews was most instrumental in classifying and recording Stein's collections, both for the British Museum and the National Museum, Delhi.[12]

In December 1898 Stein was offered a position in the Indian Education Service as Principal of the Calcutta Madrasah that had been founded by Warren Hastings in 1781. Bengal was not at all to his liking, however, and he was succeeded by Edward Denison Ross in 1901. Stein was transferred from the Bengal to the Punjab Educational Service.[13] Stein then spent many years working in the Education Department of the Government of India. From January 1904, he became Inspector-General of Education and Archaeological Superintendent, North-West Frontier Province and Baluchistan.[14]

In a life-long battle that Stein waged with sundry forms of authority[15], one of the rare defeats he had to accept was in 1905, after his highly acclaimed first expedition. This occurred because of the official refusal to appoint him to a post he called Archaeological Explorer. Sir John Marshall, the Director-General of Archaeology, had suggested the title of 'Special Explorer'. The Secretary of State himself was unwilling to confer this nomenclature upon Stein, and the Government of India named him as merely another 'Superintendent' in the Archaeological Survey.[16]

Stein accepted the post of Superintendent in the Archaeological Department in 1910, but found himself once again posted where he was most unwilling to be — Bengal — "it is to me personally most uncongenial — or to put it plainly — distinctly hateful". But this posting was a mere formality, owing to the need to fill a vacancy on paper. By 1911 he had been given the one position in the Archaeological Department that was likely to bring him at least partial satisfaction: Superintendent of Archaeology in the North Western Frontier Province. He only worked at this post for a few months.[17]

Stein made many shorter expeditions to areas other than Chinese Central Asia. He had been to Swat in 1896 and then accompanied the curiously named Sir Bindon Blood's Expeditionary Force to Swat in 1898.[18] He had wished for long to follow the tracks of Alexander the Great, and he achieved this in explorations in 1911-12 on the North West Frontier.

From about 1926 to 1936, Stein's tours took him to Swat for the identification of Mount Una as the Aornos of Alexander's campaign; to Waziristan, Baluchistan and Makran for two explorations in 1927-1928 to investigate the likelihood and nature of links between the Mesopotamian and Harappan civilisations; he undertook four Iranian expeditions from 1932 to 1936, when he visited Iranian Baluchistan, the Persian Gulf coast, eastern Fars and Iranian Kurdistan. In his sixties in 1938, he pioneered the use of aerial photography in archaeology to study the old Roman limes from rather conveniently situated Royal Air Forces bases in Mosul in northern Iraq. In 1940-41, the dried-up course of the so-called 'lost river' Sarasvati was surveyed.[19]

Stein had doggedly sought permission to explore in Afghanistan, particularly, the remains of the Graeco-Bactrian civilisation in the then Balkh province, from the 1890s onwards. In a letter in 1923, Stein wrote, "My hope of reaching Bactria made me take to Oriental Studies, brought me to England and India, gave me my dearest friends and chances of fruitful work." He had thrice been refused entry into Afghanistan: in June 1902, in October 1912 and in October 1922. In a tragically uncanny rounding of life, he was eventually invited by the Afghan government two decades later. He died only a week after arriving in Kabul on 26 October 1943, a month shy of his eighty-first birthday.[20]

The Methods

Sir Aurel Stein's character and temperament were impressively suited for a career of more than forty years of archaeological and cartographic activity. He possessed inordinate physical strength and stamina, that some have found remarkable for a short-statured individual of five feet and four inches. His disdain for personal safety and his immense physical capacity to bear pain were phenomenal even by the contemporary yardsticks of the stiff British upper lip. His first expedition was not abandoned after he suffered from frostbite while surveying the headwaters of the Yurung-kash River and went on to lose all the toes on his left foot, and nor was the third when the Badakshi stallion he was riding reared back and crushed his leg.

Stein's singularities, that some consider his angularities, marked him out among his explorer peers. A lifelong bachelor, Stein's emotional impulses were rarely, if ever, of a romantic nature. One of his biographers, Annabel Walker, considered that 'His attitude towards the opposite sex, like his view of a conventional social life, was coloured by his commitment to work... it seems perfectly possible that a man such as Stein experienced no sexual passions".[21] Likewise, Fred Andrews wrote that his "principle of regarding his work as the first consideration under all circumstances governed his life".[22]

Sir Aurel Stein's entire working life was in the service of the Government of India, albeit occasionally in positions he felt unjustly confined to. Unlike Sven Hedin, whose political involvements were markedly fascist[23] or Baron Mannerheim, who achieved highest office in Finland,[24] Stein's life was one of archaeological exploration, the academy and museums.

He made a series of temporary sojourns wherever his brother's family or his circle of friends were, or where his books and papers happened to be; home was never a place that possessed either fixity or luxury. Stein was powerfully impelled by a quest for acceptance by his adopted country, which came with British nationality and a knighthood. He was also strongly driven by a yearning to gain the recognition of his scholastic peers by overshadowing the discoveries and archaeological collections of his German and French rivals. Money was important more as a means to finance expeditions and to support his brother's family than as the basis for a comfortable personal life.

His biographers have described his working methods as meticulous and methodical. Stein excavated carefully and intelligently, and if he had a weakness for spectacular relics, he was also strongly drawn to the 'refuse — antique dirt and litter, still pungent after so many centuries'. Stein claimed to be able to identify earlier Tibetan occupation of a site like Miran by the especially loathsome, excretory quality of their rubbish: in 1932, Stein wrote, "I have had occasion to acquire a rather extensive experience in clearing ancient rubbish heaps and know how to diagnose them. But for intensity of sheer dirt and age-persisting smelliness I shall always put the rich 'casings' of Tibetan warriors in the front rank."[25]

His letters and books make clear his preference for being at archaeological sites rather than preparing his notes for publication. The volumes he authored after each of the three expeditions, nevertheless, are testimony to his fastidiousness with accuracy, his insistence on exhaustively presenting his readers with both essential and supportive knowledge, and are arguably better mines to seam by students of Chinese Central Asia than the records left by von Le Coq or Grunwedel.

The Desert and the Oases

The northern and southern Silk Routes skirt the rim of the Tarim Basin, extending over an area of 530,000 square kilometers across Xinjiang/Sinkiang ('New Dominions'), China's largest and westernmost province. It stretches for about one thousand miles latitudinally and is about 600 miles at its greatest longitudinal span. The basin is almost completely enclosed by mountains: the T'ien Shan to the north, the Kunlun to the south, and the Pamirs to the west. Geographically, Kashgaria is the Tarim Basin, a great pear-shaped depression extending for about 900 miles from Kashgar in the west to Lop-nor in the east, and over 300 miles from the Tarim River in the north to the gravel glacis of the Kunlun mountains in the south.

Within the Tarim Basin is the Taklamakan Desert spreading over some 337,000 square miles. In Turkic, Taklamakan means 'go in and you won't come out' or 'the place from which no living thing returns'. Ancient Han records inform us that the Chinese knew the Taklamakan as the *Lui Sha*, or `Moving Sands,' for its ever-shifting dunes driven by the relentless winds. Sir Clairmont Skrine, British Consul-General at Kashgar in the 1920s, wrote that the dunes "seem to clamour silently... for travelers to engulf, for whole caravans to swallow up, as they have swallowed up so many in the past".[26]

Xuanzang, who passed through it on his way to India, described the demons that the Chinese believed inhabited the desert and lured men to their thirsty deaths: "When these winds rise, both man and beast become confused and forgetful, and there they remain perfectly disabled...it is all the work of demons and evil spirits". Sven Hedin, one of the few Europeans to have crossed it, called it "the worst and most dangerous desert in the world". Stein, who came to know it even better, considered the deserts of Arabia "tame" by comparison.

THE EXPEDITIONS

The First Expedition: May 1900 – July 1901

In a letter of 2 February 1899 to his brother Ernst Stein wrote that "an archaeological exploration" into Chinese Turkestan "has been in my thoughts since 1897". On 10 September 1898 he sent a proposal to the Lieutenant Governor of Punjab, intended for Calcutta, for assistance in sanctioning and funding a tour of archaeological exploration to Khotan in the Tarim Basin. Drawing on the Xuanzang account, Stein emphasised the early and highly distinctive nature of Buddhism in that ancient kingdom.

The immediate prompting for Stein's request stemmed from the collection of the so-called Bower Manuscripts, named after Lieutenant Hamilton Bower, a British intelligence officer in the Indian Army who was in the Kashgar region in the late 1880s seeking the assassin of a fellow Great Gamer and ostensible trader, Andrew Dalgleish. From the early 1890s, a stream of manuscripts had been acquired by George McCartney and Nikolai Petrovsky, the British and Russian Consuls in Kashgar from Gulan Qadir and Islam Akhun. These, along with others obtained by the French cartographer Jules Dutreuil de Rhins and the Moravian missionary, Weber, eventually found their way to Dr. Augustus Frederic Rudolf Hoernle at the Asiatic Society of Bengal in Calcutta by the services of Bower and others. By 1899, the collection of manuscripts was large enough for Hoernle to publish his findings on it.[27] Although some were written in Sanskrit using the Brahmi script, and others in Kharoshti, till then known only in inscriptions and coins, most were written in scripts that were unknown and hence undecipherable. Having identified the language and studied the contents of the manuscripts that were readable, Hoernle discussed the possibility that the manuscripts might be forgeries; scholars at the British Museum wondered similarly and Hoernle eventually rejected the notion of the manuscripts being forgeries. Stein referred to these documents and suggested, in his application, that if the casual search of native treasure-seekers had yielded these, then systematic exploration might be expected to produce others of greater importance and quantity.

There were several stated objectives of this expedition: to substantiate Khotan's links to India through Mahayana Buddhism; to undertake "a semi-antiquarian, semi-judicial enquiry" to authenticate (as genuine or forgeries) the birch-bark manuscripts"; and, to survey the Mustagh Ata massif and the glaciers in the Nissa valley that feed the headwaters of the Yurung-kash (White Jade) branch of the Khotan river. To add an irresistible 'Great Game' flavour to a proposal directed at Calcutta, Stein mentioned that the Russians were planning on sending three 'savants' to Turfan and that Sven Hedin was planning to resume his expeditions.[28]

On 31 December 1898 Stein received the news that the Home and Finance Departments of the Government of India had sanctioned the Khotan expedition and that the Foreign Office had agreed to arrange for a passport and assistance in China.[29] The expedition was allotted a sum of Rupees seven thousand for travel and the purchase of antiquities. In June 1900, Stein was placed on special duty by the Government of India for the purpose of archaeological explorations...in the region of Khotan.

Stein entered Chinese territory in the Tagh-dumbash Pamir area via the Kilik Pass. This was where he started the triangular and plane survey which continued throughout the expedition. The desert sites explored from Khotan were Dandan-oilik, Niya, Endere and Rawak.

Stein's first Taklamakan site was Dandan-uilik/oilik ('the place of houses with ivory' in Uighur). This monastery complex on the eastern edge of the Khotan oasis was located to the north of the Southern Silk Route. The town flourished from the fourth

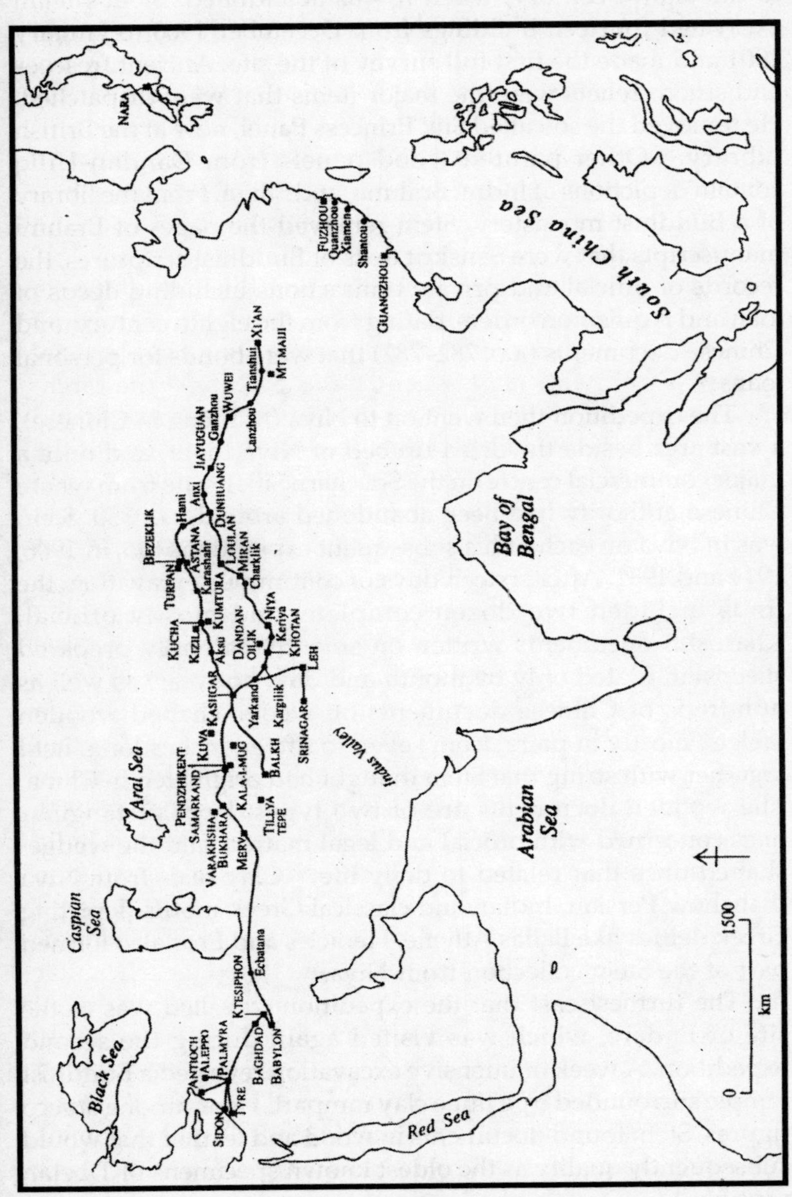
NARA
South China Sea
FUZHOU
Quanzhou
Xiamen
Shantou
GUANGZHOU
XI'AN
MT MAIJI
Tianshui
Lanzhou
WUWEI
Ganzhou
JIAYUGUAN
Anxi
DUNHUANG
Hami
LOULAN
MIRAN
Charklik
BEZEKLIK
TURFAN
ASTANA
Karashahr
KUMTURA
KUCHA
KIZIL
Aksu
NIYA
Keriya
DANDAN-OILIK
KHOTAN
LEH
KASHGAR
Yarkand
Kargilik
SRINAGAR
Indus Valley
BALKH
KUVA
PENDZHIKENT
SAMARKAND
KALA-I-MUG
TILLYA TEPE
VARAKHSHA
BUKHARA
MERV
Aral Sea
Bay of Bengal
Arabian Sea
Caspian Sea
Ecbatana
KTESIPHON
BAGHDAD
BABYLON
ANTIOCH
ALEPPO
PALMYRA
TYRE
SIDON
Black Sea
Red Sea
0
1500
km

to the eighth century, when it was abandoned. Stein's team excavated fourteen buildings from December 1900 to January 1901 and made the first full survey of the site. Ancient frescoes and stucco reliefs were the major items that were dispatched. He removed the so-called Silk Princess Panel, now at the British Library.[30] Other painted wood panels from Dandan-Uiliq contain depictions of Indra, Brahma, and Shiva. From the library of a Buddhist monastery, Stein removed the pages of Brahmi manuscripts that were Sanskrit texts of Buddhist scriptures, the records of official and private transactions including deeds of loan and requisition orders, dating from the eighth century, and Chinese documents (A.D. 782–787) that were bonds for personal loans.[31]

The expedition then went on to Niya (Minfeng in Chinese), a vast area beside the dried-up bed of Niya River, and once a major commercial centre on the Southern Silk Route from where Chinese authority had been abandoned around A.D. 350. Stein was in Niya on each of his subsequent expeditions too, in 1906, 1914 and 1931. After sixteen days of continuous excavation, the finds included two dozen complete, and mostly official, Kharoshti documents written on smooth, carefully prepared sheepskin (dated only by month and day, not year) as well as hundreds of Chinese documents on wedge-shaped wooden tablets, mostly in pairs, from seven to fifteen inches long, held together with string that Stein thought had originated in China. The wooden documents are of two types: large rectangular ones concerned with official and legal matters and the wedge-shaped ones that related to daily life.[32] Clay seals from Niya that show Persian, Indian and classical Greek motifs depicting Greek deities like Pallas Athene, Heracles and Eros also formed part of the Stein collection from Niya.[33]

The furthest east that the expedition travelled was to the site of Endere, which was visited again during the second expedition. A week of intensive excavation revealed a Buddhist temple surrounded by a huge clay rampart. Here, among stucco figures, Stein found documents in wood and leather that would subsequently qualify as the oldest known specimens of Tibetan writing.[34]

Rawak or 'high mansion', north-east of Khotan, is believed to be one of the largest and most important sites in Chinese Central Asia, with the largest stupa on the Southern Silk Route. Stein discovered the site in April 1901 and in eight to nine days, uncovered about ninety sculptures adorning both sides of the wall of the stupa court. They were mostly life-sized painted stucco images of standing Buddhas, carved in relief, as well as four guardian figures and many Boddhisattva figures. Realising that the delicate and large statues could not be transported, Stein photographed them and recorded their precise position. This was fortunate because when Stein returned to Rawak about five years later, he found that the sculptures had been smashed.[35]

After these perambulations, Stein returned to Khotan in April 1901 to complete the expedition. Islam Akhun met Stein on 25 April 1901 and described how he had forged and aged the documents that had flowed out of this region for several years: the paper was bought locally; it was then stained yellow or light brown with the addition of a substance called *toghruga*; text was added to it by hand or block-printing; the pages were hung over a fire and bound up in crude imitation of European volumes; finally, the manuscripts were encrusted with sand before being taken to Kashgar.[36]

On 2 July 1901, he delivered the antiquities he had returned with to the British Museum and personally began the task of recording the details of the two to three thousand objects that formed this collection as they were unpacked: details like precisely where and at what depth on the site they were found and their numerical order. Stein saw to the development of nearly a thousand photographic plates.[37]

The Second Expedition: April 1906 – November 1908

By the end of 1901, Sir Aurel Stein had established a commanding and diverse reputation: as an intrepid explorer, an archaeologist of near peerless ability and a European citizen who was able to effect the transfer of considerable quantities of Chinese cultural wealth with dispatch and thoroughness. These achievements were acknowledged over the years to come: British citizenship, a knighthood, several awards from the relevant institutions and the respect of his peers. A special resolution that was passed at the Thirteenth International Congress of Orientalists in Hamburg in 1902 congratulated Stein. This acclaim also started what Peter Hopkirk terms 'the international race' into Chinese Central Asia. A small group of monks left Japan in early 1902 and by August the first German expedition had left Berlin bound for Kashgar and its environs.[38]

In September 1904, Stein conjured up 'the spectre of Russo-German competition' and argued that it seemed 'scarcely possible to foresee whether such favourable conditions [in Chinese Central Asia] will prevail for a prolonged period...which would close that field to researches from the British side' in his formal application to the Government of India for a second expedition. This expedition was to last two years and seven months. It was jointly sponsored by the Government of India (sixty per cent) and the British Museum (the rest) on the understanding that the material that Stein brought back should be divided *pro rata* between the two sponsors.[39]

Journeying through Swat, Dir, Kashgar and Khotan, the expedition's first archaeological stop was at Niya. An archive of documents left behind by a Chinese magistrate named the Honourable Cojhbo Sojaka was discovered as well as nearly three dozen perfectly preserved deeds on double rectangular tablets, with their seals and fastening intact, and an abundance of classical seals.[40]

Stein followed approximately the same route as Marco Polo had done, across the Lop Nor desert to Loulan. Along the route he picked up large numbers of Chinese coins, arrowheads and other small objects. In one such find he discovered a neat line of over two hundred Han dynasty copper coins, extending for about thirty metres along the road. This garrison town was the principal target of the expedition. It had been discovered and cartographically recorded by Sven Hedin in 1900.[41]

The excavations at Loulan continued for eleven days. One of the most important discoveries was a single bale of yellow silk, forty-eight cm wide. The discovery of wooden measuring devices and an inscribed fragment of fabric led Stein to conclude that this was the standard size for the bales of silk that were traded along the Silk Routes. In a huge rubbish dump, wedge-shaped and rectangular documents written on wood, paper and silk in Chinese and in Kharoshti, dating to about A.D. 260–330 were found that provide an insight into the administration of the Chinese garrison at Loulan. Among the larger objects found were wooden architectural fragments, similar to those at Niya. Stein also found figural sculpture dated to around the third century of Buddha and the Boddhisatvas.[42]

Miran had been a flourishing Buddhist and commercial centre of immense vitality and importance and then a fortified town of the Shanshan kingdom from the Han dynasty until the fourth century, when it was abandoned. It had been under Tibetan occupation from about 775 to 860 when the Tibetans effectively controlled all traffic along the Southern Silk Route.

During three weeks in Miran, Stein identified fifteen buildings including three stupas, several towers, smaller structures and the Tibetan fort. The documentary remains included office papers written in everyday Tibetan of the eighth and ninth centuries, a palm leaf manuscript fragment and a packet of papers in Runic Turkish that was testimony to the fact that the Western Turks shared with the Tibetans the conquest of the Chinese-held Tarim Basin in the eighth century. Among the unearthed artifacts were several lacquered leather scales from Tibetan armours, several fine stucco heads and huge seated torso figures and a delicately painted fresco that Stein dated to the third century A.D. Many of the frescoes, of great beauty, were sent to India while those that were impractical to remove were photographed. After conscientiously probing the debris at Khadalik, Brahmi tablets, excellently preserved Chinese texts (including a roll that was thirty inches long) and texts on birch-bark in Sanskrit were found, the expedition left with these and stucco and fresco objects that filled six large boxes.[43]

Stein's last destination on this excavation was the one that earned him both the acclaim of his peers and the greatest excoriation from the Chinese: Tun-huang ('blazing beacon') and the nearby Caves of the Thousand Buddhas (Ch'ien-fo-tung). The northern and southern silk routes had converged at Tun-huang before moving as a single route to Xian; the Caves that had once numbered more than one thousand constituted China's greatest and most complex rock-temple and chapel complexes. Stein was there for twenty-three days between 21 May and 13 June 1907.

The location and numbers of the caves, and their extraordinary frescoes had been described by Professor Lajos de Loczy, head of the Hungarian Geological Survey, who had visited them in 1879 as a member of Count Czechenyi's expedition as also had the Russian Prejevalsky.[44] They were a storehouse for copies of Buddhist texts and paintings and contained over forty thousand documents. They had been sealed in the eleventh century by an unknown person(s) but were discovered by accident in 1900. When Stein arrived in 1907, Wang Yuanzhuan/Wang Yuanlu (Abbot Wang), the caretaker of the cave complex, who had already given away some of the manuscripts and paintings to local officials, was happy to part with several cartloads more for "such a number of silver ingots or horse-shoes" as Stein thought was "enough to satisfy his honest conscience and the interests of his cherished shrine". Stein removed camel-loads of booty from the caves, for which he had paid a mere 130 pound sterling.[45]

These paintings and manuscripts formed the world's earliest and largest paper archive. Most of the documents are Buddhist texts in Chinese from the fifth century A.D., Tibetan leaves from the eighth and ninth centuries, texts in Sanskrit and other indigenous languages of Buddhist Turkestan. The town had been under both Chinese and Tibetan control during the first millennium. A shortage of paper meant that the other side of many of the documents had already been used for mundane purposes, that later, within the discipline of Dunhuangology, were valuable to understand social patterns and economic life. Among the documents are early *feng-shui* texts, military reports about the altitude sickness suffered by soldiers fighting in the Pamir Mountains, prescriptions for arthritis and period pains, letters apologising for getting drunk at a dinner party and tax documents, besides a host of other subjects.

The most famous item to emerge from the so-called Cave 17 was *The Diamond Sutra*. This is the document that has probably drawn the greatest Chinese ire against Stein. In the original Sanskrit it was called *Vajracchedika-prajnaparamitasutra*, or, more simply 'Prajna-Paramita'. It was translated into Chinese by Kumarajiva (384–417) and called *Jin gang ban ruo bo luo mi jing* or 'Chin kang ching'. It was a large, block-printed scroll that measures 16 feet in length. The colophon at the inner end *dates* it, precisely, to the 13th of the 4th moon of the 9th year of Xiantong (or, 11 May 868 A.D.) and provides the *name* of the man who commissioned and distributed it, Wang Si.[46]

The value of the paintings from Tun-huang, that Arthur Waley has dated to a period between the seventh and tenth centuries, is enhanced by the fact that in the mid-ninth century, Buddhism and other 'foreign religions' were outlawed and suppressed in China and much Buddhist art was destroyed. The paintings of Tun-huang escaped this fate. Most of the banners from Tun-huang removed by Stein and his team are of silk, either fine gauze, resembling modern fan gauze, or of ordinary plain weave. Others are of cotton or linen. The painted banners did not cover as wide a span of time as the wall-paintings in the caves, for the earliest grottoes in the valley of the Thousand Buddhas were carved from the cliffs in the fourth century A.D. and devotees began to decorate them not long afterwards.[47]

The manuscripts from Tun-huang filled seven cases and the more than three hundred paintings and embroideries, another five; they left Tun-huang in five horse-drawn carts. Stein acquired five more cases of manuscripts from Wang in Tun-huang on his third expedition when he also bought a further six hundred scrolls in a neighbouring town. About half of the manuscripts and almost all the paintings of the entire British Stein Collections are from Tun-huang, which Stein visited during this and the next expedition.[48]

The "caves" was Stein's name for the basement rooms in the British Museum where the collections of the second expedition first arrived. As before, Stein entrusted the unpacking, arranging, photographing, and the Descriptive List, the detailed summary of each item of art and artefact, to Andrews. Because of his position at the Battersea Polytechnic Institute, Andrews could only work half-time. It was then that Miss F.M.G. Lorrimer (nicknamed 'the Recording Angel') began her long association with Stein, one that continued when she moved to India. By the early spring of 1910, the more spectacular finds were ready to be exhibited at the British Museum.[49]

The Third Expedition: 1913 – 1915

Stein's request for "for a journey of archaeological and geographical exploration in Central Asia and chiefly within Chinese Turkestan" was sent in November 1912 and the Government of India sanctioned the proposal in 1913. The Third Expedition left Srinagar in July 1913. It lasted for two years and eight months and covered nearly eleven thousand miles from "westernmost China across the whole Tarim Basin [and back] to the uppermost Oxus and to Iran, from the Hindu-Kush valleys in the south to Dzungaria and Inner Mongolia in the north-east". The route on this expedition differed from those of the earlier expeditions. Stein and his team passed through the recently formed kingdom of Drarel, never before visited by a European, and by way of the Darkot Pass, the Taghdumbash Pamir, the valley of Tash-kurghan, and the Kara-tash River Gorges, reached Kashgar. They entered the Taklamakan at its eastern end, from Maral-bashi.

Stein returned to the ruins of a shrine in Miran that he had excavated in 1907. On the platform supporting the stupa was a series of niches containing the remains of colossal stucco sculptures, including five large seated figures of Buddha. Stein removed a head from the third of the five Buddhas, measuring fifty-four cm in height, and it is now in the British Museum. He wanted to extricate and remove some of the paintings he had seen here in 1907, but he found that a clumsy attempt by the Japanese had destroyed them. His photographic record of what remained is, hence, valuable. Smaller paintings like one of the Buddha and six disciples passing through a forest, and fragments of others have survived and are in the National Museum, Delhi.[50]

Kara Khoto (The 'Black Town', Heicheng or Etzina), was situated on the edge of the Gobi Desert at the northern border of the Xia state in northwestern Inner Mongolia and was one of their principal cities. It was at its artistic zenith between the twelfth and fourteenth centuries. The sculpture and paintings here represent the earliest expression of Sino-Tibetan art. The site had been discovered by the Russian explorer Colonel Petr Kozlov, a protégé of Prejevalsky's, in 1908.[51]

Stein was sure it formed the remains of Marco Polo's thirteenth-century city of Etzina. Evidence remained within the walls of the old city of Buddhist shrines and stupas and there was a good deal of archaeological relics that remained after the Russian expedition of 1908. Stein found drawings and prints on paper (now in the British Museum), many pieces of silk, quantities of fallen pieces of stucco decoration, painted and gilded, frescoes, fragments of glazed pottery and other objects, and plenty of records in the old Tangut language, Chinese, Tibetan and Uighur.[52]

The Turfan region was very rich in archaeological sites. By the end of the fifth century, Turfan was a thriving centre on the northern silk road. The oases of the region held the remains of both Manichaean and Buddhist cults, as well as literary and artistic elements from Persia and India. It had been part of the Uighur Empire (847–1031) that had maintained some autonomy from the Mongols. The late adoption of Islam by the Uighurs meant that the pre-Islamic remains lasted longer than elsewhere in this region, aided also by the extreme dryness of the climate. Xuanzang had stayed in the region on his way to India. The sites had been visited by Dmitri Klementz and his botanist wife in 1898, by the German expeditions, and there had also been three Japanese expeditions sent by the explorer Count Kozui Otani, the spiritual leader of the *Jodo Shinzu* ('Pure Land Sect') in 1902, 1908 and 1910.[53]

Among the sites that Stein visited in the Turfan region were Kara-khoja, from where he removed small fragments of painted plaster and other small objects, and Toyuk, from where he took away fragments of manuscripts and sections of the domed ceiling described below in the section on the National Museum, Delhi.[54]

Stein also visited Bezeklik, north-east of Turfan, at the end of 1914. The caves here were first explored by von Le Coq in

1905 and by the Japanese in 1908-09. Andrews wrote that "Observing the extent of the progressive damage the still-remaining (after the German expeditions) paintings were suffering from local vandalism, (Stein) decided to remove as many as possible to save them from total destruction".[55]

Returning to the Turfan region from an official visit to Urumchi, Stein removed what remained of magnificent frescoes decorating a series of cave temples at Murtuk after Grunwedel had, in an act of gross vandalism that the Chinese are yet to come to terms with, removed some sixty cases of fresco panels.[56]

The expedition then travelled to the great cemetery of Astana, where both Han and other ethnic groups of Gaochang had been buried from the late third century A.D. in over four hundred tombs. Being located merely forty kilometres from Turfan, the same arid climate preserved the mummified bodies as well as interred artifacts like paper hats, belts and shoes; a female tomb figure has arms made from recycled pawnshop tickets!

Although some of the contents of the tombs had been robbed, the objects that meant the most to Stein had not been taken. In the first place, inscribed in Chinese on a special funeral brick was the name and date of each coffin's occupant, as well as biographical data. The silk textiles that Stein cut away from the mummified and discrete bodies are important historically because they can be dated with exactness from the inscriptions on the bricks.[57]

It was while he was near or at Astana in February 1915 that Stein heard that the Chinese authorities had demanded that he stop all archaeological work immediately. After ensuring the dispatch of more than 140 cases of antiquities (he had sent numerous cases of antiques to Kashgar in the previous winter already), Stein left the Turfan region on 16 February 1915, and after travelling 938 miles in fifty-five days, he arrived in Kashgar on 31 May. It took a month to pack the 182 cases of findings from this expedition in Kashgar; the haul from this expedition was more than double than that garnered by the second expedition.[58]

The 'Fourth' Expedition: August 1930 – June 1931

Stein realised that the Archaeological Department would not be able to support another expedition, so in his search for support, he applied for funds to the Boxer Indemnity Fund, which represented the balance of the indemnity claimed by Britain from China as damages related to the Boxer Uprising. The Professor of Chinese at Oxford, W.E. Soothill, suggested in a letter to him in March 1925 that Stein might win Chinese approval by offering them first choice of his finds, since they were concerned about the 'wholesale exportation of their treasures', and by helping to establish a School of Chinese Archaeology. A week later, Eric Teichman, Chinese secretary to the British Minister in Peking, recommended that Stein visit China to explain his objectives, and that he carry out his work under official Chinese auspices rather than Indian ones since there was 'a growing (and very natural) feeling against the carting off of these things to foreign museums'.

Since Stein had left Central Asia in 1915, no archaeologist had removed anything from there for a variety of reasons: the European war; the political fragmentation of the country by warlords; and the emergence of conspicuous anti-Westerner feelings in China. The first post-war expedition, in 1923-24, was an American one comprised of Langdon Warner, Curator of Chinese Art at the Fogg Art Museum at Harvard and Horace Jayne of the Museum of Pennsylvania. They had visited Karakhoto in November 1923 but found little of extractable interest other than fresco fragments; Kozlov and Stein had already been there. At Tun-huang, Warner removed a three-foot high T'ang figure of a kneeling saint, today one of the most prized items in the Fogg Museum) and about a dozen modestly sized frescoes directly off the walls. Warner returned in 1925 but, facing fierce anti-foreigner demonstrations at Tun-huang and elsewhere, had to abandon the expedition. He returned with photographs of some of the less important cave temples.

Since Warner could scarcely return to China in the near future, the Trustees of the Fogg Museum decided to ask Stein to do so instead. In August 1928, the Lowell Institute of Harvard University had invited Stein to give a course of six lectures on his expeditions for a fee of six hundred dollars, and Stein had tentatively planned to go in the autumn of 1929. By December the lecture series had been extended to ten lectures and, in addition to a handsome fee, Stein was to receive financing to lead an expedition for Harvard to Central Asia. Despite the Wall Street crash, some 20,000 pounds were raised, of which about half was provided by the Harvard-Yenching endowment.[59]

Stein arrived in Nanking in April 1930 to negotiate one final expedition. Despite fierce resistance from the National Council for the Preservation of Chinese Antiquities in Peking, Stein managed to gain permission to travel eastwards in August 1930. But he was not allowed to do much other than wander around some two thousand miles among the Silk Route sites for some five and a half months, mapping and gathering for his Harvard sponsors what scant material he could find despite continual obstruction. During this time his passport had been recalled and he had been prohibited from any excavation. But the price of official Chinese sanction had been a last-minute condition, that everything he found must be submitted to the authorities before agreement could be given to its removal from China. Thus, his few acquisitions, which included a third-century manuscript from Niya, had to be left behind in Kashgar. After seven futile months, Stein abandoned this expedition and returned to India. He seldom referred to it and none of his obituaries mentioned it.[60]

The Stein Collections:

A. The British Collections

All the material was first sent back to London for division between different departments of the British Museum and the Government of India. Britain holds a collection of about forty thousand manuscripts, paintings and artefacts, as well as historical photographs.

The British Library Stein Collection contains over thirty thousand manuscripts and printed documents on paper, wood and other materials in many languages. When the British Library (BL) was founded in 1973, textual material from the Stein Collection, mainly in Chinese but including documents in

Tibetan, Sanskrit, Kharoshti script, Khotanese, Uighur and Turkic, was transferred from the British Museum's Department of Oriental Manuscripts and Printed Books. In 1982, the India Office Library (IOL) was transferred from The Foreign and Commonwealth Office to the British Library, joining the Oriental Collections to form the Oriental and India Office Collections. The transfer included collections of materials mainly in Tibetan and Sanskrit but also material in Chinese, Khotanese and the Kharoshti script.

Today, the Chinese collection consists of c. 14000 scrolls, c. 1000+ paper fragments and c. 3000 wood-slips; the Khotanese collection, c. 50 scrolls, c. 1600 paper fragments and c. 100 wood-slips; the Tibetan collection, c. 1400 paper fragments and c. 2300 woodslips; Sanskrit/Prakrit (including Brahmi and Kharoshti scripts), c. 1500; in addition to c. 300 Kuchean, c. 100 Uighur, c. 50 Sogdian and 26 Mongolian manuscripts.[61]

Incidentally, the British Library also holds smaller collections from other scholars and travellers to Chinese Central Asia, such as Dr. A.F. Rudolf Hoernle and Sir George McCartney *and* the documents forged by Islam Akhun and his associates! The collection contains paintings on hemp and paper and artefacts such as sutra wrappers, paper cuts and paste brushes, along with over ten thousand prints, negatives and slides taken by Stein from about the 1890s to 1938 in India, Pakistan, Chinese Central Asia, Iran, Iraq and Jordan. Over fifty thousand manuscripts, paintings, textiles and artefacts from the Stein Collections have been digitised on an integrated Chinese/English International Dunhuang Project (IDP, founded in 1994) website that was launched on 11 November 2002. The IDP website is accessible via a single interface in Chinese and English (http://idp.nic.gov.cn/ and http://idp.bl.uk/).

Some of the manuscripts are on display, and changed regularly to avoid excessive exposure to light, in the John Ritblat Gallery. The Stein Collection on permanent display in the Hotung Gallery consists of a mere four cases of archaeological finds. When this gallery was first opened in 1914 as part of the British Museum's Edward VII Wing, Stein's collection represented almost the entirety of the inaugural exhibition. The need to prevent damage from exposure has meant that paintings, works on paper and textiles are not displayed in the Hotung Gallery but are stored in the basements (Stein's 'caves') where they were first unpacked; without special permission, their contents can be known only from their catalogue entries. Annabel Walker pertinently points out that "For decades, hardly anything from the huge collections of his finds at the British Museum has been on permanent display".[62]

Earlier this year, in what William Dalrymple calls "making amends" for confining much of the Stein Collection away from public viewing, the British Library organised a three-month long exhibition, 'The Silk Road: Trade, Travel, War and Faith'. Of the four hundred treasures that were exhibited from June to September, two hundred and fifty were Stein finds, and the rest comprised British Library items and others on loan from China, Japan, Germany and France. Items such as early medieval silk paintings, the carved marble funerary monument of a Sogdian trader from sixth-century Samarkand and an eighth-century fragment showing Jesus Christ as an unbearded Manichaean prophet were on view.[63]

Stein had done post-doctoral research in Oxford while he was in England in 1884–1886. He had spent long periods of time staying with Percy Stafford and Helen Mary Allen there at later stages of his life. There is a smaller British depository of Stein-related material in the Department of Special Collections and Western Manuscripts of the Bodleian Library, University of Oxford (www.bodley.ox.ac.uk/dept/scwmss/). This consists of photographs (1894–1938) and 'other papers' (1903–1944) bequeathed by F.H. Andrews to the Ashmolean Museum in Oxford and then given by the Museum to the Bodleian Library in 1988 and a large collection of assorted Stein material within the Bodleian itself. Much of this material was catalogued by M. Clapinson and T.D. Rogers in their *Summary Catalogue of Post-Medieval Western Manuscripts in the Bodleian Library Oxford. Acquisitions 1916–1975*, Volume 2 (Oxford, 1991).

There is a small and compact collection of about seven hundred artefacts in the Stein Loan Collection of the Victoria and Albert Museum in London: textile fragments, some sixty stucco, terracotta and ceramic pieces, individual items on painted and carved wood and tempera work on plaster and cloth.

B. The National Museum, New Delhi Stein Collection

The Central Asian Antiquities Collection or the Stein Collection, containing almost twelve thousand artefacts is, qualitatively and quantitatively, the richest non-Indian collection in the National Museum. It may also be the largest single Stein repository outside England. It consists of wall paintings; painted silk and cotton banners; sculpture in wood, stucco and terracotta; coins; porcelain and pottery; objects of metal, leather, glass and fibre; precious items of gold and silver; and, religious and secular documents written on paper and wood in seventeen languages and twenty four scripts.[64]

At the end of his third expedition, Stein received a letter from Sir John Marshall in June 1916, informing him that the Government of India had decided that his collections of 1906-08, as well as his new ones were to be installed in a museum to be built in Delhi.[65]

From about 1918, Stein began to visit Delhi regularly. The Ethnological Museum was to be the ultimate destination for the third expedition collection. The frescoes were transferred to Delhi while the rest of the collection left Srinagar in 1924. Stein and Andrews oversaw the construction of a separate building for a Museum of Central Asian Antiquities where they were eventually mounted and where they remained until they were shifted to the National Museum.

The finds from Stein's three expeditions were first divided between the British Museum and the Archaeological Survey of India in New Delhi. The Stein Collection was originally housed in the Central Asian Antiquities Museum administered by the Archaeological Survey of India, and transferred to the National Museum between 1958 and 1962. The large murals were shifted in 1996-1997.

In his exhaustive catalogue, Andrews described the objects from Stein's second and third expeditions, which he writes were discovered on the sites of ancient Buddhist shrines, secular buildings, military stations, burial grounds and camping places on or near to the old trade routes.[66]

In 1968, the Central Asian Antiquities Department was created under the charge of a Keeper. Dr. Chhaya Bhattacharya-Haesner was appointed the first Technical Assistant in 1969 and she carried out a partial verification of the antiquities. During the 1980s all the antiquities were recorded, after further verification, in twelve registers. The items were provided with accession numbers, and information concerning the type of object, material, the site of the find, its chronological provenance and measurements was included. For items falling outside the Archaeological Survey of India, on the one hand, and the National Museum, on the other, lists were compiled in three additional registers.[67]

The earliest wall paintings from Chinese Central Asia in the National Museum are from Miran and Kara-khoja. The paintings, from Balawaste, Farhad-beg Yailaki and Khadalik in the Domoko region (about 500 miles west of Miran), are probably about 300 years later in date than the Miran specimens. With the war-time destruction of a substantial part of the Berlin wall paintings, the National Museum collection has gained heightened prominence, being the only collection that houses relatively intact wall paintings from the Turfan region. The pictorial block prints in this collection are mostly illustrations to Buddhist canonical texts and are reproductions of outline drawings evidently intended originally to be coloured either by hand or, less probably, by colour blocks.[68]

A considerable proportion of the painted plaster that Stein cut from the walls of cave and structural shrines at Karakhoja, Toyuk, Bezeklik and other sites visited on the third expedition were reassembled, mounted on aluminium backing and arranged by Andrews in the Central Asian Antiquities Museum.

The Indian collection of silk, wool and cotton textiles is particularly rich in quantity and diversity. The collection contains many fragments of woollen carpet from Loulan and Niya, representing both the tapestry type (Andrews likens them to the *darri*) and the pile carpet, as well as several samples of richly coloured polychrome silk objects, including some of the earliest known silks woven to fine designs and in beautiful colouring.[69]

As for the sculpture and pottery segments of this collection, the earliest examples of stucco pottery are from the Niya and Miran sites, Astana, Karakhoto, Pei-ting, Ming-oi, Dunhuang; Sorchuk, Khotan and Turfan. Numbering some two thousand objects, the stucco items are in very fragile condition, prone to vibration damage. Some from the Astana area have lost their glaze. A large proportion of the objects retained in Delhi from Khotan and Yotkan consists of terracotta fragments of vessels and more or less complete figurines. Much of the wooden stationery that Stein had packed in Niya in 1900-01 was allocated to the National Museum. Apart from the pre-historic stone implements, there is very little of stone in the collection. The collection also holds beads of glass, stone, bone, ivory and metal; fragments of metal mirrors and several examples of complete mirrors; and many types of finger rings.[70]

In another work, Andrews draws attention to some individual acquisitions by the Central Asian Antiquities Museum that belong outside the categories surveyed above. Thus, Stein skillfully removed a part of the beautifully painted domed ceiling, with floral scrolls supporting a series of seated figures, from a rock-cut shrine in Tuyuk in small sections on his third expedition. Andrews reconstructed this in Delhi. During the same expedition, Stein removed, in sections, paintings from Bezeklik, which Andrews reassembled, mounted and installed in this museum.[71]

C. The Dunhuang Manuscripts

The manuscripts from Dunhuang are now largely housed in four major institutions, namely the National Library of China, Beijing; The British Library, London; The Bibliotheque Nationale, Paris; and the Institute of Oriental Studies, St. Petersburg, with smaller holdings elsewhere. In early 1896, a *Reuters* report from China stated that Mr. Duan Wenjie, Director of the Tun-huang Research Academy and Curator of the caves, had expressed a plea for the return of the forty thousand precious scrolls of manuscripts which had been removed to repositories in Western Europe, like those just mentioned. He expressed the hope that Tun-huang could be reconstituted as a single unit: outside China, apart from the c.10,000 scrolls in the British Museum and the c. 8,000 in France, about 20,000 scrolls from Tunhuang are now to be found in over a dozen countries.[72]

These collections await complete and inter-related catalogues, and, as an additional impetus to scholarly exertions, none of them offer full access to their respective collections.[73] Most of the paintings and artefacts have been reproduced in three volumes, *The Art of Central Asia: The Stein Collections at the British Museum.*

D. The Stein Collection at the Hungarian Academy of Sciences

Throughout his life, Sir Aurel Stein maintained contact with friends and colleagues at the Hungarian Academy of Sciences (HAS) after his first visit to it in 1897. He presented over three thousand volumes of his own, as well as personal and professional correspondence and over forty-five thousand photographs to its library from 1922 onwards. He explained why he sent a large number of his books to this Library in a letter of April 1922: it was because it was "in [that] fine Library I first started my Sanskrit and other philological studies as a school boy. The Librarians have ever since been kind friends to me."[74]

The HAS undertook a three-year project (1999–2002) to produce an English-language catalogue of the HAS Stein Collections to parallel British catalogues. Apart from its Hungarian members, like Eva Apor, Agnes Kelecsenyi, Agnes Karteszi and P. Balazs (librarians with Oriental Studies expertise) the team was an admirably international one: John Falconer (British Library), Susan Whitfield (IDP), Tim Rogers (co-editor of the Bodleian Library Catalogue of Stein Papers), Lilla Russell-Smith (The Circle of Inner Asian Art) and Helen Wang, (Editor, with Eva Apor) *Handbook to Stein Collections in the UK* (British Museum Occasional Paper No. 1129, 1999.) Wang and Apor also edited *Catalogue of the Collections of Sir Aurel Stein in the Library of the Hungarian Academy of Sciences.*

This section on The Stein Collections is necessarily *suggestive* of the range, magnitude and dispersion of the collections rather than exhaustive and precise. Being based in India, I have been obliged into a reliance on material available on the Internet and published sources that are far from adequate. The processes of systematisation of the collections, meanwhile, proceeds apace.

A Note on the Sources

Stein published the narrative of his first expedition in three works. *Preliminary Report of a Journey of Archaeological and Topographical Exploration in Chinese Turkestan* (1901) was written almost immediately upon his return to England as a succinct statement of about forty pages of the expedition expected of a government official; essentially, it supplied details of where he went and what he did.

Sand-Buried Ruins of Khotan: Personal Narrative of a Journey of Archaeological and Geographical Exploration in Chinese Turkestan (London, 1903), is the 'popular' account that was meant to introduce a little-known region to a wide public; five hundred copies, amounting to two-third of the print-run were swiftly sold. It was compiled from his diary, field notes and letters to family and friends, and it told the *story* fully: plans and procedures, obstacles, lessons learned, troubles and triumphs.

Ancient Khotan: Detailed Report of Archaeological Explorations in Chinese Turkestan (Oxford, 1907) was the scholarly account in two volumes with precise inventories of the sites excavated. It had to be a cooperative enterprise and was, with Andrews compiling a list of all the antiquities and contributions from many scholarly specialists: the French sinologist Edouard Chavannes on the Chinese documents from Dandan-Uiliq, Niya and Endere; L.D. Barnett of the British Museum and A.H. Franke from the Moravian Mission on the Tibetan manuscripts and graffiti; the Hungarian geographer, Lajos Loczy on the sand and loess specimens from Khotan; S.W. Bushell, a Sinologist and E.J. Rapson, from the British Museum, on the coins; and A.H. Church, on the stucco fragments.

The second expedition was presented to the world in *Ruins of Desert Cathay: Personal Narrative of Explorations in Central Asia and Westernmost China*,(London, 1912) in two volumes of 1,000 pages and 350 photographs, plates and maps. The scholarly report, entitled *Serindia: Detailed Report of Explorations in Central Asia and Westernmost China* (Oxford, 1921)—after the term 'Serinde' which French Orientalists had invented to describe Chinese Central Asia—was similarly massive; it consisted of five volumes, three of text (including contributions from a number of other scholars), one of plates and another in the form of a box containing ninety-six map sheets.

Arthur Waley, later to become known as a prolific translator of Chinese poetry, worked on the paintings from Dunhuang while employed in the British Museum's Department of Oriental Prints and Drawings, reading and interpreting their inscriptions and identifying the subjects portrayed: his detailed catalogue, *A Catalogue of Paintings recovered from Tun-huang by Sir Aurel Stein* was published in 1931. Lionel Giles published the results of his study of the Chinese manuscripts, *Six Centuries at Tun-huang* (The China Society) in 1944.

Innermost Asia: Detailed Report of Explorations in Central Asia, Kensu and Eastern Iran (Oxford, 1921), in four volumes, two of text with pictures, one of photographs, and one of maps, was the erudite record of the third expedition. This was the only one of his expeditions of which he wrote no popular account. While he did give a number of lectures, and his address to the Royal Geographical Society was long enough to fill a short book, he felt that this wide coverage of his activities excused him from writing another version for the non-scholastic public.

On Ancient Central-Asian Tracks: Brief Narrative of Three Expeditions in Innermost Asia and Northwestern Kansu (London 1933) is Stein's compact and popular account of his three expeditions. The book originated as the Lowell Lectures given at Harvard University in December 1929. After an initial survey of the geography of Chinese Central Asia and the history of Chinese influence there, the chapters follow in a geographical rather than a chronological sequence. Apart from these essential themes, the book gains value from Stein's descriptions of the finding and excavation of major sites.

The fourth expedition was a fiasco and was never substantively recorded.

There are two major biographies of Aurel Stein. In *Sir Aurel*

Stein: Archaeological Explorer (Chicago and London, 1977), Jeannette Mirsky constructs an extremely detailed narrative that draws heavily on the voluminous correspondence that Stein directed to his family and friends. Her account is replete with minutely constructed stories of the expeditions that are often hauntingly evocative of the natural environment, the sites and Stein's personal tribulations and triumphs. Annabel Walker's *Aurel Stein: Pioneer of the Silk Road* (London, 1995) is intended for a less specialised reader. There are frequent and relevant meanders into the other expeditions of the time and general conditions in Chinese Central Asia and rather fewer probes into Stein's inner world.

Jonathan Tucker's *The Silk Road* (New Delhi, 2003) is an extensive and scholarly treatment of an almost lifelong fascination with the region, the roads, sites and artefacts. It ranges over the entire complex of roads between China and the Mediterranean, and has descriptions of all the major towns and oases. It is also beautifully illustrated with maps for each segment of this arterial network.

Peter Hopkirk recounts how the principal *Foreign Devils on the Silk Roads* rediscovered lost cities and removed vast treasures in an account that was for almost two decades the best source on the exploits of the European, Japanese and American archaeologists in the region. Drawing on her prodigiously impressive work within the domain of Dunhuangology, Susan Whitfield skillfully uses contemporary accounts to animate *Life along the Silk Road* from A.D. 750 to 1000 by semi-fictively reconstructing ten characters.

The Notion of Conservation by Removal

Like their counterparts in Africa, Greece, South America and elsewhere in Asia, the nineteenth and early twentieth century 'Silk Roaders' were profoundly convinced of both the wisdom of removing cultural treasures from their historic homes and the legitimacy of transporting them to their own countries or elsewhere in the West or in East Asia. Their accounts are resonant with the belief that Oriental antiquity was best studied by and where the whole panoply of European skills and intellectual apparatuses could be brought to bear upon it: they often wrote about how the local inhabitants, in their ignorance, superstition or greed, had destroyed buried treasures. By way of a conclusion to this essay, it might be apt to ponder upon the felicific calculus that necessarily brings both morality and academic investigation into congruence with each other. Hopkirk poses the question of the morality of depriving a people permanently of their heritage, however sound the reasons for 'rescuing' it may have seemed at the time.[75]

In her book concerned with *The Return of Cultural Treasures,* Jeannette Greenfield has usefully identified the three issues involved: the perennial one of conservation; the contemporary ones of the illicit trade in them; and the commercial and historic one of the return of cultural property.[76] The first of these was deployed to justify the expeditions; purchases at Tun-huang and elsewhere implied the play of the second; the Chinese have always resented, often protested, but never formally requested the return of their lost heritage.

In his proposal to the Government of India for the Third Expedition in November 1912, Stein raised the possible charge of "foreign exploitation" that might be levelled against him. He justified his archaeological work with the claim that Chinese Turkestan was a field "in which India may justly claim a predominant interest" by virtue of the fact that "the spread of Buddhist religion and literature over Central Asia and into the Far East is the greatest achievement by which India has influenced the history of Asia in the past". Jeannette Mirsky has argued that Stein's scholarly endeavours elided into his being "deluded into thinking that Chinese Turkestan was his personal preserve".[77]

While Stein was in Chinese Central Asia in 1930, nineteen Chinese academics united under the aegis of the National Commission for the Preservation of Antiquities and invited Stein's sponsors, Harvard, the Archaeological Survey of India and the British Museum to consider whether in the interest of science and international good feeling they should continue their support promised to Sir Aurel Stein. They claimed that Stein had used his interest in Hiuen-Tsang to conceal the fact that he intended to take archaeological objects from Silk Road sites and had thus obtained his passport dishonourably; and, that he had engaged in "commercial vandalism" in Tun-huang.[78]

However much Stein, his competitors and many of his colleagues respected the antiquity of Chinese culture, which they sincerely and deeply did, they also believed unequivocally that these remains were best off where they could be recorded, studied, displayed and published—outside the Orient. In removing treasures from "the hidden library" in Tun-huang, Stein wrote, "My main care was how many of them I might be able to rescue from their dismal imprisonment and from the risks of their present guardian's careless handling. To my surprise and relief [Wang Yuanzhuan] attached little value to these fine art relics of T'ang times'."[79]

In entitling his lecture to the Chicago Literary Club on October 2, 2000, *The Vanishing Trove: Reviled Heroes, Revered Thieves*, Ray H. Greenblatt captured some of the uncertainty that pervades judgement on whether the extraction of Chinese Central Asian treasures was beneficial because they were protected and made available for study and display. Likewise, Mirsky implies that if Stein had not taken what he did, the treasures may not have survived as a collection but drifted (as, she writes, a good many pieces did when some ten thousand manuscripts were being brought to Peking) piece by piece into dealers' hands and by such circuitous routes reached Western collections. Certainly none of the items Stein brought back to the British Museum wandered into private hands or was cut up or lost. Like Greenblatt, who prefers to reserve judgement on whether his protagonists were heroes or thieves, Mirsky remained undecided about whether Stein should be "condemned or excused". Walker has trenchantly observed that "Many of the items which Stein *resurrected* (my emphasis) from the desert arrived in the West only to be buried yet again".[80]

Stein's colleague Arthur Waley, disagreed with the established positions from his own one of knowledge and prestige. He invited his British readers to imagine how they would feel if a Chinese archaeologist discovered a hoard of medieval manuscripts in a ruined English monastery and bribed (the custodian of the Tun-huang caves) in order to carry it off to Peking. Walker places herself in circumspect alignment with Mirsky and the apparently clear bulk of opinion: It seems glib to condemn a man for acting in a way entirely consistent with the period in which he lived and the western world in which he was raised.[81]

Precisely? The jury might well remain out for much longer on whether the ethics are meretricious or scholarly.

Note: This essay is based on research data that was available till December 2004, when it was presented at the seminar. It does not incorporate data on developments in the Stein Collection since then.

NOTES AND REFERENCES

1. Sir Leonard Woolley's claim to fame rests on his uncovering the royal tombs at Ur. He also worked on Stein's British Museum collection and made a highly critical official assessment of the Archaeological Survey, the *Woolley Report* in 1939. Sir Leonard may have wished to distinguish between Stein's necessarily brief forays into Chinese Turkestan and his own prolonged excavations in the less punishing climes of Mesopotamia. Peter Hopkirk points out that Stein's expeditions, akin to raids in their extractive goals, had to achieve a maximal result from sparse funds and limited supplies, undertaken within stated periods of leave from the Government of India. Peter Hopkirk, *Foreign Devils on the Silk Road: The Search for the Lost Cities and Treasures of Chinese Central Asia.* (1980), pp. 88-89.
2. Annabel Walker, *Aurel Stein: Pioneer of the Silk Road*, London, 1995, pp. 6-9.
3. Walker, pp. 10-13; Jeannette Mirsky, *Sir Aurel Stein: Archaeological Explorer*, Chicago and London, 1977, p. 16.
4. Pausanius, in the second century A.D., was the author of the *Itinerary of Greece*, an extremely graphic description of historical topography. Xuanzang had travelled from China to India in the seventh century in search of scriptural texts missing from the Chinese version of the Buddhist canon, and he wrote a precise account of his travels (629–645) after he returned to China, *Record of the Western Regions (His Yu Chi).* Stein relied on Xuanzang's account to match with towns named in Chinese annals among many of the hundreds of ruined desert sites that he excavated. Stein's knowledge of Xuanzang was to prove greatly beneficial in his negotiations with the Chinese Amban at Yarkand on his

first expedition, and with Abbot Wang at Tun-huang on his second expedition. Stein had read William Marsden's *Marco Polo* in his childhood and had been much taken with it. See Mirsky, p. 29.

5. Mirsky, pp. 16-17; Walker, pp. 36-37, 74; Susan Whitfield, *Life Along the Silk Road*, London, 2000, p. 3.
6. Mirsky, pp. 18-19; Walker, pp. 13-14.
7. *Ibid.*, pp. 21-22.
8. Walker, pp. 17-18.
9. The term, the 'Great Game' was first used by Lieutenant Arthur Connolly of the British Indian Army when he was travelling in Russia, Persia and Afghanistan in c. 1830 and was popularised by Rudyard Kipling in his novel, *Kim* (1901). It was used to describe the rivalry and strategic conflict between the British and Russian Empires for supremacy in Central Asia, from around 1813 to the Anglo-Russian Convention of 1907. As Imperial Russian expansion, particularly after the conquest of the Khanates from the 1860s, threatened to collide with increasing British interference in Afghanistan, the two empires played out a subtle 'great game' of exploration, espionage and imperial diplomacy throughout Central Asia. The conflict never erupted, however, in warfare. For accounts of the Great Game, see Peter Hopkirk, *The Great Game: The Struggle for Empire in Central Asia* (1994) and Karl Meyer and Shireen Brysac, *Tournament of Shadows: The Great Game and the Race for Empire in Asia* (2201). The most notable of Stein's cartographic productions was the *Memoir on Maps of Chinese Turkestan and Kansu from the surveys made during Sir Aurel Stein's Explorations, 1900-01, 1906-08, 1913-15.*(1923). See Mirsky, p. 31; Walker, pp. 19-24.
10. Stein had met Sir Henry Rawlinson, 1810–1895, in the London home of Dr. Theodore Duka (1825–1908), the author of a biography, *The Life and Works of Alexander Csoma de Koros*, in 1884.
11. Stein published his work on the *Rajtarangini* in three moments: the first was his critical edition in Sanskrit in 1892; the second, *Memoir of the Ancient Geography of Kashmir* (1899); and the third was the masterly two-volume *Rajtarangini: A Chronicle of the Kings of Kasmir, Translated with an Introduction, Commentary, and Appendices* (1900; Repr., New Delhi, 1961. The latter two works were translations in English. See Mirsky, pp. 24, 36-37; Walker, pp. 27-28, 34-36, 69.
12. On the nature of the friendship between Stein and Andrews, see Mirsky, p. 43; Walker, pp. 38-39, 113-114. On Andrews work on

the Delhi Collection, see the section below on the Stein Collections: The National Museum, Delhi.

13. He arrived in Calcutta in May 1899 and, appalled by the heat (140°F in the shade) and much else, moved to Darjeeling and Sikkim eight days later for about eight weeks.
14. Mirsky, p. 208; Walker, pp. 61-62, 64-66, 122.
15. Among the phrases Stein used to describe government authorities and their methods were: "a mixture of red tape, classical dilettantism and – whitewash!", or "that center of intellectual sunshine'. Walker, pp. 123-124.
16. Mirsky, p. 336.
17. Walker, p. 193-4.
18. Walker, pp. 58-59. See also Stein's description in *Detailed Report of an Archaeological Tour with the Buner Field Force*, Lahore 1898.
19. Mirsky, pp. 447, 512-514.
20. Walker, pp. 248, 1.
21. *Ibid.*, p. 57.
22. *Ibid.*, p. 57, citing Fred Andrews, 'Sir Aurel Stein: The Man', in *Indian Art and Letters*, XVIII: 2 (1944).
23. Sven Hedin advocated rearmament in Sweden in 1911-14, was a war correspondent writing pro-German articles from the Western and Eastern Fronts during 1914-15, often met Nazi leaders in Germany in 1936 and was involved in 'personal' diplomatic missions to Germany and in pro-Nazi publishing activity between 1939 and 1943. The historian David Gilmour described Sven Hedin as "a ruthless and sinister figure whose principal hero (until he met Hitler) was the last German Kaiser."
24. Baron Mannerheim was made Regent of Finland in September 1918, Commander-in-Chief of Finland's military in November 1939 and he served as the President of Finland from 1944 to 1946.
25. Walker, p. 157, citing Stein, *On Ancient Central Asian Tracks*.
26. Tucker, p. 139, citing Skrine, *Chinese Central Asia*, 1926.
27. A.F.R. Hoernle, 'A Collection of Antiquities from Central Asia', *Journal of the Asiatic Society of Bengal*, Part 1, 1899. Part 2 was published in 1901.
28. Mirsky, p. 79.
29. *Ibid.*, p. 86.
30. Xuanzang recounts the legend about the Silk Princess, current at the time of his visit in 644, and her role in the introduction of sericulture: Before silk was known in China, the king of Kustana (Khotan) sent an embassy to the 'eastern country' (China), where it was known, for a marriage union with a princess of the eastern

country. Despite the king's instructions, the bride smuggled in both the mulberry seed and the silkworm eggs and that is the legend of how silk may have made its first appearance in China. For the full story, see Jonathan Tucker, *The Silk Road: Art and History,* New Delhi, 2003, pp. 181-182; Walker, pp. 100-102.

31. Tucker, 183; Mirsky, pp. 160-161; Hopkirk, pp. 83-86.
32. Wooden stationery did not become obsolete with the invention of paper by the Court eunuch T'sai Lun (or Cai Lun), which, Stein thought, had happened in China in A.D. 105 but Stein found no paper documents in Niya, perhaps because of the slowness of diffusion of paper. The use of bamboo as a medium for writing continued, however, even after the discovery of paper, and wood remained the official writing material to about the end of the third century A.D. in China.
33. Mirsky, pp. 171-172; Walker, pp. 103-106; Hopkirk, p. 89; Tucker, p. 177; F.H. Andrews, *Wall Paintings from Ancient Shrines in Central Asia recovered by Aurel Stein.* (Oxford, 1948; repr. Bangkok, 1998), viii.
34. Tucker, p. 175; Hopkirk, pp. 93-94; Walker, p. 106.
35. Tucker, pp. 184-185; Hopkirk, pp. 96-97.
36. Hopkirk, p. 102; Walker, pp. 108-109.
37. Mirsky, p. 191; Walker, p. 113.
38. Hopkirk, pp. 109-110; Walker, p. 126.
39. Walker, p. 127; Hopkirk, p. 147.
40. Mirsky, p. 242; Walker, pp. 147-148.
41. Walker, pp. 150-151.
42. Walker, pp. 153-155; Hopkirk, pp. 151-153; Tucker, pp. 169-170.
43. Walker, pp. 157-160; Mirsky, pp. 248-9, 241.
44. *Ibid.*, p. 227.
45. Wang was trying to raise funds for the repair of the paintings and sculptures decorating the hundreds of other caves in the complex. For eight nights, Wang carried the documents out of the cave at night. Whitfield, 5.
46. The value of the version in the British Museum may derive from the fact that it proved to be the oldest known example of a block-printed book *that bears an actual date* (not the earliest example of block-printing *per se*); block printing techniques had already been in existence for more than a century before the production of this book. See Tucker, p. 131; and Jeanette Greenfield, *The Return of Cultural Treasures*, (Cambridge, 1984), p. 167, citing *Encyclopedia Sinica*.
47. Walker, pp. 196-7 citing Arthur Waley, *A Catalogue of Paintings recovered from Tun-huang by Sir Aurel Stein* (1931); for a description

of the Tun-huang banners, see Fred H. Andrews, *Descriptive Catalogue of Antiquities recovered by Sir Aurel Stein.* (Delhi: Asian Antiquities Museum, 1935), p. 27).

48. Mirsky, p. 279; Walker, p. 170; Hopkirk, p. 207; Whitfield, p. 5.
49. Mirsky, pp. 340-341.
50. Walker, pp. 218-221; Tucker, pp. 173-174.
51. Tucker, pp. 120-121; Hopkirk, pp. 201-2.
52. Walker, pp. 223-224; Andrews, *Wall Paintings,* x-xi; Mirsky, p. 371.
53. The Japanese also excavated at Karakhoja, Loulan, Charkhlik, Niya, Khotan and Kucha. Apparently the Japanese were the first to stumble upon the treasures at Kyzil. They had collected Buddhist texts, fragments of wall paintings and sculpture. The members of the Japanese expeditions, two monks in the first one, Zuicho Tachibana (a naval officer) and Eizaburo Nomura (an army officer) in the second and third ones were not trained archaeologists skilled in recording provenance and compiling lists. The size and contents of the artifacts they returned with, consequently, cannot be accurately known. In addition, the identity of the objects that found their way to museums like the Tokyo National Museum and the Kyoto Museum from their first repository in the home of Count Otani remains unascertained. The collection has never been thoroughly catalogued. For details (and their absence), see Hopkirk, pp. 198, 190-192, 232; see also Mirsky, pp. 376-377.
54. Andrews, *Wall Paintings,* p. xi.
55. Andrews, *Ibid.*, p. xii. These were among the paintings that Andrews catalogued in Delhi.
56. Mirsky, pp. 376-377.
57. Tucker, pp. 143, 144; Mirsky, pp. 378-379; Hopkirk, pp. 207-208.
58. Walker, p. 228; Andrews, *Wall Paintings*, xii; Mirsky, p. 382.
59. Mirsky, pp. 463, 465-466.
60. Hopkirk, pp. 225-226; Mirsky, 466-469; Walker, 286.
61. See *IDP Newsletter No. 12,* Winter 1998-9, for a list of the major catalogues.
62. Walker, p. 3.
63. William Dalrymple, 'Sands of Time', *The Guardian*, Saturday June 19, 2004.
64. For details, see Fred H. Andrews, *Descriptive Catalogue of Antiquities Recovered by Sir Aurel Stein during his Explorations in Central Asia, Kansu and Eastern Iran*, Delhi, 1935, pp. 1-30. Andrews had been involved in the preparation for storage of

Stein's finds from the first expedition at the British Museum. Walker, p. 113.

65. Mirsky, p. 382.
66. Andrews deployed a dual and comprehensive mode of listing: first, the sites are listed with the objects found at them as in Ast. for Astana followed by a number for the object; pp. 37-353. Then, the objects are listed by category and all the sites of their discovery are provided: viii; pp. 354-445. My summarised account of the National Museum holdings relies on this work.
67. This information is from an unpublished paper by Dr. Chhaya Bhattacharya-Haesner for the Conference on The Documentation of Central Asian Antiquities, UNESCO and IGNCA, New Delhi, July 1997.
68. Andrews, *Descriptive Catalogue*, pp. 2-3, 30.
69. *Ibid.*, pp. 17-19, viii.
70. *Ibid.*, pp. 5, 12-14.
71. Fred H. Andrews, *Wall Paintings From Ancient Shrines in Central Asia Recovered by Sir Aurel Stein*, Oxford, 1948; repr. Bangkok, 1998, p. xi-xii, xxv. This work, that death prevented Stein from writing himself, contains descriptive details of painted fragments from Miran, Farhad-beg-yailaki, Khadalik, Balawaste, Toyuk, Kara-khoto and Murtuk; and, paintings from Farhad-beg-yailaki, Bezeklik and Dandan-oilik.
72. Greenfield, p. 167.
73. For introductory information on the major collections of Dunhuang manuscripts, please refer to the following issues of *IDP News, Newsletter of The International Dunhuang Project* (London): IDP News 2 (January 1995) for the Institute of Oriental Studies, St. Petersburg; IDP News 3 for the Staatsbibliothek, Berlin; IDP News 4 for the Bibliotheque Nationale Paris; IDP News 6 (November 1996) for the National Library of China, Beijing; IDP News 10 for private and public collections in Japan and IDP News 12 (Winter 1998-99) for the Taipei Collection.
74. Mirsky, p. 413.
75. Hopkirk, p. 6.
76. Greenfield, p. 254.
77. Mirsky, p. 355.
78. Walker, p. 287.
79. Greenfield, p. 167; Walker, p. 170.
80. Mirsky, p. 254; Walker, p. 352.
81. Walker, p. 265, citing Waley, *Ballads and Stories from Tun-huang*, 1960; p. 364.

14

Kyrgyzstan in History: Accounts of Russians Scientists and Travellers

Ruby Roy

The history of a country is based primarily on archaeological and written sources. The study of the history of the Kyrgyz people is challenging, as there is a dearth of historical evidence. Archaeological sources are important for knowing about the Kyrgyz in ancient and medieval times. Academician Bartold says that there is no concrete information about the Kyrgyz till the fourth century A.D. when the Turkoguz nomadic empire was found. The South Kyrgyz people were mentioned in written sources for the first time in A.D. 1635. Prior to this, there was hardly any information about them.[1] Written sources improve from the eighteen century onwards as several Russian scientists, administrators, travellers and others visited present-day Kyrgyzstan and have left valuable accounts.

Archaeology is the primary source for knowing about the Kyrgyz in antiquity. However, there is hardly any information about the politico-economic condition of the tribal society in these sources. Monuments, memorials, pertoglyphs do not give substantial information historically about the socio-economic and political situation. This is true even about Saimaly Tash,[2] the foremost petroglyph site in the South. It is one of the most significant and largest finding of rock art in Central Asia. There are about ten thousand boulders with engravings dating back to the beginning of the Third Millennium B.C. Various themes represented in the petroglyphs include animals, hunting scenes, men ploughing the land with oxen, the sign of swastika, etc.

The rock paintings have been studied by several scholars, the most famous being A.N. Bernshtam. His study points to links between Southern Kyrgyzstan and Iran.[3] Archaeological excavations have revealed that agricultural settlement existed in the Southern Kyrgyz city of Osh during ancient times.[4] However, archaeological sources are not substantial for ascertaining certain facts about the ethnic background of the Kyrgyz, the ethnic elements which led to the formation of Kyrgyz nationality and the territory where Kyrgyz nationality took root. Ethnographic sources, art and legends can provide some of these answers.[5]

A connected history of Central Asia and its people in proper perspective was hampered by difficult and remote geographical terrain, and widespread illiteracy. There was no state with a given territory and an ethnic or linguistic group.[6] These factors tended to exclude the history and cultural heritage of Central Asia from the mainstream of historical attention. Yet, Central Asia was the cradle of early civilisation, which saw the major emergence of historical forces—from sedentary civilisation around the Oases of Zerafshan (Samarkand and Bukhara) and the Syr Darya (Fergana, Kokand and Andijan).[7] It was the main area, which saw the synthesis of Turko-Persian culture which gradually spread to Kazkhstan and Kyrgyzstan of today.[8]

Written sources for the study of the Central Asian history are scarce and fragmented. They can be found in different ancient languages, such as Persian, Sogdian, Chinese, Latin.[9] This points to the fact that the ancient world knew about this region and the people inhabiting this area. Information about the people of Central Asia came to Greece through Persia and from Greece to countries near the Black Sea. It is not surprising therefore, that ancient texts contain references to the people of this region. Many Greek writers referred to all the nomads of Eurasia, including those of Central Asia as 'Scythians' while the Persians called them 'Sakas'.[10] The initial parts of *Avesta* refers to the Central Asian nomadic tribes as 'Tura', who were seen as the enemies of sedentary Iranians who owned 'fleet-footed horses'.[11] The *Avesta* also mentions the existence of major political units in Central Asia.[12] Scholars believe that as early as the first millennium B.C. an urban civilisation grew up in the irrigated parts of oases areas such as that of ancient Hyrcania, south-west of modern Turkmenistan.[13] Firdawsi's *Shahnama* (eleventh century) contains information about Turan.[14] Strabo, the famous ancient Greek historian, wrote that under Greek rule, Central Asia experienced such unprecedented urban growth that it became famous as the land of a thousand cities in the West.[15] Russian scholars such as V.V. Radlov, N.M. Yadmitsev and D.A. Khvolsan interpreted and analysed writings in Syrian and ancient Turkic languages engraved on grave stones in Semeriche Aulieata (Talas).

Ancient Chinese sources also mention the Kyrgyz people. According to Bartold, the *History of Tang Dynasty* gives information about the Kyrgyz, their physical appearance, territory, relation with other tribes, language, etc.[16] Bartold states that Chinese sources for the first time mentioned the word Kyrgyz.[17]

The Origin of the Kyrgyz

The territory of present Kyrgyzstan has been conquered by different people throughout history. The nomadic Kyrgyz people are one of the oldest in Central Asia.

The history of the ancient and medieval world to a great extent was shaped by movements of people in the 'heartland of Eurasia'—the vast area stretching from the Caspian Sea in the West to the borders of China in the East. The movement of Turks into Central Asia en masse in the eighteenth century[18] was part of this general movement of people in the region. This was not in the nature of any invasion but was the displacement of tribes which often led to the establishment of tribal confederations, the building of empires, like the Karakhanid empire[19] extending from Transoxiania to present-day Xinjiang.[20] The last migration of Turkic tribes was that of the Kyrgyz[21] who occupied their present country in the sixteenth-seventeenth centuries. Scholars therefore opine that the origin of the Kyrgyz cannot be understood without taking into account the history of the Turkic population in Central Asia.[22] There is hardly any historical evidence about the period and place of the formation of Turkic tribes and it is extremely difficult to define the ethnographic affinities of the Turks.[23] It is generally accepted that ancient Turkic tribes hailed from Central Asia.[24] According to the famous Central Asian scholar Mahmud Kashgar, "the Kyrgyz were pure Turks".[25]

The ancient group of Kyrgyz people was formed in the area far from their modern territory.[26] This formation took place in the area around River Yenisei in Siberia and was the result of a prolonged intermixture of local tribes with Central Asian Gun tribes. This process of development of the Yenisei Kyrgyz led to the gradual emergence of state and specific cultural features, such as Yenisei — Runic writing.[27] Through military campaigns the Yenisei Kyrgyz extended their territorial limits. During such campaigns, some of the Yenisei Kyrgyz came to the Tien-Shan mountain area and helped the Tien-Shan Kyrgyz to develop and establish economic relations with the neighbouring regions.[28]

Therefore, reference to the Kyrgyz people in antiquity, is to Kyrgyz who inhabited the region near River Yenisei.[29] The Yenisei region, which is present-day Tuva, was the power base of the Kyrgyz.[30] According to Bernshtam, the history of the Kyrgyz has two main stages: formation of Yenisei Kyrgyzes, and their disintegration due to political, economic and tribal problems and the 'beginning of Kyrgyz nationality in the Tien-Shan region'.[31]

Kyrgyz nationhood may have been a late development but the concept existed among them despite their numerous clan wars, and fights against the Chinese, Kalmyks and Mongols.[32] This concept was reflected in *Manas* and in the activities of tribal chiefs such as Muhammad Kyrgyz. Historical and concrete references to the idea of Kyrgyz statehood are found in the famous Kyrgyz epic *Manas* (ninth-tenth century).[33] The hero Manas urged fellow Kyrgyz to sink all differences and set up a united country.[34]

The desire for statehood was also reflected in the activities of popular Kyrgyz leaders, the most popular being Muhammad Kyrgyz.[35] In the beginning of the sixteenth century, Muhammad Kyrgyz led the Kyrgyz tribal communities of Tien-Shan. His headquarters was at Barskoon on the banks of Lake Issyk-Kul. His entire life was devoted to the struggle of the Kyrgyz people. During his time, for the first time Kyrgyz emerged as an independent community.[36]

Russian Sources

Writings of Russian scientists and travellers on the history of the Kyrgyzes since the late Middle Ages form valuable source material for the study of the country and its people in antiquity.[37] The numerous notes, reports, diaries memoirs of these scholars help in the understanding of Kyrgyzstan's past. They were pioneers in the distribution of information about the Kyrgyz. Documents and archival materials in Russian are important in constructing a connected history of the Kyrgyz. Archival materials in Russian are found in the Central State Archives of Uzbekistan and Kazakhstan, Omsk and Orenburg Oblasts, USSR Central State Military Historical Archive and others. These archival materials and documents include reports, notes, reviews of Czarist governments officials which throw light on Kyrgyzstan in the eighteenth century — like the establishment of first Russian — Kyrgyz diplomatic ties at the end of the eighteenth century, the relation between the Kyrgyz and their relations with neighbours and about Kyrgyzstan and the struggle between the Kyrgyz and Kokand Governments. The Historical Institute of Kyrgyz USSR between 1976 and 1983 gathered about six hundred documents in Arabic, Turkic and Tajik languages. These documents give general information about the people during this period — their social interests, intellectual level, and moral values. The Czarists government used this information while dealing with foreign powers.

Central Asia is a geographical expression. As a geographical expression it covers Mongolia, the northern part of China, Siberia, Iran, Afghanistan and the present Central Asian Republics. But today it is more of a geopolitical expression, and includes the five Central Asian Republics of Turkmenistan, Uzbekistan, Kazakhstan, Kyrgyzstan, and Tajikistan. Russian Orientalists and geographers were instrumental in defining the geographical boundaries of Central Asia.[38] Nikolay Khanikoff and Ivan Mushketov were pioneers in this respect.[39] Khanikoff's theory states that in defining the geographical limits of Central Asia, the criteria should be common geographical features: the absence of flow of water into the open sea is a good criterion. Mushketov's definition of Central Asia comprised the region which had Altai mountains in the north, Tibet in the South, Pamiirs on the West and Mt. Khinganin in the East. Central Asia as presented by the Russian geographers roughly corresponds to Mackinder's heartland region which he describes as the geographical pivot of history.[40] The Russians knew about the Tien-Shan Kyrgyz long before the establishment of formal diplomatic relations between the two. Concrete information about the Kyrgyz people began to reach Russia from the eighteenth century onwards. This was due to the efforts of Czar Peter I (1682–1725), also known as Peter the Great. Right from the beginning, scientific explorations and categorisation was part of Peter's project. He took interest in scientific expeditions and research. Florio Benevene, the Russian ambassador to Bukhara, in his secret dispatch of March 10, 1722 informed the Czar about Central Asian feudalism and the local people—Uzbeks of Bukhara and Khiva and Tashkent, Kazakhs and about the Kyrgyz. A more in-depth information about the Kyrgyz a year later appeared in the travel accounts of Ivan Unkovsky, the Czar's ambassador in the court of the Junagadh leader, Tsevan Rabtani. In May-June 1723, Unkovsky visited the eastern parts of Lake Issyk-Kul in the north. Lake Issyk–Kul is a drainless lake in the Issyk–Kul Oblast (province) of Kyrgyzstan. Situated in the northern Tien-Shan mountains, it is one of the largest mountain lakes of the world and the second highest navigable lakes of the world. It is one of the ancient lakes on this planet and is estimated to be approximately 25 million years old. It is known as the 'Pearl of Central Asia'. Unkovsky found about 5000 wooden huts which had a proper security system. He gave information about Lake Issyk-Kul and that the northern Kyrgyz did not recognise the authorities of the Jungars.

The accounts of Peter Ivanovich (1712–1777) for the first time outlined the general characteristics of Tien-Shan Kyrgyz.

He also dealt with the origin and meaning of the Tatars. He gives a brief description of the Tatars and their contemporary condition. But this work was not published. This is highly rated as an original encyclopaedic work. Vassily Nikitich Tatishef (1686–1750), another historian from Orenburg, published a book called *Histories* based on the information's given by Richkov[41] (Archives of Academy of Sciences, USSR). This book gives information about the Tien-Shan Kyrgyz, their movements, how they differed from the Kazakhs and their relation with their neighbours.

Richkov's information about the population of Southern Kyrgyzstan was updated in detail since it was based on the travel accounts of Philip Sergevich Efremov, a Russian Corporal. Efremov visited several parts of Central Asia, Kashgar and other countries. He went to South Kyrgyzstan, the city of Osh and the Terek–Devan pass on the route to East Turkestan. After travelling for several years (1774–83), Efremov returned home and penned his travel accounts entitled *Wanderings*. According to this, the Kyrgyz led a nomadic life and lived in the area between Osh and Kashgar. Till the late eighteenth century, the Kyrgyz were independent of the Kokand Khanate as they had their own prince. But they maintained barter trade relations with the Kokand state. The travellers took special note of the large number of feudal lords among the Kyrgyz. This book also throws light on the household activities of the Kyrgyz and their Central Asian neighbours. Efremov's *Wanderings* was so popular that it went through four reprints in 1786, 1794, 1894, and 1911. This book was perceived as an adventurous account but it was an authentic narration of the countries of the East.

The most inclusive and rich information about the Kyrgyz in the eighteenth century and beginning of the nineteenth century was given by Captain I.G. Andriev, a Siberian military engineer and erudite scholar. The Siberian authorities were interested in knowing about the history of the Kyrgyz and Kazakhs for administrative purposes. This task was entrusted to Andriev in 1784, who had good knowledge about the nomadic neighbours. In 1785, Andriev had prepared a history and ethnographic sketch of the Kazakhs which was rejected due to some historical rules. He was asked to prepare shorter accounts for the purpose of local administration. Andriev then wrote about the Kazakhs after gathering information from local traders, officers, general people and travellers. He also used documents available in the archives of Siberia which mentioned the relation between Russia and the Kyrgyz and Kazakhs. Andriev's work contains a separate chapter on the Kyrgyz. He gives a detailed and fairly accurate description about their inner life, foreign relations and political history in the eighteenth century. He names the chapter on the Kyrgyz as *'Wild and Hardy'*. His information dispelled myths about the origin of Kyrgyz and Kazakhs. They were ancient people and belonged to one tribe. But the Kyrgyz moved beyond Kazakh territory. He mentions that at the time of war, it was possible to organise fifty thousand Kyrgyz people at short notice. The author was particularly impressed by their valour in safeguarding their freedom. From Andriev's accounts we also learn about the first Kyrgyz embassy in Russia which was set up in 1785. He also mentions that their economy was based on cattle grazing and agriculture. He makes special mention of horses owned by Kyrgyz. At the same time, he took note of negative social phenomena, like feudalism. Andriev's accounts form an important source for the reconstruction of the historical past of the Kyrgyz. Andriev's work can be found in the archives of Russia. It was not available to specialists of Central Asian Studies till the mid-twentieth century, when it was published.[42]

The accounts of Richkov and Andriev expanded historical knowledge of the Kyrgyz people in Russia in the second half of the eighteenth century. The emergence of Kyrgyz nationhood in the nineteenth century marked a new stage in the pre-revolutionary study of the Kyrgyz and their history. The conquest of Kyrgyzstan by the Kokand Khanate in the beginning of the nineteenth century adversely affected diplomatic and trade relations between Russia and Kyrgyzstan. In spite of difficult situation, sketchy information about the Kyrgyz was available through the communications sent by merchants and officers travelling through the Tien-Shan. We can find brief and fragmented information about the Kyrgyz during that time in separate notes and articles of N. Potanin and P.A. Slovtsov.

A.U. Levshin's special article is most informative about the Kyrgyz of that time. However, all these writings did not portray a general picture about the domestic and external condition of Kyrgyzstan. If, in the second quarter of the nineteenth century, there was a temporary break in trade and diplomatic relations between the two countries, by the 1840s Russian scientists, Orientalists and geographers once again started taking keen interest in Kyrgyzstan. In 1849, the Russian Geographical Society published a rather extensive review of the Kokand state and the fast changing political scenario there. Within two years the same society published a more detailed account of the Kyrgyz. It was considered a fundamental work about the Kyrgyz people in Russian meant for general readers. This publication contained a variety of information about the Kyrgyz, their origin, movements, social and economic life, dependence on Kokand Khanate, including the wide-spread anti–Kokand revolt in 1842. Such information was not mentioned in earlier publications.

There were several Russian scholars who wrote extensively on the Kyrgyz and their history. Two of the most outstanding scientists in the nineteenth century who did seminal work on the subject were Chokhan Valikhanov and A.P. Fedchenko. Chokhan Valikhanov[43] (1835–56) was a scientist and traveller who visited Issyk-Kul in 1856 with a military scientific expedition and in 1857–58 on his way to Kashgar and in 1864. He wrote extensively about the Kyrgyz during ancient and medieval times, especially in the first half and mid-nineteenth century within a chronological framework. He evaluated events as a scientist and did not give a militaristic review of the country. Valikhanov's *Diary* gives valuable information about the history and ethnography of the region. His dairy is based on personal observations and interaction with local people during his journey. He left a good account of the Kyrgyz, their movements and relation with neighbours including the Kazakhs. His details about their household and general economic condition with special reference to agriculture, cattle breeding, trade routes through Kyrgyzstan, lead to a deeper understanding of the country and the people. He wrote on diverse subjects, including historical legends, entertainments, games, customs and music of the Kyrgyz. His diversity is also reflected in his notes on the *Manas* in the Kyrgyz language. He was probably the first Russian scientist to write in the Kyrgyz language. Such original work makes Valikhanov's accounts a primary source for the study of Kyrgyzstan in historical and contemporary perspective. Therefore, it is of special interest and utility for historians and ethnographers.

A.P. Fedchenko was the first scientist who widely explored the southern region of Kyrgyzstan during his travels in Turkestan in the mid-nineteenth century. It was a difficult and dangerous mission, as Kokand was under the powerful and despotic rule of the Khans. His information in the form of short reports about South Kyrgyzstan and the Kokand State was used by several authors in their books. Fedchenko's history of the Kokand Khanate[44] and South Kyrgyzstan are of great political importance. He deals with the oppressive feudal situation and the suffering of the Kyrgyz people. He wrote in detail about the deplorable condition of the Alai Kyrgyz because of feudal oppression. This led to a series of popular revolts against the Kokand Khanate.[45] Fechenko mentions the revolt of the Kyrgyz in Alai in 1871 and Sokh in 1873. Khudair Khan suppressed it with extreme cruelty.

He also mentions the struggle between the Kyrgyz and Kipchak feudal lords for political domination. He notes that the development of the Kyrgyz was impossible under the feudal Kokand State. He also wrote about their economic condition: cattle breeding, domestic production, and handicrafts.[46] His experience was published in the book, *Travels in the Kokand State* in 1872.

There were several other scientists and travellers whose accounts are good sources for understanding the history of Kyrgyzstan. Peter Petrovich Semerov's accounts aid in the study of the complex past of the century. His writings on history, archaeology and ethnography, especially about the Issyk-Kul Kyrgyz and their relation with Russia, China and

Kokand helped future scholars to know the country better. His travels to Tien-Shan also mentions the underwater ruins of Lake Issyk-Kul.

Nikolai Aleksevich Severtsov, a famous Russian scientist, came in touch with the Kyrgyzes during his period of imprisonment in the Kokand State. In 1864 he acquainted himself with the lifestyle of the Chui Kyrgyzes, specially certain tribes, like the Saribagish. His travel accounts (*An Essay About Pamir Mountain Country 1886*) were published in book form and widely read in Russia and other countries. Severtsov's accounts of Kyrgyzstan in the mid-nineteenth century was not just a register of events. It had an analytical approach. He wrote about the voluntary desire of the Kyrgyz to join Russia in order to escape from the feudal oppression of the Kokand khans.[47]

M.I. Venukov's accounts give rare information about the relation of the Kyrgyz with their neighbours: Kazakhs, Kokand and Kashgar, the trade relations of Asian countries with Russia and their voluntary union with Russia. Venukov's writings for the first time gave details about the plans of Pishpek and Tokmark.[48]

The study of the fortresses of Fergana Valley, one of the most ancient historical and geographical regions in Central Asia, is very important. This valley[49] is located on the intersection of three important states.[50] This makes it crucial in the political, economic and particularly in international relations of these states. The valley has attracted the attention of many scholars for centuries because of it natural beauty and wealth. It has been a trade and political centre for East Turkestan and adjoining areas. The pre-revolutionary history of Fergana Valley is vast. Russian travellers, scientists and Czarist government officers visited the valley. Such visits increased in the second half of the nineteenth century after its conquest by Russia. The Russian visitors collected important materials on ethnography and history of the valley. These works have a historical importance as they were in the nature of eyewitness accounts. Russian travellers Fedchenko and Mushketov toured the valley extensively. Fedchenko spoke highly of the artificial irrigation system supported by the two rivers, Naryn and Syr

Darya. Local newspapers and journals also[51] described the problems of the valley, and about the coming of the Russians in 1875 when the Russian army attacked the Kokand Khanate.[52]

Academician Vassily Vladimirovich Bartold (1869–1930) was the most eminent Russian scholar on Central Asia. His views on historical processes became a source work, which inspired future scholars. His works were translated into several languages—English, German, French, Turkish, Persian Uzbek and Kyrgyz. In 1894, he came to Central Asia for the first time with a scientific expedition. He visited Talas, Issyk-Kul, Tien-Shan. After that he visited the region several times. He wrote a *Report* about his scientific expedition in Central Asia. In this report he wrote about trade relations from the ninth to the twelfth century, towns and villages of Central Asia and about historical events of this period. Bartold was interested in the history of Kyrgyzstan as a young scholar. In his book entitled *Turkestan*, he wrote about Kyrgyzstan. This book is about the people of Central Asia, which includes details about the Kyrgyzes and their history. He used source materials in Arabic and Persian languages.[53] He, for the first time, used information written during ancient times. He wrote about the history of the Kyrgyzes from ancient times till the nineteenth century in the book named *Kyrgyzes* (1927).

Bartold is known for his pioneering work on the Karakhanid State which is one of the least studied periods of the history of Central Asia and East Turkestan.[54] Written sources of a later period give historical information about the Karakhanids. Bartold critically analysed the main written sources in the 1920s. His information on the history of the Karakhanids remains the most reliable source even today.[55] A great merit of Bartold's work lies in the extensive use of numismatic material for studying the commercial activities of Karakhanid empire. It is generally said that Bartold made a greater contribution then any other Russian scholar for knowing the history of Central Asia in the proper perspective.

Conclusion

Written sources concerning the history of Kyrgyz are not very informative and lack a chronological perspective. Historical interpretation is often controversial. A proper perspective emerges from the eighteenth century onwards in the writing of Russian scholars and travellers who visited Kyrgyzstan and Central Asia. Until now hardly any original writings in the Kyrgyz language have been translated into Western languages. Scholars working on Kyrgyz history, therefore, rely on Russian language works as primary historical sources. Russian sources focused on a wide-range of subjects, such as geographical setting, ethnicity and many others. Though nations-state and empire are popular historical subjects, the Russians were motivated by their desire to know the country better for academic and administrative reasons.

NOTES AND REFERENCES

1. U.A. Zadneprovosky, 'Archeological Monuments of South Kyrgyzstan and the origin of the Kyrgyzes' in G.F. Debaetsh, General Editor, *Works of Kyrgyz Archeological and Ethnographical Expedition (KAEE) Vol. 3 Academy of Sciences, Frunze U.S.S.R. 1959*, p. 23.
2. Saimaly Tash is the Kyrgyz name for 'patterned stone'. It is 5,000 years old. The site is on Fergana range of Mount Tien-Shan in South Kyrgyzstan near Osh. On Suleiman Mountain in Osh there are numerous drawings on the rocks and inscriptions, connected with ancient beliefs and cults. Ertabyldy Sulaimanev, *Holy and Sacred Places of Mountain Sulaiman of Osh: History of Development of Religious Beliefs Project*. Unpublished, p. 5.
3. U.A. Zadneprovosky, "Archeological Monuments of South Kyrgyzstan and the Origin of the Kyrgyz, in *KAEE* p. 25. Bernshtam has extensively; studied the monuments of South Kyrgyzstan. His works inform us about the history of this area.
4. U.A. Zadneprovosky has studied such archaeological sites in the south. He was the first to say that Osh is 3,000 years old.
5. S.M. Abramzom, 'Ethnic Genesis of the Kyrgyz People' in *KAEE*, p. 31.
6. Mansura Haider, *Medieval Central Asia*, Delhi 2004 and B.A. Litvinsky and others (ed.), *History of Civilisation of Central Asia (HCCA)*, Vol. III, UNESCO, 1992. First Indian edition, New Delhi,1999, p. 489.
7. See *Medieval Central Asia*.
8. *HCCA*, Vol. III, pp. 477-78.

9. Bartold in his book *History of Civilization in Turkestan* wrote about the people of Central Asia and the Kyrgyz. He found information about them in Persian and Arabic languages sources.
10. Abetekov and H. Yusupov, 'Ancient Iranian Nomads in Western Central Asia' in Janos Harmatta and others (ed.) *HCCA*, Vol. II, p. 24.
11. Historians believe that this could be a reference to modern-day Turkmenistan, well known for its horses. Ibid. p. 23.
12. M.A. Dandamayev, *Media and Achaemenid Iran*, Ibid. p. 41.
13. Ibid. Land between two great rivers of Central Asia the Amu Darya and the Syr Darya was known as Turan in ancient time. Later it came to known as Turkestan and after invasion of Arabs as 'Maverau nnehr'.
14. H.B. Paksoy (ed.), *Central Asia Reader: The Re-Discovery of History. London*, NY, 1994, p. 11.
15. P. Bernard, 'The Greek Kingdoms of Central Asia', *HCCA II*. p. 23.
16. B.A. Litvinsky, and Zhang Guang—*'Historical Introduction'*, *HCCA*, Vol. III, p. 23, Tang Dynasty (1618–907 A.D.) expanded till Eastern Turkestan in the West.
17. V.V. Bartold, *The Kyrgyz and their History*, p. 127.
18. Oliver Roy, *The New Central Asia: The Creation of Nations*, I.B. Tauris, London, NY, 2000, p. 5.
19. Karakhanid: a Turkic word meaning 'Big King'. Best period of this empire from end of 10th Century till 11th Century A.D. It included area that approximately covered what are today the Central Asian Republics.
20. According to another source the habitat of the original Turks was in the Altai and from an early period they began to migrate towards China and Turkmenistan. Francis Henry Skrine and Edward Dension, *History of Russian Turkestan and the Central Asian Khanate*, pp. 12 – 13.
21. *The New Central Asia*, p. 7. The Kyrgyz migrated after their defeat by the Buddhist Oyrats.
22. History of the Kyrgyz was closely connected with the Turkic population and their movements.
23. *The Heart of Asia....* p. 124.
24. *'Turkic people of Central Asia and Origin of the Kyrgyz people'*, *KAEE*. p. 18.
25. *Medieval Central Asia*, p. 356.
26. Fn – 19, p. 14 notes, p. 5.
27. J. Junu Shalev, A. Ch Kaker and V.M. Ploskikh, *Historical Stages of Kyrgyz Statehood*, 2003, p. 10. Translated from Russian. Runic

texts found in the Yenisei area belonging to 6th–7th century A.D. mention an ancient Kyrgyz state and the head of this state was called Ajo.

28. Written sources testify to this. Istakhri, famous Arab geographer and author of *Khudt-al-Alam,* mentions that the Kyrgyz came to Tien-Shan area in the 10th century. Quoted in 'Turkic People of Central Asia and Origin of the Kyrgyz People', p. 21. Book translated by V. Monrsky, Reprint edition, 1970, London. Bartold also mentions that the Kyrgyz were connected with the Yenisei group of Kyrgyzes who come to Tien–Shan area but at a later period—15th-16th centuries. *The Kyrgyzes,* Frunze, 1927. The Tien-Shan is on the north-east of the present Kyrgyz Republic. Some others opine that in A.D. 1290 the Mongols defeated the Yenisei Kyrgyz and then they fled to Tien-Shan.
29. *Historical Stages of Kyrgyz Statehood,* p. 10.
30. D. Sinor and others, 'The Uighurs, the Kyrgyz and the Tangut' in M.S. Asimov and C.E. Bosworth (ed.) *HCCA,* Vol. iv. , p. 200.
31. *Turkic People of Central Asia and Origin of the Kyrgyz People, KAEE.* p. 22. According to *Bernshtam* the Kyrgyz are the heirs and successors of all cultural developments of their predecessor in Tien-Shan, part of which became a component of Kyrgyz nationality, *Ibid.,* p. 22.
32. Following the death of Chingiz Khan (1242), his grandson Batu organised his domain into a separate Khanate within the Mongol Empire called among other names Kipchak or Golden Hordes in later Russian and European sources. Roger Barlett, A *History of Russia,* Palgrave, Macmillan 2005, p. 27.
33. Epic *Manas* has 500,000 verses. Manas and his followers defeated their enemies and finally secured the territory that was to became later Kyrgyzstan. Manas was the most important figure of Kyrgyz Struggle for national identity during the Middle Ages. S.I. Lipkin, Russian poet and translator completed the Russian translation of *Manas.*
34. These tribal clashes came to an end in the 19th century with the coming of Russians to present-day Kyrgyzstan. The Kyrgyz were known for their fighting spirit. *Haider Dughlat* (16th century), *Medieval Central Asia,* p. 376.
35. Kubat–bi (18th Century), Ormon Khan (19th Century) Kurmanjam Datka (late 19th century) were some other leaders.
36. V. Ploskikh and others (ed.) *Kyrgyz and their Predecessors,* Bishkek, 1994, pp. 42-50 : Translated from original Russian.
37. The section is primarily based on two Russian books: (*i*) V.M.

Ploskikh, Chief editor, *History of Kyrgyz Soviet Socialist Republic*, Frunze, Kyrgyzstan, 1984. There are total two chapters besides the introduction and conclusion. The introduction consists of two parts (*a*) Historiography, pp. 23–52 and (*b*) Sources, pp. 53–76. (*ii*) V.M. Ploskikh and others, *Source of the study of History of Kyrgyzstan (Ancient to 19th Century)*. Published by National Academy of Sciences, Kyrgyzstan and Institute of History, Bishkek, Humanitarian University, 1996. Part (*iv*) Chapters–iv and v include works on Russian Travellers and Scientists: 18th–19th Century pp. 468–492 and Documents and Sources 18th–19th Century pp. 493–506. I had fruitful discussion on the subject with Academician V. M. Ploskikh, Kyrgyz Slavonic University, Bishkek and Prof. Ertabyldy Sulaimanov, Department of History, Osh State University, Kyrgyzstan. I am thankful to them. The English translation was done with the help of M.S. Lousia and Yulia Gorbunova, students of Center for Indian Studies, OSU. My thanks are due to them also.

38. For an understanding of the term 'Central Asia', see L.I. Miroshinkov's article in A.H. Dani and V.M. Masson (ed.) *HCCA Vol. I*, pp. 477–79. German geographers *Alexander Von Humboldt and Ferdinand Richthofen* in the first half of the 19th Century were pioneers in this field.
39. *Memoirs, Paris, 1862 and Turkestan, St. Petersburg 1886,* Ibid. pp. 477 and 478.
40. Denis Sinor (ed.) *The Cambridge History of Inner Asia,* Cambridge University Press, 1990. Mackinder's 'Heartland' concept tried to explain the geopolitics of the region.
41. Richkov of Orenburg was a scientist and encyclopaedist.
42. Russian military-engineers have left rich documentary materials in the form of reports and notes. These are considered quite extensive, especially on issues such as the Czarist government's policy in Central Asia in the XIX century. These are kept in the Central State Archive of the Republic of Uzbekistan.
43. Valikhanov was a friend of the great writer Fyodor Dostoevsky.
44. 'Khanate', a Turkish word meaning State. The Russian version is 'Kaganat'.
45. The South Kyrgyz revolted against the oppressive Kokand State several times in the 19th century, especially during Khudair Khan's rule. *Kyrgyz and their Predecessors,* p. 46.
46. Even today the South is known for its handicrafts.
47. Both Fedchenko and Severtsov wrote extensively on the architecture of Osh and Uzgen in South Kyrgyzstan.

48. Pishpek was the capital which was named Frunze during Soviet times. Mikhail Frunze was the famous revolutionary who led the Kyrgyz during the Revolution of 1917. The capital was renamed Bishkek after the collapse of USSR. Tokmark is in the north.
49. Accounts of Fergana Valley by Russian scientists are based on their travels from second half of the 19th century till the beginning of the 20th century. *All About Osh* (1998). Papers Presented at Conference in Osh in 1997. Conference organised by Osh State Administration, Osh State University, October 12, 1997. English translation. Unpublished.
50. Tajikistan, Kyrgyzstan and Uzbekistan.
51. *Military Collection, Historic Bulletin* etc.
52. *Turkestan Collection and Historiography of Russian Conquest of Central Asia*, pp. 129–140 in E. Sulaimanov and others (ed.) Papers presented at the First Regional Sciences Conference on the "Social Economic and Cultural Development", Osh, 1997. English Translation.
53. In the University he was a student in Faculty of Eastern Languages. He studied several languages—Turkish, Arabic, and Persian.
54. E.A. Davidovich, *'The Karakhanids'*, in M.S. Asimov and C.E. Bosworth (ed.), *HCCA Vol. iv*, p. 119.
55. Ibid. pp. 119–142.

Traversing the Silk Road

15

Shifting Frames: Cultural Crossroads of the Past and Present

Rajeev Sethi

The only lesson human history, or the evolution of the species, with its diverse flora and fauna teaches us so well, is that no civilisation has ever continued to survive without absorbing influences from values, cultures and genes outside of itself. We can ask: what is this self beyond the outside? Indeed, what is this other? While some of us scholars make a living out of unravelling such issues, I have often been seduced by unfinished puzzles and pieces that do not seem to fit. I can shape and place them as I please, unhindered. This need to create my own mosaic, resonant with texture and forms, can be analysed as a post-modern predicament, or perhaps even as the philistine wavering of an undisciplined mind.

If you would allow me, I would go up in the air and hold up a frame, like the borders of an ancient carpet to view what floats in. We can shift the frame in any direction or enlarge it to any size. Once a carpet-maker in Kyrgyzstan told me why a carpet has a border. "It is our point of reference ... what we see within the frame is all that human eyes can observe, the rest and beyond, is for the Almighty".

My problem with framing anything runs the risk of being myopically conceived. Two years ago, our so-called far-sighted saffron brigade projected a major national initiative for dialogue between the South Asian civilisation and what they saw that as the not so equal 'others'. Their attempt to define

Hindutva as an exclusive ancient pedigree has denied our subcontinent the vitality of its own diversity and the 'Ganga Jamuni *tehzeeb*' born from the interface of parent civilisations.

While working on the Silk Route at the Smithsonian in Washington, I began looking at the transnational production of culture as encounters of fate on the crossroads of trade. The Spice and the Silk Routes, pre-dating the Internet, chasten us to believe that we are not so unique, and then chasten us further to recall that our connections in the past were not merely commercial. Evidence of this old motion and past exchange is still to be found, indeed to be celebrated, in the living arts and life of Asia.

Continental Connections

As a South Asian, the influence of our ancient cross-connections is a part of my living reality. Our challenge is to embrace this wondrous diversity, even in all its opposing forces from an unparalleled vantage point, to remain alive and mindful to the ever-evolving humanity that links us all. For me it is a creative expression: roots that become branches. Like a banyan, its spread is wide and widening, seeking similar ethos and sensibilities. I begin to understand who I am as an Asian, not just as an Indian, and what we as Asians mean to each other and to the world. In search of this comprehensible and meaningful Asian identity, I was most inspired by the resonance of one part in the other and of a present placed so tentatively in a shared past.

Contemplating the scenography of the festival at the Smithsonian in a country in the aftermath of 9/11, I travelled through what seemed to be a seamless journey from Italy, Turkey, Iran, Uzbekistan, Turkmenistan, Kazakhstan, Kyrgyzstan, (countries that most Americans have barely heard of) into China and Japan up to the borders of Mongolia and Korea. All along the journey, South Asia appeared to me like the missing piece of the puzzle I spoke about, resemblances that I merely snipped and shaped. I do this to fit my own creative landscape, mindscape, soundscape and spiritual space. I wanted to do a morphing of forms and faces on the geographical route, like a gentle relay, blurring boundaries and races. Looking at the medieval squares of Isfahan, Samarkand and Delhi, I understood Soviet style plazas in China and Central Asia. Indeed, I have used the deflection and reflection of terracotta and stone in my own work as an architect, inspired by their use at the Topkapi of Istanbul, the gates at Xian, and the fort in Gwalior. I am not an architect trained in the occidental discipline, but I do work in design which takes architectural dimension and I learnt much about defining space by learning to dance. I found Uzbek blue pottery similar to what you find in Khurjha and Jaipur. I even found two century-old cotton *rumal* from Masulipatnam with dates written in Telugu and an empty space left out generously by the Indian artist for his counterpart, the Persian *kalamkar* in Isfahan to put his signature. This unabashed, often spontaneous give and take motivated by trade, would give ulcers to purists and jobs to scholars in the future as the global village protests homogenisation. But history, as I said earlier, absorbs and redefines. Change alone defies rigor mortis.

I bought several eighteenth century chain-stitched rugs from Bukhara, identical to what is produced in Srinagar today. In a centre of handmade silk needlework at Bukhara, I bought a *chador* made with special needles and hooks which created the effect of colour enrichment much as we do in Kashmir, Gujarat and Banjata Tandas of Andhra. The Persian *boota*, the gold *darakh* and our *kalpavriksh* have now taken new directions in designer clothes and soft-furnishings. Their *dastarkhans* and our *dastarkhans* can provide new inspirations to an innovative table linen designer. Handkerchiefs and mirror bags have common motifs of *badam* (almonds), *guldasta* (bouquet) and *gulhazara*. There is a rich repository of resonant symbols, ready for use in many reincarnations, from the erstwhile 'Roos' to Hindustan.

The Future of Human Skills

As people involved with change, I think we need again and again to ask this question, not just about our engagement with Central Asian culture but about the future of human skills themselves in the post-industrial scenario. In a country with shared journeys, what is really the future of work and livelihood in the fast-changing concept of work? Asia has a phenomenally huge unorganised sector, that I prefer to call self-organised and in India itself it is the second largest sector after agriculture. How do you self-empower the unemployed youth? How does one govern the uncounted? How do micro, small and big enterprises find a balance for co-existence? When you read official pamphlets from Uzbekistan asking for many popular masters to work within the companies of the Ministry of Light Industries, just as we do our little *melas* and subsidised cottage industries, you know how rarified and completely precious this craft has become and that very soon we are bound to see the death of many legacy industries.

What is the future of the most vulnerable—the under-employed, the handicapped, children, women? How do you map the force, whom we consider artisans? Is a woman working at her home making a *suzni*, an artisan who will qualify as adding anything to the GDP? Is there any census that could help us prepare the required statistics about such skilled people for future planning initiatives? The aging population and demography compound the politics of work. There is also, of course, the issue of devalued cultural industries and the future of vulnerable traditions, the future of skills of the hand, body and mind, the future of making, doing and being. Today, our abilities to do so much shrink and disappear like the whales, tigers and penguins that we rightly make a lot of fuss about. These are issues that I think Central Asia will have to look into really soon because they woke up to it very late. In India we had people like Kamaladevi Chattopadhyay and Pupul Jayakar linking their movements to the pursuit of freedom, but I see these questions being raised now in the blurred horizon out there. I see a lot of hope too. I would end with a mention of some of the fine initiatives being created there, such as the Central Asia Craft Support Association, a network of almost forty associations in all the five countries that are helping to map Craft Initiatives. Young designers are going to work with felt, leather and silver, to create a new vocabulary and to make it as meaningful and as dynamic as it was before. These initiatives are as important, not just for Central Asia but for the whole of Asia ... indeed for the whole world !

16

The Silk Road Re-Visited

Rta Kapur Chisti

The story of silk is a compelling one of the earliest instances of knowledge turned to practical advantage. Just as the needs of food and shelter compelled people in various parts of the world to discover ingenious ways of cultivation, preservation and developing the building arts, so also their need for clothing led them to explore and find various natural fibres. Silk was the most valued of these finds. There are myths and legends about a silk-producing variety of worm existing initially in the wild. They speak of the discovery of the purest and most precious filament that was drawn from the silk cocoon to weave clothes for their gods and goddesses initially and only then for themselves.

The story of the different types of silk is related to the species of silkworm that feed on specific trees and plants of a region. Of these, the cocoon of the domesticated Bombyx mori silk moth, which feeds on the leaves of *morus alba*, the white mulberry, yields the finest, longest, and most lustrous filament. The other varieties of silk moths produced what are referred to as 'wild' silk. These have glorious textures, colours and warmth but cannot be obtained in filaments of matching length, fineness and lustre.

The varieties of silk varied from the cotton, like white of Eri that feeds off the castor oil tree (*Ricinus Communis*) or Kessera (*Heteropanax Fragrans*); to the beige to dark browns of upto twenty varieties of tussar that live off the Oak (*Quercus*) in the hills, the Sal (*Shorea Robusta*) and the Arjun (*Terminalia Arjuna*), or Phutuka (*Melastonia Malabathricum*) in the plains; the sheer gold of Muga feeding on the Sualu (*Litsaea Polyantha*) or Som (*Machilus bombycina*) and the luminous white Bombyx mori that thrives on the mulberry tree (*Morus Alba*). It was the rearing and breeding of the latter that provided the Chinese the impetus to perfect the quality, length and the smooth evenness of the mulberry silk filament.

Sericulture and silk weaving spread along the Silk Road, from China to Western Europe through Japan, India, Mongolia, Pakistan, Bangladesh, Uzbekistan, Syria, Kyrgyzstan, Kazakhstan, Turkmenistan, Turkey to Italy. It overtook the many regional, and more anonymous, traditions of wild silk. Nurtured outside the realm of court-recorded history, these 'wild' varieties suffered the predicament common to the progress of civilisation everywhere: a continuing movement towards uniformity of material culture built on the neglect of natural diversity.

Legacy of the Past

The culture of mulberry silk, invented and perfected by the Chinese, brought inquisitive travellers and traders from within and beyond to the East, to learn the secrets of this rare art and spread its magical spell along what came to be known as the Silk Road.

It was this two-way traffic that turned their knowledge and expertise with the breeding, spinning and weaving of silk into practical advantage for over two thousand years. There were other areas in the world, including India, where the mulberry variety was found, but none could compete with the uniform perfection and length of the Chinese filament. Even well into the twentieth century after the Communist revolution of 1949, the Chinese succeeded in standardising the length and quality of the mulberry silk filament by destroying various strains of silkworm that could not produce filaments of even length. They propagated the worm strains that could produce an undisturbed filament of upto a thousand metres. Though it set a high enough standard for them to dominate the world market for silk at least in the form of yarn, if not fabric, they had not foreseen the growing demand for texture as well.

In the past ten years alone, the previously known 'wild' varieties, some of which have been cultivated since the nineteenth century, have not only grown in stature but have also brought into focus the need for 'variety' in sustaining marketability. So much so, that we find the Chinese re-introducing the Tussar worms into cultivation to compete with their South and Central Asian neighbours.

The Silk Road has come full circle as it were, providing its own clues to sustainability and regeneration. It is the wide open space between uniformity and diversity; the smooth and the rough; the fine and the coarse; the light and the heavy. In a world of globalising markets, it is difficult to sustain the shades of variation possible. Often enough the variant exists only due to compulsions of poverty and unavailability of an alternative. Not necessarily because it is recognised for its own worth.

The Silk Road brings into focus the sheer beauty of diversity; the immeasurable contribution of being yourself, not necessarily in relation or comparison to another. Much like the complexity in nature, there is a harmony created by the myriad image, the difference in perception and expression, though human instincts and emotions are shared.

The Silk Road recalls the ambience of a world that had learnt to communicate and understand without language and celebrate the diverse without the compulsion to subjugate. That was the wonder of the Silk Road as it existed originally.

In this multi-faceted democracy of ours, many centuries co-exist simultaneously and no matter how rapidly the islands of well-being may grow, with our attempt to industrialise, catch up with the world and more recently, liberalise and globalise, the catch words of the last fifty years, the sea of poverty or at least segments of it remain out of reach. It is when the starkness of this reality strikes, that the need to look for a self-sustaining means of livelihood with dignity reasserts itself.

The challenge today is that such communities are being pushed to the brink as being 'under productive', and referred to as 'a legacy of the past', when they are in fact the finest example of harmonious development. Their sustenance in economic, social and cultural terms is a challenge, both philosophical and literal, for all societies in transition. Ultimately we are all in process of transition, both in the 'developing' and the 'developed' world. We need to find ways to recognise the worth of the human 'hand' even as the human 'mind' seeks to relieve it from the drudgery of constant application. In doing so, we lose not only the great resources of 'hand' skills but also their intrinsic contribution to human development.

In the case of the Central Asian Republics that came into their own with the disintegration of the Soviet Union, the situation is more ambivalent. The communist state had helped the textile arts and crafts to survive on a 'museum and visitor market' if not a mass one. With independence and the re-discovery of their neglected ethnicity, a new found interest arose in maintaining of their historical textile techniques. Though a vast resource of skill and expertise has already been lost, the revival of the international tourist trade has unearthed the old samples of textiles and the continuing production of these at whatever level is possible now.

Plight of Weavers

In India the most recent survey of handlooms in ten districts of eastern Uttar Pradesh (September 2004) reveals the dire conditions weavers are facing because there is a sudden decline of production orders especially in the last year at least of handloom fabrics. This is a direct fallout of cheaper machine made fabrics from other parts of south Asia, particularly China. In the rural and semi-rural areas, as most weavers are landless, starvation-like conditions are evident everywhere. If there is a choice of moving towards a bigger city because of some family member already being there, the more able-bodied are migrating. In cities such as Banaras, only those traders who have found markets in the metropolitan cities and beyond are able to give work to weavers while the rest have already left weaving for becoming street vendors or rickshaw drivers. We are told there is approximately 25,000 metres of plain Chinese silk entering the market every day, which is either sold after dyeing or is embellished with embroidery both for saris or other garments. The Chinese strategy seems to be to consciously provide subsidised fabrics to flood the Indian market if it can help in capturing it. If Chinese chiffon can be sold in India at Rs. 9 to Rs. 16 a metre, we can only estimate the 'no cost' or 'low cost' at which raw materials are being procured for state owned factories and the labour and finishing costs for this.

It is wake-up time for the hand skill sector or even pockets of it, if we want them to survive or find a foothold in the Indian or international market. Pockets of high skill can certainly be maintained but even these will require design and quality support on an annual basis in order to chart out a reasonably sound future. For those who will be eliminated from the profession, there could be alternative industries that could benefit from their skills. Just as the IT hardware industry received the talents of whole families of jewelers in Karnataka in the 1970s, weavers too could be considered a vast skill resource for an alternative sector.

The patterned fabric and product range is our greatest asset which no market including the Chinese can compete with, if we were to judiciously plan, develop and promote its inherent skills. With the collapse of the sari market in India, and the increase in the wearing of the stitched garment, a careful and concerted planning and effort is required both in design and marketing of patterned fabrics for varied use in the national and international markets.

A revised role is now required, if any, from the government and most certainly a complete withdrawal from the actual production and marketing process. However, there are specific areas in which its actual involvement is not only necessary but can be mutually beneficial both for itself and the producer. The areas that require government intervention may be listed in the following categories:

(*a*) Health and education for the artisans.
(*b*) Raw material outlets supplying relevant materials.
(*c*) A small design development and technical advisory group for each region of not more than four persons per region.

All the above may need government support only for an initial period of two to four years and should thereafter be supported by the producer community, especially the trader and exporter who has benefited the most from the handcrafted skill sector.

There is no need to castigate increased mechanisation in principle either socially or economically and in reality it need not be in conflict with the hand skill sector. The hand skill sector is in effect the base R&D laboratory for developments that can take place both within it and the increasingly mechanised systems of production. It provides the ideal space for both design and technical innovations which may not receive the attention they deserve in a faster production mechanism, preoccupied with higher turn-overs in less time.

The mechanised production sector is relatively organised and able to milk the system, both government and market, for its own benefit. The hand skill segment of production is not only unorganised but also exploited at all levels from the single unit of the spinner/weaver/dyer/printer to successive stages of entrepreneurs/co-operatives, financiers, wholesalers, agents and exporters. To add to this confusion is the complex production and distribution system of raw materials that unleashes the full ferocity of market forces on the producers, without vision or perspective as to the future course of this most vulnerable sector. With the result, that to keep the demand/supply chain active, the single unit producer must buy what is available in terms of raw materials, at high financial risk in order to survive. In the last twenty years and more so in the last five, we have seen the decline of indigenous varieties of cotton, silk, wool with cheaper bulk supplies from China, Korea, and Mongolia. This is largely because cultivation of indigenous varieties is increasingly neglected and their advantages being overlooked in comparison to the easier import mechanisms available. We have already lost:

(*i*) More than sixty varieties of indigenous cottons including naturally coloured cottons to the longer staple hybrid variety. Though hybrids may be beneficial for high-speed spinning in the mills and for finer counts, they require more water, pesticide protection and fertiliser inputs in the long run, whereas the *desi* indigenous varieties are hardier and ecologically more suited for difficult conditions. Moreover, we have areas such as Andhra Pradesh, which have been able even before the advent of Gandhiji and till today spin up to 150 counts from these relatively short staple varieties. This in the context of the highest count mill yarns being 120s count produced worldwide today emphasises the capabilities and high quality skills of the hand-spinning sector. In the semi-mechanised hand spinning sector production on the Amber Charkha, India is producing a limited range of 120s to 500 counts, which also reveals a potential as yet untapped and unprecedented. The employment potential of hand spinning and weaving for textured varieties of fabrics is formidable in the Indian and international market if we were to look at it not as a slower means of production but as a branded variety of fabrics in which we could have virtually a monopoly in world market terms.

(*ii*) In terms of silk, India has been the home of nearly 40 varieties of Tussar silk worms, upto four varieties of Eri, the golden Muga in the Brahmaputra valley and at least two varieties of Mulberry silk. Since Independence we have lost more than half the varieties of Tussar, at least two varieties of Eri, Muga is fast declining in terms of production area and the two indigenous variety of Mulberry in Kashmir and Bengal are facing their most difficult challenge from Chinese imports.

The Indian Context

The planned growth of cultivation in specific climatic and soil zones of specific varieties of silk can not only regenerate a neglected rural economy but with the added potential of machine and hand reeling of these silks and weaving can unleash an unprecedented variety of textured and naturally coloured silks. The Chinese have won over world markets in the production of uniformally long filaments of Mulberry and in the last 10 years have been scouring India, Vietnam, and other

South Asian countries for other varieties of silks that they had virtually banished in their quest to propagate and promote the long smooth filament producing Mulberry. This search for reintroducing other varieties of silk was primarily in order to find a foothold in the colour, texture variations available in the non-Mulberry sector.

The advantages of our democracy are negated by the disadvantages of a lack of full view vision in the development of potential resources, both natural and human. Even when they are realised, there is an inability in implementing them across states and regional interests, despite economic and social advantages that can be seen both at state and central levels.

(*iii*) The case of wool is even more complex, as the base of the raw material production comes from the numerous nomadic herding communities that are involved in the rearing, breeding, moving along from north to south in search of appropriate pastures, sheering and sale of wools of varying range and variety. These routes are now significantly threatened by ongoing developments, especially the proliferation of settled village, town and city communities that no longer accommodate the nomadic presence. The animals themselves vary from the goat, sheep, camel providing the coarsest hairs for tent coverings, floor coverings to the finest wool of the Pashmina goats in the high mountain ranges.

It is not only a question of the decrease in traditional utility items such as floor and tent coverings but an inability to look at this area as a potential resource for other applications. The coarse varieties of wool which were traditionally the biggest export from a state like Rajasthan to Iraq and the West Asia region for indigo-dyed tent fabrics and felts are now facing extinction as their alternative application is not even considered worthy of development potential.

In the case of the finest soft wools, such as Pashmina, the benefit to the herding, rearing communities is so small and so precarious that the series of middlemen and traders cannot help in the development of its production and scope of improvement.

(*iv*) The scope for development in the natural resources of the textile industry and its cross-fertilisation with the manmade fibre industry for specific fabric and product development has not even been considered in the present phase of prospective development. This aspect of development can only be addressed if natural raw material resources and manmade fibres are not necessarily seen as representing separate interest groups. They are to be seen in the totality of their functional utility and their scope for economic and social development.

(*v*) On this mapping and development of natural resources across the country along with the base skills of hand and machine reeling/spinning rests the overlay of specialised hand weaving skills and their associated support systems. Including preparatory processes, dyeing and maintenance facilities often provided by specialised skilled communities within a given region.

For instance, there are coarse count cotton areas with expertise in handling metallic yarn warp patterning or floss silk patterning in the borders or fine count areas that not only use metallic yarns in a similar way but have the capability of handling metallic yarn right upto the selvedge edge with a minimum cotton thread edging. There are areas that can still handle over 150 counts of fine cotton and still have access to sizing methods that give a smooth uniformity to the yarn. Similarly, there are silk areas that have the expertise of handling untwisted silk partially in warp and completely in weft to weave a range of patterned textiles from the sheerest drapes to the rich and heavy. These are apart from the well-known weaving areas in and around Banaras, Bangalore, Chanderi, Paithan, Yeola, Malikarmur, Kancheepuram, Gadwal, etc. which are facing a series of specific problems in the availability of raw materials, production and marketing which do not know to whom these issues must be addressed.

In terms of wool, there are areas adept in the tapestry technique for the weaving of coarse wool rugs, floor coverings, patterned felts, and carpets. There are areas capable of tweed development in the hand skill sector which have lost ground to the mill-made suiting industry. In the fine wool sector, patterned weaving has lost its area of expertise to embroidery. Though mill-woven Jacquard weaves provide cheap volume production, there is no attempt to regenerate even this area, with design and innovation in the hand skill sector. A sustained hierarchy of skills is the only way to provide for growth, regeneration, innovation within the textile sector, both hand and mechanised.

All the aforementioned examples are instances that offer immense scope for unique developments within India which could give it exclusive advantage both within the country and international market. Instead, they are facing the final threat of extinction and with the impending WTO implementation, the situation will become only worse. Therefore, a single-window addressable body of concerned individuals with the power to direct energies, activate systems and maintain an overview is necessary, if we are to sustain and develop even a part of a present potential which is steadily being extinguished.

Trade Without Boundaries

In the context of trade on the ancient Silk Route and the North–South interaction with the subcontinent, there is a noticeable decline since the nineteenth century. This was partly initiated by the British as Afghanistan was treated as a buffer area between the subcontinent and central Asia and trade was not encouraged along this route. The ancient links were further weakened in the first half of the twentieth century and there was no direct access to the central Asian Republics of the Soviet Union. The socialist system has transformed them socially and economically by providing them access to better physical infrastructure but their predicament in terms of finding access to world markets in terms of their inherent hand skills remains similar to the Indian experience.

In a sense, the example of the ancient Silk Route and the parallel Spice Route, give us insights into the concept of global trade without boundaries. Yet the means of its functioning and its relation to prevalent political systems is what is at variance with the circumstances the world is faced with today. The major change in trading patterns seems to have occurred in the colonial period when large portions of the world became the raw material providers for countries in Europe and America. Their skills and their products had exchange value only when they did not threaten or intrude upon the production systems prevalent in those countries. Their import was either ruled out or restricted if they affected the parent economies. The dropping of trade barriers in the process of globalisation is the logical conclusion to the economic liberalisation of the world. It however, does not take into consideration the variations in technological production systems, the social and economic circumstances that limit production capabilities and the disparities that sustained and fuelled economic and social progress till now. The competitive edge is now more about producing the cheaper substitute than about the original variant. It also causes a levelling out of market variations so that fewer variations remain worldwide.

17

Reviving the Silk Route: Problems and Prospects

Meena Singh Roy

The relevance of trade routes and corridors for nation states is undisputable. While they have opened up opportunities and prospects for political, economic, scientific and cultural cooperation, they have also created a number of complex problems. On the one hand, they are proof of how transportation and communication networks have linked the communities of the globe; how they have spread religion, art, painting, peace and prosperity; how the physical features of the land have influenced the location of the trade route, growth of settlements and cultural diffusion along those routes. On the other hand, these routes explain how empires have used these routes for wars, destruction, diplomacy, advancing their national interests and for expanding their influence.

It is in this context that an attempt is made to understand various dynamisms related to the famous Silk Route[1], the trans-Asian trade network linking the Mediterranean with the Asian continent. The paper argues that the process of reviving the Great Silk Route and developing new transport networks, which is underway in the region, is conditioned by three factors: economic and geopolitical interests of regional and extra-regional powers; security fears and political differences among the states; and geographical and economic constraints of the Central Asian Republics (CARs). In the changing geopolitical paradigm, Silk Road diplomacy is being used by these players to gain a foothold in this region and to push their political, economic and strategic interests. However, in this process CARs have been able to garner some economic and political gains. The construction of new corridors is opening the Central Asian region to the world market and offering new prospects of economic cooperation.

The term 'Silk Road' was coined by Ferdinand von Richthofen. Since then the word has come to epitomise a sense of exoticism and adventure and has captured and captivated the Western imagination. One writer has described the Silk Road as the "catch phrase of vaguely defined beauty".[2] Was the Silk Route then a myth or a reality? By the first century B.C., the Silk Road was the longest network of land trade routes in the ancient time, connecting cities in over a dozen countries, China, CAR, Afghanistan, and ancient Taxila on the Indian subcontinent, Iraq, Alexandria, and Rome. In fact, the Silk Route was not one but many.[3] For centuries bazaars all along these routes were filled with crowds of people speaking diverse languages. Long caravans went along these dusty roads carrying precious gems and silks, spices and dyes, gold and silver, exotic birds and animals to European countries.[4] Merchant cargoes also included salt, wool, jade and many other items.[5] This was also the route through which Buddhism travelled to other parts of the world. It was in nineteenth century that the Central Asian region became the region of barriers and conflict rather than the area which used to connect the economies and people all along the famous Silk Route.

Today, the Silk Route has also become the road map for major powers to enhance their own interest and gain a foothold in the strategically important, resource-rich region of Central Asia. It is also about oil diplomacy. In this new unfolding geo-strategic situation, the new Silk Road strategy is being used by various regional and extra-regional powers, to advance their economic, political and military interests in the Central Asian region. It has become the route of competition and cooperation, engagement and containment, and finally the route of information technology.

The Current Transport Scenario

Before we examine the regional and international initiatives which are underway in the Central Asian region, it is important to understand the current status of CAR's transport sector. Central Asia inherited the transport system which was developed with an orientation to Moscow, mainly northwards, but post-independence, the need to meet the political and economic requirements of these states was felt. Roads and rails are not in great shape. According to international experts, 1,500 km of roads in the region are deteriorating each year.[6] Corridors between Central Asia and Xinjiang are limited and the passage between CARs and South Asia is even more restricted. Prior to their independence, the CAR's roads were used to serve the monolithic Soviet economy where links with neighbouring countries had no priority. But after independence, trade flows are being reoriented, with implications for investment in transport infrastructure. Regional traffic in Central Asia is overwhelmingly carried by rail, as shown in Table I. Even within the CARs, roads carry only 22% of traffic. On the other hand, roads carry significant amounts of imports over long distances from China and other countries (50% or more). In Central Asia, the most developed modes of transportation are railways and motorways (Foreign Trade Carried by Rail and Road in the CARs shown in Table I and Table II indicates Transport Networks in the CARs). It covers over 90% of the transit traffic.[7] Under the framework of the Economic Commission for Europe (ECE) and the Economic and Social Commission for Asia and Pacific (ESCAP), the UN has determined five Eurasian corridors:

1. Western Europe-Russia–Korean Peninsula directly, or via Kazakhstan and China, or via Mongolia and China-(West-East-Trans-Siberian corridor)-Northern corridor of Trans-Asian railways.
2. Europe-Southern and Southeastern Asia via Turkey and Iran.
3. Southeastern Europe-Turkey-Iran-Central Asia-China (Central Corridor through the CARs–Kazakhstan,

Uzbekistan, Turkmenistan. Southern corridor of the Trans-Asian railways.

4. Europe-Caucasus-Asia (via the Black Sea–Caucasus-via the Caspian Sea-Central Asia).
5. Northern Europe–Russia-Central Asia-Persian Gulf—North-South Corridor.[8]

Four of the above mentioned routes (1, 3, 4, and 5) involve the Central Asian states' transport network. The road network in CARs consists of 66,000 km of roads, of which about 29,000 km carry most of the regional traffic. In overall terms, Kazakhstan is by far the dominant player in regional transport, carrying not only its own trade but also considerable volumes of CARs' transit traffic. There is one major paved road corridor connecting the countries in Central Asia: the East-West highway that links Tashkent with Almaty. This road runs to the southwest of Uzbekistan, with further links to Turkmenistan, to the Kazakhstan-China border at Horgos and onward to Urumchi in the east. Portions of the roads have been upgraded in Xinjiang, but major reconstruction of several sections of the road is still needed.

The rail networks in Central Asia have about 22,100 km of main line, of which about 5,000 km are double track and 4,000 km electrified. The existing rail network already links the major cities and industrial centres of the region. The conditions of these rail tracks have been deteriorating, and maintenance has been poor because of declining revenues. In recent years several new lines have been constructed in the region, mainly in Turkmenistan and Uzbekistan. More such lines are planned, although most are long-term projects because of financial constraints. In the short term, considerable priority is given to rehabilitating the regional rail network and promoting regional traffic.[9]

Table I: Foreign Trade Carried by Rail and Road in the CARs

(In thousand tonnes)

Country Group	*Imports into CARs*				*Exports from CARs*			
	Rail	*Road*	*Total*	*%*	*Rail*	*Road*	*Total*	*%*
Within CARs	3,705	1,037	4,742	35	3,705	1,037	4,742	11
Russia-Belarus	5,361	965	6,326	46	25,711	567	26,278	62
Europe	1,454	144	1,598	12	4,234	130	4,364	10
PRC-Mongolia	167	173	340	2	3,429	227	3,656	9
Japan-Korea	106	12	118	1	835	14	849	2
Others	174	418	592	4	1,753	683	2,436	6
Total	10,968	2,749	13,716	100	39,666	2,658	42,325	100
%	80	20	100		94	6	100	

CARs=Central Asian Republics, PRC= People's Republic of China
Source: *http://www.adb.org/Documents/csps/CARE/2004/appendix9.pdf*

Table II: Transport Networks in the Central Asian Republics, 2004

(1000 km)

	Railways	*Roads*
Azerbaijan	2.1	25.0
Kazakhstan	14.3	89.0
Kyrgyz Republic	0.4	18.8
Tajikistan	0.5	12.5
Uzbekistan	4.0	43.5
Total	21.3	188.8

Source: *http://www.adb.org/Documents/Reports/CA-Trade-Policy/Chap5.pdf*

Today the Great Silk Route is being resurrected like the Phoenix. With the 1994 Samarkand Declaration, sixteen countries along the old route revived the Silk Road for tourism. Now it is motor vehicles that traverse this ancient road instead of camels. All along this route, luxury hotels house the travellers instead of inns, and the commodities they seek in exchange for their money is not silk or horses or technology but the sights and sounds of the Silk Road itself. An international organisation, like UNESCO has introduced the international programme, 'The Great Silk Road — A Road of Dialogue, Understanding and Rapprochement of Cultures'.[10]

There are a number of new routes which are being considered for development. The efforts by regional countries like Iran, China, India, Pakistan, Turkey and Russia are being made to either revive the old routes or to develop the new transport corridors. The European Union (EU) and the United States (US) have also been involved in various projects in the region. An international financial institution, the Asian Development Bank (ADB), has also been considering such plans. There are some which are under construction, and a few others, which have been operational. In general, the development of the regional transport system can be categorised in four geographical directions. The most important ones are:[11]

1. Russia, Europe and the Baltic region.
2. China, Japan and the South East Asian region.
3. Trans-Caucasian Republics, Iran, and Turkey.
4. Afghanistan-Pakistan and India.

There is already a set of highways and waterway routes, which exist in three of the above-mentioned directions. It is mainly the Afghanistan-Pakistan-India route which needs to be connected to the Central Asian region. Considerable moves have been made in this direction. In April 2004, the long-awaited attempt to revive the ancient Silk Route project known as the Asian Highway,[12] first proposed in 1959, and delayed due to the Cold War, was finally approved. The new treaty was signed by 23 nations at the United Nations' 60th meeting in Shanghai. Under this agreement multiple land links between Khabarovsk and Tokyo in Asia would be created, spanning 140,000 km of roads before arriving in St. Petersburg, Finland, and the old Western terminus of Istanbul. This route would alleviate the isolation in landlocked countries, including Bhutan, Kazakhstan, Kyrgyzstan, Laos, Mongolia, Nepal and Uzbekistan.[13] Although this project is extremely ambitious, if realised, it would serve as a network of corridors connecting the entire Southern Asia-CARs with Europe and Russia. However, significant obstacles like problems of political differences and investment remain before the full potential of this project can be realised.

The new transport routes passing through Central Asia started developing in the 1990s.[14] In 1991, the railway between

Kazakhstan and China was joined, and the international 'Druzhba-Alashankou' control post was opened. In October 1994, Railway Ministers of China, Russia and five Central Asian countries held a conference in Beijing, during which they formulated a railway transport development programme between them, improved transport organisational measures and signed a joint communiqué to guarantee unimpeded passenger and cargo transport on the continental bridge.[15] In 1997, the railways in Meshkhed-Serax-Tedjent section were connected. Thus trans-continental transport corridors were formed in two directions—the Eurasian and the Trans-Asian railways.

The active study of the Transport Corridor Europe-Caucasus-Asia[16] (TRACECA) started in 1995 on the proposal of the European Union. This is a well-known project prepared within the framework of Technical Assistance to Commonwealth of Independent States (TACIS). This project is supposed to connect Europe through a transportation-communication corridor reviving the Great Silk Route. It is also meant to create the condition for the transportation of oil, oil products and cotton to Europe through the development of unified documentation, customs procedures, loading and unloading mechanisms etc. The TRACECA would be formed in three stages by 2010 and would include 9 corridors with 13 branches.[17] During this 10-year period, TRACECA has implemented 53 projects, 39 technical assistance and 14 investment projects, for a total of over Euro 110 million.[18] However, due to certain bottlenecks[19] this corridor is ineffective at present in serving transit transportation.

Another important route is the Central Corridor of the Trans-Asian Railway, which coincides with the Silk Route. This corridor lies along the route from China's eastern port, through Alashankou, Druzhba, Chengeldy (Kazakhstan), Tashkent, Bukhara (Uzbekistan), Chardzhou, Tedjent (Turkmenistan), Meshkhed (Iran) with the outlet of Istanbul (Turkey) and further along the route to Europe. However, the capacity of this corridor at present is practically not realised, the traffic volume on this route does not exceed 0.2–0.3 million tonnes. The most active at present is the Northern corridor of the Trans-Asian Railway that unites China with Russia, Baltic and European countries through Kazakhstan. Special importance in providing international transportation by the Trans-Asian Railway is attached to the development of the Druzhba station on the Kazakhstan–Chinese border. This route is of great significance because of the increasing volume of traffic which passes through this route. It is expected that traffic passing through this cross will be about 7–8 million tonnes. It is planned that the Druzhba-Alashankou cross would carry up to 40% of the total containers shipped by China to European Countries.[20]

The ongoing development in the creation of North–South Corridor linking South Asia with Europe via Iran and Russia is a significant attempt to restore the historic trade links connecting Europe with the Gulf region, the Indian Ocean and South Eastern Asia. This inter-governmental agreement between India, Iran and Russia was signed in St.Petersburg on 12 September 2002.[21] This agreement has been ratified by all the three signatory states and has come into force since 16 May 2002. Kazakhstan, Belarus, Oman and Tajikistan have also joined this corridor. Armenia, Azerbaijan, Bulgaria, Turkey, Ukraine, Kyrgyzstan and Syria are on the verge of accession to this agreement. This corridor will facilitate easier movement of goods along the corridor connecting India through the sea route to Iran and then via the Caspian Sea to the Russian Federation and to Europe. This route is expected to offer both quicker and cheaper transportation than the primary alternative — the shipment of goods from South Asia through the Mediterranean and Suez Canal and then into the Atlantic and North Sea to the Baltic ports. Usage of this corridor will provide 20-30 per cent economic saving in time and costs.[22] Experts believe that the volume of traffic on this sector may reach 20–30 million tonnes of cargo per year. However at present the volume of cargo which passes through this corridor is insignificant. Some experts believe that this route has more prospects in the middle term,[23] whereas others are of the opinion that the strategic significance of this route is more for Russia, India and Iran. This may therefore act as a counterweight to the competing Baku-Tbilisi-Ceyhan project that suits the interests of the US.[24]

The new transport corridor (the construction of Chinese-Kyrgyz railway) to China through Kyrgyzstan (Bishkek-Balykchi-Jalalabad-Torugart-Kashgar) has been approved and would be joined to Uzbekistan's railways through Jalalabad. This route would provide the shortest way from the port in China to the Gulf and South European countries. It is opined by a few experts that this route can deprive Kazakhstan of certain economic and political benefits. It would also mean that Uzbekistan, by using this route, could significantly decrease its dependence on Kazakhstan's transit services.[25] Along with the railways, the motor traffic were also opened between CARs and their neighbours. These were five between Kazakhstan and China, two between Kyrgyzstan and China, and three between Turkmenistan and Iran. There are several other routes which are operational connecting Central Asian Republics with Pakistan and Gulf as well. Uzbekistan and China are building the Osh–Kashgar highway.[26]

A new Silk Road between China and Tajikistan became operational on 25 May 2004. This road links the Xinjiang Autonomous Region in the West of China and the Gorno-Badakhshan oblast in the east of Tajikistan. This will open the route for China through Tajikistan to the heart of Central Asia, Russia, the Caspian Sea and onwards. This route provides opportunity to Tajikistan to get an exit into Pakistan, India and further towards the Pacific. Iran has offered Tajikistan a $31million package to upgrade infrastructure, including building an important tunnel on the Anzob pass between Dushanbe and Khojend.[27]

Another important project in the southern direction is that of the Turkmenistan-Afghanistan-Pakistan route (this includes both railway as well as a route to export energy from Central Asia). This is the shortest route from Central Asia to South Asia.[28] There are serious problems with this route; as far as the railroad is concerned there is competition between Turkmenistan and Uzbekistan. While Uzbekistan wants this railroad to pass through Termez, Turkmenistan wants it to start from Kushka. Moreover, the situation in Afghanistan is also not conducive for the realisation of such a project. There are serious security concerns related to this route, both for the transport corridor and pipeline to India because of differences between India and Pakistan. However, the recent dialogues between India and Pakistan have raised some hopes for this pipeline. Some experts are of the view that such cooperation between India and Pakistan would be the biggest confidence building measures (CBMs) for peace between the two countries.[29] But the possibility of such a route would depend on how India–Pakistan relations evolve in the future.

Twenty-two additional international passenger and cargo road transport routes between China and Kazakhstan were added in September 2006. This will bring the total highway passenger transport routes between the two countries to 64 where highway passenger transport routes between China and Kazakhstan will total 33. There will be 31 road cargo transport routes between the two countries.[30] During the Japan and Central Asia dialogue in June 2006, Japan proposed a joint project to build a road linking Central Asia and the Indian Ocean region through Afghanistan.[31] Another route connecting CARs would be the Islamabad–Peshawar motorway (M-1). This motorway would provide connectivity from CARs, China and Afghanistan to the ports and industrial areas of Pakistan. The Islamabad–Charsadda section of this motorway will be opened for traffic from August 2006 whereas the last section of this project (Peshawar-Charsadda) would be completed by January 2007.[32] The Japanese business community is toying with the idea of building a railway across Sakhalin to the mainland. Japan would like to see Central Asia as an economically developed region, very much along the lines of the East Asian pattern.[33] Russia and Turkmenistan have reached an agreement to build a railway that would connect Russia with Iran via Kazakhstan and Turkmenistan. Kazakhstan is trying to build a missing railway link which will link China with Europe via Kazakhstan, Turkmenistan and Iran. Rail road between Afghanistan and Uzbekistan is also under consideration.[34]

Regional Initiatives

One of the recent regional initiatives is the proposal of Trans-Afghan Corridor.[35] In January 2005 Tashkent hosted the first session of an interstate coordinating council for setting up a trans-Afghan transportation corridor that will link Uzbekistan (Termez city), Afghanistan (Mazar-i-Sharif and Herat), and Iran (Bander-Abbas and Chabahar ports). This council will prepare recommendations on financing, mapping, and constructing the 2,400 km road.[36] Another important regional initiative, facilitated by ADB was the establishment of Central and South Asian Transport and Trade Forum (CSATTF) by Afghanistan, Pakistan, Tajikistan and Uzbekistan. These countries signed a protocol in Manila in August 2003 to establish a North-South and East-West trade and transport corridor linking Central Asia with the warm waters of Indian Ocean. Iran attended the ADB-sponsored meeting as an observer and Turkmenistan was invited for the next meeting. Pakistan has offered three ports for integration with the proposed corridor: Karachi, Port Qasim and Gawadar. Iran has offered Bander Abbas and Chabahar. This corridor would dovetail as an interface for the North-South corridor initiated by Russia and India and TRACECA project promoted by EU.[37] There are several bottlenecks which exist, and joint effort would be required to address these bottlenecks.

Pakistan is also trying to improve its connectivity to CARs through China and Afghanistan. ADB has offered $2 billion to Pakistan Railways network which will enable Pakistan to become the most accessible international trade route to CARs, Iran and China. Pakistan and Afghanistan have already agreed to lay railway track of about 103 km between Chaman and Kandahar and this track would be extended to Turkmenistan and other CARs. The feasibility study of the Quetta to Kandahar railway track has been completed and Pakistan would construct 10 to 12 km railway track from Quetta to the Afghan border. The track from Afghan border to Kandahar would be the responsibility of the Afghan government.[38] Pakistan has also proposed to construct a $ 90 million road through the Boroghil Pass in the Yarkhun Valley to link Pakistan with the CARs. Of the thirteen passes which lead to Afghanistan from Chitral district, the Boroghil Pass is the easiest and lowest in altitude. This pass remains closed for very short period late in winter. Wakhan is a 13 to 65 km wide strategic strip in the northeast of Afghanistan with a length of about 300 km. The area links Afghanistan with Pakistan in the south, Tajikistan in the north and China in the east. The Wakhan-Boroghil route has been preferred against the one passing through the central parts of Afghanistan due to the security situation in the neighbouring country. This road will connect the 12,484 foot-high Boroghil Pass at the northwest of the Yarkhum Valley in Chitral with Sarhad-i-Langar in Wakhan at a distance of about 95 km and move on to Iskashim in Tajikistan leading to the Tajik capital Dushanbe via the Korung-Kalai Chumb and Kulob areas. From the Boroghil Pass, the road will traverse down the over 300-km-long valley and reach Peshawar. The distance from Tajikistan to Peshawar via the Wakhan-Chitral route is estimated to be 700km.This road will also branch off to the northern areas via the 10,500-foot-high Shandur Pass and merge into the Karakoram Highway. A number of road projects that seek to interlink northern areas and Chitral have already been sanctioned by the Pakistan government.[39]

The land route from Bishkek to Karachi and vice versa through Province of China is also under construction. The quadrilateral agreement signed by Pakistan, China, Kyrgyzstan, and Kazakhstan is expected to give boost to the trading activities among member nations through the Karakoram Highway.[40] Pakistan has also offered Gwadar deep-sea port to CARs which can serve as the hub of trade for Central Asia. During President Askar Akaev's two day visit to Pakistan on17-18 January 2005, it was agreed between the two countries that Pakistan would import electricity from Kyrgyzstan and both countries would build roads to improve trade. It was decided to strengthen the links through Kashgar in China and onto Bishkek through the Karakoram Highway. The road which is being constructed on Karakoram Highway to link the two countries would be completed by 2006, promoting Pak-Kyrgyz trade.[41] Establishment of a railway link from Gwadar to Taftan in Iran via Saindak is also being planned. A road from Gwadar to Sandak, running parallel to the Iran-Pakistan border, will make it the shortest route to reach Central Asia from the warm water of the Arabian Sea. Another 515-km long highway connecting Gwadar via Pangur, Khaan, Chaghi and Rabat up to Herat in Western Afghanistan is being planned. This would link up Pakistan by road directly with the CARs.[42]

Multilateral Initiatives

Various multilateral institutions, like Asian Development Bank (ADB), World Bank, European Bank for Reconstruction and Development (EBRD), and Islamic Development Bank (IsDB) have provided support in developing the road, rail, air, and port sectors in CARs. The Shanghai Cooperation Organisation (SCO) has also taken some initiative in this respect. Transport is one of the focus areas of SCO. Recently an agreement was signed in Shanghai on a highway project connecting Tajikistan and Uzbekistan.[43] The EBRD has been the lead donor with 11 loans worth 364 million Euros in all four sectors. The World Bank has financed 4 loans worth $240 million in the road and urban transport sector in Kazakhstan, Kyrgyzstan, and Uzbekistan. IsDB has financed 9 loans worth $100 million—mostly in road and air transport sectors—in Kazakhstan, Kyrgyzstan, Uzbekistan, Turkmenistan, and Tajikistan. ADB has provided lending and non-lending support since 1996 in road and railway sectors. ADB has extended eight loans worth $317 million to Kazakhstan, Kyrgyzstan, and Tajikistan for the rehabilitation of roads and two loans amounting to $140 million to Uzbekistan for the rehabilitation of railways. The major projects supported in the road sector are the development of following corridors:

- Bishkek–Osh (Kyrgyz)
- Almaty–Akmola (Kazakh)
- Almaty–Bishkek(Kazakh-Kyrgyz)

In the railway sector, ADB is supporting the rehabilitation of the 641 km Chengeldy-Khodhjadavlet corridor in Uzbekistan under the two projects. Since 1994, ADB has provided a grant worth $20 million for project preparation, addressing policy and institutional issues, human resources development, and commercialisation and cooperation of transport enterprises. A total of eleven projects worth $327.1 million are proposed for the road and railway sector in Kazakhstan, Kyrgyzstan, Mongolia, Tajikistan, Uzbekistan, and Azerbaijan during 2004-2006.The major projects likely to be supported in the road and railway sector are:

Road Projects

- Aktau–Atyrau (Kazakhstan)
- Borovoe–Petropavlovsk corridor (Kazakhstan)
- Kyrgyz Southern transport corridor (phase I and II)
- Central and Southern corridors (in Azerbaijan)
- Dushanbe-Kyrgyz corridor
- Regional road development (Mongolia)

Railway Projects

- Regional railway development project (Uzbekistan–Afghanistan railway link)
- Bekhabad–Khanebadam railway link (Tajikistan)

In addition to the above, a grant worth $6.35 million has been proposed during the same period for developing regional studies for road and railway transport, policy and institutional issues, capacity building of the executing agency, and harmonisation of cross-border issues.[44] In January 2005, ADB signed an agreement to provide Kyrgyzstan with a US$ 32.8 million (Euro 25 million) loan for 31years, to reconstruct a road linking Kyrgyzstan with China. A 124-km section of the road that links the Southern Kyrgyz town of Osh with north-western China will be reconstructed. This same road also connects Kyrgyzstan with neighbouring Uzbekistan.[45]

Another important regional initiative has been taken by Central Asian Regional Economic Cooperation (CAREC). A Transport Sector Coordinating Committee has been set up under CAREC programme to develop transport services in the member countries and improve their transport links with each other and the rest of the world. The CAREC member countries have recently agreed on the Regional Transport Sector Map. This formulates the strategic priorities for regional cooperation in the transport sector. Finally, transport is one of the priority areas of regional cooperation among Azerbaijan, Kazakhstan, Kyrgyzstan, Tajikistan, Turkmenistan and Uzbekistan under the UN Special Programme for the Economies of Central Asia.[46]

Impediments in Reviving and Developing New Corridors

There are inherent constraints limiting the progress of developing the regional transport infrastructure. In this respect some scholars believe that "it is an irony that Silk Route is no longer a bridge but an obstacle for cooperation".[47] The main impediments for building the new transport corridors are:[48]

- Geographical constraints
- Security fears and political differences
- Economic constraints

First and the foremost constraints in developing these new routes is geographical constraints. Central Asia inherited a network of transport routes linking the region to Moscow, but with very little alternative options for its links to the outside world. During the early years after independence CARs were unable to maintain even the Soviet time infrastructure. Various factors starting from poor economic conditions, civil war in Tajikistan, lack of funds to a breakdown in inter-economic ties led to the decline in internal transport infrastructure. Out of five republics, Uzbekistan had a relatively developed transport network. It still has the highest density rail and road network in Central Asia.[49] It also has a good international air links, though its regional air links remain limited. As compared to Uzbekistan, Kazakhstan and Turkmenistan, the transport network in Tajikistan and Kyrgyzstan is poor and needs urgent upgrading. In Kyrgyzstan, nearly 70% of roads are believed to be in urgent need of upgrading. Over 50 per cent of bridges do not meet the existing requirements in terms of the vehicles size or axle load. In Tajikistan this remains extremely limited. There is a lack of direct road connections to state capitals, production centers, markets, and ports. In addition, there are non-physical barriers as well. These include unjustified delay while crossing the border, bureaucratic trammels, frequent changes in transit regulations, arbitrary practices while weighing goods, high transit charges (especially for foreigners) as well as official and unofficial taxes imposed by authorities controlling international shipments. With respect to rail transport, the key issues affecting the region are:

- The dislocations caused by the breakup of the railways into national units have resulted in numerous cross-border operational obstacles. Among these obstacles are a lack of track-sharing agreements, lack of joint planning of infrastructure investment, frequent changes of locomotives and crews at borders, time consuming and expensive train remarshalling at borders, complicated documentation requirements, and inter-railway payment delays.
- Technology is obsolete and poor in quality, and management lacks a developed marketing orientation. This has contributed to excessive tariffs for international traffic, tariffs that do not separate movement and terminal costs, lack of convenient billing systems, and lack of consignment information for shippers.

Security fears and political differences within Central Asian states and among the countries interested in developing these new routes are an important impediment. There are inherent border disputes between the Central Asian states. Examples of border clashes between Uzbek–Tajik, Uzbek–Kazakh and Uzbek–Kyrgyz can be cited in this respect. Despite the improved security situation after the end of Taliban rule in Afghanistan, there has been very little improvement in the border regimes between these republics. The issue of border delimitation remains unresolved, which has very often ended in border disputes. This has restricted the possible development of regional trade development. Security fears emanating from Afghanistan has further hampered the development of these new corridors. The long-term investments in developing various transport networks and pipelines have slowed due to the political differences among countries who are interested in the region. Political differences between Iran and US and India–

Pakistan are some of the examples.

Insufficient economic growth in the region and low level of investment have also hampered any meaningful progress in developing the transport infrastructure. Since economic conditions are unlikely to improve rapidly in Central Asia (with the exception of Kazakhstan and Turkmenistan due to their energy exports) in the short term, the major investment in transport infrastructures would be low. Perhaps Kazakhstan and Turkmenistan would be able to fund significant transport improvements from their own financial resources.

In order to arouse the interest of foreign shippers in the current and planned transit routes, Central Asian Governments will have to establish closer and more efficient cooperation in customs and tariff policy.[50] It is also important to note that the transit rates are different in different republics causing problems. The transit rate in Uzbekistan and Turkmenistan are $460 and $740, respectively, whereas in Kazakhstan it is $66.[51] In this respect Kazakhstan has asked other countries to consider abolishing the transit permit fee for automobile transport. It has reached such an agreement with Russia and Kyrgyzstan. For any effective progress in the development of the transport network, greater regional cooperation is required.

Strategic Significance of Transcontinental Corridors

These initiatives bring us to the question of why these transcontinental corridors should be developed. Are these initiatives a part of the grand strategy adopted by the international community for the economic development of Eurasia or are these initiatives used by countries to promote their own interests and influence in this resource rich region? The current developments indicate two trends: First, the struggle among the major powers to control the resources and pipelines in the region is underway. But it is also interesting to note, that development of these corridors are also helping CARs improve their economies. It is also providing enormous opportunities to the neighbouring countries to enhance their trade with this region. A similar argument has been provided by Jonathan Tennenbaum in his article. According to him by integrating the two poles,[52] Europe and Asia through a network of high-efficiency infrastructure corridors,[53] and using these corridors as instruments to promote the rapid development of the relatively backward interior areas between them, has the potential to unleash a sustained period of real economic growth over the next 30–40 years. Such a project would have a worldwide economic impact, mainly due to the concentrations of the human population (which is about three-fourth of the total population on this planet) all along this corridor which connects Europe, southern and eastern Asia.[54] Once these corridors are fully operational, they will not only promise considerable saving in transport cost, as compared to sea routes, but will promote greater regional economic development, and establish political stability in the region.

The 'New Great Game' among the major players (Russia, China and US) has brought about the geo-political competition for enhancing their influence and gaining a foothold in the region to control the energy resources of CARs. While this power play in some ways has helped the region by bringing investment in the energy sector, it has also brought about the threat of conflict among the major players. This geopolitical competition among major players is not only hampering the progress of developing these new transport corridors but also in constructing the oil and gas pipelines in the region.

The growing involvement of the US[55] in and around the Central Asian region reflects the elevated significance of CARs in the US global strategy, hardly imaginable before 11 September. While Russia and China have supported the US war against terrorism and endorsed US actions in the region, they have expressed their concern about the long term US military presence and its implications for the region. The entry of Americans into Central Asia is not only undermining the Chinese influence, it is also posing a challenge to the Russian influence in their own backyard. This has led both China and Russia to bolster political, military and economic ties with the Central Asian States to reclaim their position. The current trends also indicate that despite US military presence and its growing involvement in the region CARs are deepening their ties with both Russia and China. In this New Great Game the Central Asian states are pursuing a "multi-vector" approach to foreign policy, to balance and manage the major powers who are trying to enhance their influence in the region.

China has used the Silk Route to expand its political, economic and commercial interests.[56] In the past twelve years China has used the Silk Route to increase its trade, and extract natural resources from the Central Asian region. China stands to gain maximum benefit from the corridors which are being developed in and around CARs. China's linkages with CARs have been mentioned in the previous section. Central Asia is of great significance to China.[57] In 2000, China unveiled its 'go-west' policy, which represents a shift in focus of the development from coastal areas to the country's inland and western regions, including Xinjiang Uygur Autonomous Region and Inner Mongolia Autonomous Region. This strategy shift has accelerated the trade volume between the China and CARs. In addition to its 'go-West policy', China also sees the Central Asian region as a future source of its energy supply.[58] The expanding US strategic presence in Central Asia over the past two years has dramatically raised the stakes for Beijing. China imports nearly half the oil it uses, most of it from the unstable Middle East. With demand growing and domestic production unable to meets its needs, China now sees Central Asia as a vital energy source. China's Ministry of Finance estimated that by 2010, the country's annual energy needs will require the country to import 130 million tonnes of oil per year, up from the 60 million tonnes it imported in 2002.[59]

Though Central Asia may not figure as importantly and significantly as the oil-rich Gulf region, in recent years the US has developed important stakes in and around Central Asia. This region is embedded with 'strategic concerns' that lie at the core of the United States interests.[60] As expressed by Secretary of State Colin L. Powell, "America will have a continued interest and presence in Central Asia of a kind that we could not have dreamed of before."[61] Post 9/11, officials in the US felt that larger US interest lay in ensuring that Central Asia does not become the next Afghanistan.[62] In addition to increasing its military profile, the US is also strengthening its economic ties with the region. It signed a Trade and Investment Framework Agreement (TIFA) with all five Central Asian states in June 2004. This agreement is intended to provide a forum for various trade issues and would increase and diversify trade and investment opportunities between the United States and Central Asia. The agreement also sets up a US–Central Asia trade council. The United States imported $571 million goods from Central Asia in 2003 and exported $548 million.[63] Post-Andijan violence in Uzbekistan, the US has strained its relations, resulting in the withdrawal of its military base in Uzbekistan. But its interests are very much intact and there are no signs of Washington's withdrawal from this region.

Russia cannot be indifferent to the fact that the former Soviet republics of Central Asia have become an area of competition. Russia's rule over this region has lasted for more than a hundred years.[64] Russia has major stakes in this region. Given the geographical proximity, historical links and the presence of multimillion Russian diaspora in Central Asia, it considers this region vital to its interests.[65] In recent months, Russian profile (economic, political and military) has been increasing in CARs.[66]

In such a scenario, the development of Central Asian transport corridors would be conditioned by the emerging relations among the major players. The complex relations between of US–Iran–Russia, US–China and US–CIS are likely to have significant implications in the building of these corridors and pipelines. The US wants to deny Iran any entry in the energy sector of this resource-rich region. Not so openly, but US also wants to bypass Russia in this sector. Therefore, how things unfold in the future remains to be seen. Such a relationship of rivalry and competition is likely to slow down any process of development of transport infrastructure in the region.

Indian Initiatives

India, like other regional powers has been very keen to increase its connectivity with the region. The importance of Central Asia for India goes beyond its civilisational and historical links. This region is of great strategic significance to India.[67] India's security interests in CARs emanate from its geo-strategic location. It shares its borders with China, Afghanistan and Pakistan Occupied Kashmir (POK). In fact, CARs can play an important role in maintaining peace along Afghanistan's northern border, to battle *jihadis*, drug traffickers and to stop the flow of illegal weapons.[68]

India has been exploring the possibility of a land route option through Iran and Turkmenistan. In this context, the three-party agreement on international transit of goods amongst Turkmenistan, India and Iran was signed in February 1997 at Teheran.[69] Before this in April 1995, a trilateral Memorandum of Understanding on trade and transit to facilitate the use of Iranian and Turkmen territory for trade with other Central Asian countries was signed.[70] India wants Central Asia to be part of an extended trade network through the North–South corridor. This inter-governmental agreement amongest India, Iran, and Russia was signed in St. Petersburg on12 September 2002.[71] This agreement has been ratified by all the three signatory states and came into force on 16 May 2002. This corridor will facilitate easier movement of goods along the corridor connecting India through the sea route to Iran and then via the Caspian Sea to the Russian Federation and to Europe.

During his visit to Tajikistan in January 2003, the External Affairs Minister said, "We wish to bring out the best, so that trade between Central Asia and India increases manifold. Not just in one direction, but in both directions".[72] Now India has air connectivity with all five republics. India is also trying to open a new sea and road route through Iran and Afghanistan. India is building 200 km of road in Afghanistan linking Zaranj and Delaran, which will be ready soon. This will reduce the distance from India to Central Asia by 1500 km.[73]

Another important initiative was taken during Prime

Minister Atal Behari Vajpayee's two-day visit to Tajikistan in November 2003.This visit was seen as a landmark not only in enhancing Indo–Tajik cooperation but also in improving the links with the Central Asian region. The agreements were signed on establishing direct air links between Dushanbe and New Delhi, opening up of a Tajik mission in Delhi, and forming a working group (represented by Afghanistan, India and Tajikistan) on a direct land route between two countries via Afghanistan. The desire to extend the New Delhi–Dushanbe air route to Kabul was expressed by the Indian Prime Minister. The main theme of this meeting was the importance of developing a regional transport infrastructure to improve Tajikistan's economic outlook. On the eve of this visit, the Tajik parliament endorsed a resolution to join the Treaty on International Transit of Goods, a tripartite agreement amongst India, Iran, and Turkmenistan dating from 1997. The treaty aims to facilitate trade cooperation by eliminating various import duties and customs procedures.[74] The Indian option to build land road to reach Central Asia through Xinjiang and Tibet into Ladakh or Himachal Pradesh is also being considered. China is already connected through a rail link (which is 1,350 km) from Almaty to Urumchi in Xinjiang.[75] The extension of the China–Kyrgyz route to India through road has been suggested. The opening of such a route would benefit all the countries.

Do these initiatives taken by India indicate that its foreign policy focus is shifting increasingly beyond its traditional China–Pakistan focus to Central Asia? Though it would be difficult to completely accept this argument, it would be appropriate to say that after 2000, India's policy towards this region has been more focused and coherent. This brings us to the second question: what are the options for India in CARs? In this context, India would have three options: first, to engage China and work with it in sectors where their interests converge (e.g. IT sector) and to try to negotiate for the corridor to Central Asia. India's option to reach CARs through Xinjiang and Tibet into Ladakh or Himachal Pradesh needs a serious consideration by the Indian establishment. This could significantly transform the geopolitics of the region. Second, to cooperate with Iran, Russia and Afghanistan to further its interests in the region while increasing its bilateral ties with each republic. This option seems to be the most promising, due to India's friendly relations with all the three countries. The third option is that of engaging Pakistan. Of all the corridors, the Pakistan–Afghanistan corridor is not only economically viable, but would also serve as a confidence-building measure (CBM) between the two countries. However, the volatility of India–Pakistan relations has been the biggest political hurdle in developing this corridor. This route would not only promise considerable saving in transport time and cost, as compared to the sea-land route, but would also promote regional economic development. There are serious concerns related to the security of this route. Therefore, it would be appropriate to see that this route is taken as an alternative to the existing Iran corridor. One need not put all eggs in one basket. It is also important to note that the most powerful approach to address the international and regional problems is through building strong economic ties. In the case of India and Pakistan, the opening of overland routes between them to CARs, can open an era of mutually beneficial economic relations not only for the two countries but for the entire region.

To conclude, it can be said that while opportunities for developing the new routes to the Central Asian region exist, greater regional and international cooperation is required. Central Asian states and countries involved in developing these routes need to take commensurate political and economic steps to make full use of the prospects. While elements of competition and rivalry remain the main feature of the power play in Central Asia, there lies an opportunity for these countries to advance their mutual interests in partnership to develop a cooperative mechanism and address the challenges and constraints faced by them in developing various transport networks in the region. Multilateral and regional cooperation remains the most important and effective means to manage the deficiencies of the transport sector in CARs.

Note: This essay is based on research data that was available till December 2006 when it was submitted for publication.

NOTES AND REFERENCES

1. The word 'Silk Route' in this paper has only symbolic meaning. It has been used to explain the current trends in the development of new transport routes connecting CARs with the outside world.
2. Richard C. Foltz, *Religions of the Silk Road*, London, Macmillan Press Ltd., 1999, pp. 1-2.
3. It was a network of roads, going East to West, with spurs into Southern Iran, the northern Eurasian steppe, and south over the Hindu Kush to the Indian Subcontinent.
4. 'Great Silk Road', *http://www.orexca.com/silkroad.php*
5. Susan Whitfield, *Life along The Silk Road*, London, John Murray Ltd., 1999, p. 2.
6. *http://www.adb.org/Carec/transportation.asp*
7. Igor Azovskiy, 'Railroads in Central Asian Countries: Problems and Prospects', *Central Asia and the Caucasus*, (Sweden), No.1 (25) 2004. pp. 133-135; L. Gusseva, 'Transit potential of the Central Asian region's transport complex: conditions and prospects of development', *Central Asia's Affairs*, (Almaty) No. 3(3) 2003, p. 30.
8. *Ibid*.
9. *Ibid*; also see *http://www.adb.org/Documents/csps/CARE/2004/appendix9.pdf*
10. "Great Silk Road", *http://www.orexca.com/silkroad.php*
11. Igor Azovskiy, No. 7; Shavkat Arifkhanov, 'Problems of Developing Transportation and Communication Corridors in the Central Asian Region', Paper presented in '3rd India-Central Asia Regional Conference' organised jointly by Institute for Defence Studies and Analyses and Uzbekistan's Institute for Strategic and Regional Studies at Tashkent during November 6–8, 2003.
12. The Asian Highway (AH) project is one of the pillars of Asian Transport Development (ALTID) project, endorsed by United Nations Economic and Social Commission for Asia Pacific (ESCAP) Commission at its forty eighth session comprising the Asian Highway, Trans-Asian Railway (TAR) and facilitation of land transport project. During the first phase of the project (1960–1970) considerable progress was made. However, progress slowed down when financial assistance was suspended in 1975. This route provided trans-Asian trade and communication for millennia. http://unescap.org/ttdw/index.asp?MenueuName=Asianhighway
13. 'About the Asian High way', http://unescap.org/ttdw/

index.asp?MenueuName=Asianhighway, 'The New Silk Route', http://www.Zeroballet.info/supernaut/archives/000032.html

14. Oliver Wild, *The Silk Road*, http://www.ess.uci.edu/~oliver/silk.html
15. Dashdorjiin Bayarkhuu, 'Geopolitics of the New Central Asia', *World Affairs*, (Delhi), Vol.8 (1), p. 77.
16. One of the routes of TRACECA lies through Kazakhstan and Uzbekistan with an outlet to the Caspian Sea via the Turkmenistan's port and the other direction lies directly through the central regions of Kazakhstan with an outlet to Kazakhstan's Aktau port. The TRACECA member-states are Armenia, Azerbaijan, Bulgaria, Georgia, Kazakhstan, Kyrgyzstan, Moldova, Mongolia, Romania, Tajikistan, Turkmenistan, Turkey, Uzbekistan and Ukraine; Speech of Mr.Tagiro, Secretary General of the permanent Secretariat of IGC TRACECA at the International Ministerial Conference of Landlocked and Transit Developing Countries and the Donor Community on Transit Transport Cooperation, Almaty, 28-29 August 2003.
17. The technical assistance programme is funded by the EU. The European Bank for Reconstruction and Development finances the work on ports, railway and motor highways on the TRACECA corridor for the sum of $250 million. See L. Gusseva, 'Transit potential of the Central Asian region's transport complex: conditions and prospects of development', No. 7, p. 31.
18. Speech of Mr.Tagiro, Secretary General of the permanent Secretariat of IGC TRACECA, No. 16.
19. These reasons have been very well argued in the article written by L. Gusseva, No. 7, p. 31.
20. L. Gusseva, No. 7, p. 32.
21. Amit Baruah, 'India to build key road in Afghanistan', *The Hindu* (Delhi), 21 November 2002.
22. National Report of I.R. Iran on the latest measures taken in line with promotion of multimodal Transport, Iran Ministry of Roads and Transportation, General Directorate of International Affairs, November 2004; A. Spector, 'The North-South Transport Corridor', http://www.brook.edu/printme.wbs?page=/pagedefs/e9e50344b3c7ff3b4670f6410a14146
23. *Ibid*.
24. David Lewis, 'Transportation and Communication Corridors in the Context of Central Asia', Paper presented in '3rd India-Central Asia Regional Conference' organised jointly by Institute for Defence Studies and Analyses and Uzbekistan's Institute for

Strategic and Regional Studies at Tashkent during November 6–8, 2003.

25. *The Times of Central Asia*, Vol. 5 (18) 30 April 2003; L. Gusseva, No. 7, p. 32.
26. Rustam Mirzaev, 'Transportation Communications and Geopolitics in the Great Silk Road Region', *Central Asia and the Caucasus*, No. 2 (32), 2005, p. 99.
27. David Lewis, No. 24.
28. Igor Azovskiy, No. 7, pp.133-135.
29. Hilal A.Raza, 'Potential of Trade in Oil and Gas', Jasjit Singh (ed.) *Oil and Gas in India's Security*, New Delhi, Knowledge World, 2001, pp.101–106.
30. The China Eurasia Forum Weekly Newsletter No. 21, June 5-12, 2006,www.Silkroadstudies.org
31. The China Eurasia Forum Weekly Newsletter No. 21, June 5-12, 2006, www.Silkroadstudies.org
32. 'Islamabad to Charsadda motorway opens in August', http://www.dailytimes.com.pak; also see http://www.onlinews.com.pak/details.php?id=99107
33. Rustam Mirzaev, 'Transportation Communications and Geopolitics in the Great Silk Road Region', *Central Asia and the Caucasus*, No. 2 (32), 2005, p.105.
34. 'Transport sector in Central Asia', *http://www.adb.org/Documents/Reports/CA-Trade-Policy/Chap5.pdf*
35. The establishment of a trans-Afghan Corridor that would link Central Asia with the Persian Gulf and Iranian ports was suggested by President Islam Karimov of Uzbekistan. In June 2003, during Karimov's visit to Iran, three parties signed the agreement on inter-state transport routes and directions.
36. 'Tashkent hosts inter-state council's session', *Russian Information Agency Novosti*, *http://enrian.ru/rian/index.cfm?prd_id=160&msg_id=5284059&startrow=2005-0...* , also see *http://paktribune.com/news/index.php?id=89748*
37. 'South and Central Asia to establish enormous trade and transport corridor', http://iicas.org/libr_en/all/05_08_libr.htm
38. http://paktribune.com/news/index.php?id=76900
39. http://www.chitralnews.com/Latest%20new512.htm
40. 'Pakistan-Kyrgyzstan agree to enhance trade ties', *http://paktribune.com/news/index.php?id=64865*
41. 'Pakistan and Kyrgyzstan agree to improve road links', *http://www.dailytimes.com.pk/default.asp?page=story_18-1-2005_pg7_1*; Ahmed Hassan, 'Pakistan, Kyrgyzstan vow to activate ECO: Visa

rules to be eased', *http://www.dawn.com/2005/01/19/top6.htm;* "Pakistan, Kyrgyzstan vow joint anti-terror efforts", *http://paktribune.com/news/index.php?id=91068*

42. 'The Afghan Corridor: Prospects for Pakistan-Central Asia Relations in Post-Taliban Afghanistan?' *Spotlight on Regional Affairs*, Institute for Regional Studies (Islamabad), September 2002, p. 14.
43. 'What Drives SCO forward?', *http://english.scosummit2006.org/en_spzq/2006-06/16/contest_814.htm*
44. *http://www.adb.org/Documents/csps/CARE/2004/appendix9.pdf*
45. *http://www.forbes.com/business/services/feeds/ap/2005/01/24/ap1775373.html*
46. 'Transport sector in Central Asia', *http://www.adb.org/Documents/Reports/CA-Trade-Policy/Chap5.pdf*
47. P. Stobdan, 'Reviving the Silk Route – The Way Forward', Paper presented in Seminar on 'Central Asia and Indian Business: Emerging Trends and Opportunities' organised by Confederation of Indian Industry, Delhi May 22, 2003.
48. David Lewis, n.23; Igor Azovskiy, n. 8 ; L. Gusseva, n. 7; *http://www.adb.org/Documents/csps/CARE/2004/appendix9.pdf*
49. This density in Uzbekistan is with over 6,700 km of railways. Over 80% of road surface are paved and are of higher standard than its neighbours.
50. L.Gusseva, No. 7, p. 34.
51. *http://www.interfax.com/com?item=Kaz&a=on&id=5747489*
52. At one pole there is Europe, having scientific-technologically advanced industrial potential. At the other pole there is east and southern Asia with their enormous population, vast natural resources and significant industrial capabilities.
53. By 'infrastructure development corridors', what he means is the building up of a basic network of high-efficiency, high-speed transport lines reaching into the hinterland and at the same time concentrating additional investment into creating a dense network of secondary 'capillaries' in the form of transport, energy, water, communications and other basic infrastructure within the band-like region located along the main transport lines.
54. Jonathan Tennenbaum, 'The Eurasian Land Bridge', *World Affairs*, Vol. 8 (1), p. 37.
55. Olga Oliker, Thomas S. Szayna (Eds.), *Faultlines of Conflict in Central Asia and the South Caucasus,* Rand, United States Army, 2003, pp.221-225 also See Ahmed Rashid, *Jihad The Rise of Militant Islam in Central Asia,* Hyderabad, Orient Longman Private

Limited, 2002, pp. 187–207; US governments perceived interests in the region are focused on:

- Controlling energy resources
- Fighting religious extremism and radicalism
- Creating markets for American goods
- Preventing the region from Chinese or Russian dominance
- Creating the support base for its long-term strategy in South Asia and Persian Gulf region.

56. John Calabrese, 'China's Policy Towards Central Asia: Renewal and Accommodation', *Eurasian Studies*, Vol.16, Autumn-Winter 1999, pp. 75-97; Adam Wolfe, 'China takes the lead in strategic Central Asia', *http://www.atimes.com/atimes/China/f117Ad04.html*.
57. There are three main reasons for increasing Chinese interests: oil and gas, improving trade especially in Chinese western provinces and third, security, primarily the Uighur movement in Xinjiang. Heda Bayron, 'China Flexes Economic and Diplomatic Muscles in Central Asia', *http://www1.voanews.com/article.efm?objectID=CB497C79-4AE6-4BCB-90FC85D189...*
58. Taleh Ziyadov, 'Prospects of Caspian gas and its potential markets', Central Asia and the Caucasus, Vol. 5(29), 2004, pp. 52-60;*http://www.adb.org/Documents/csps/CARE/2004/appendix9.pdf*
59. International Energy Agency (IEA) estimates that by 2020, China is projected to become the second largest consumer of oil in the world, next only to the US; *http://www.eia.doe.gov*
60. Meena Singh Roy, 'Central Asian Republics: The US factor'. Paper presented at IDSA fellow Seminar on 20 December 2003.
61. Vernon Loeb, 'Footprints in Steppes of Central Asia', *Washington Post*, February 9, 2002. p. AO1.This is Powell's statement to the House International Relations Committee on 7th February 2002.
62. 'Securing Central Asia', *The Times of Central Asia (Bishkek)*, Vol. 4 (8) (155), 21February, 2002, p. 4.
63. 'United States Signs Trade Frame work with Central Asia', *http://www.eurasianet.org/resource/uzbekistan/hypermail/200406/0006.shtml*
64. Russia has always considered this region as an extension of its own soil. During the Tsar's time Central Asia was important not only economically, but also politically. During this period Central Asia acted as a buffer between the expanding British Empire and the Russian heartland. This region acquired crucial significance during the Cold War period. After the Soviet break-up, this region did not lose its importance as an area ensuring the stability in the Russian heartland. The Central Asian region

was considered by the policy makers as an area which could serve as a region checking the infiltration of extremist forces from its southern borders.

65. Andranik Migraman, a prominent political commentator and advisor to Yeltsin, has argued that the ex-Soviet Republics are a "sphere of..... [Russia's] vital interest" and that they should not be allowed to form alliances" either with each other or with third countries that have an anti-Russian orientation". Alexander J. Motyl, *Dilemmas of' Independence: Ukraine after Totalitarianism,* New York Council on Foreign Relation Press 1993, pp. 122-23. "Russia and Central Asia" *International Affairs,* Vol. 50 (1), 2004, pp. 151-165.
66. Meena Singh Roy, 'Changing Contours of Russia Central Asia relations', *World Focus,* Vol. 125 (3), March 2004, p. 12.
67. See Meena Singh Roy, 'India's Interests in Central Asia', *Strategic Analyses,* Vol. 24 (12), March 2001.
68. Views expressed by former Director Jasjit Singh, IDSA in Rahul Bedi, 'India dabbles in the new "Great Game" ', *Jane's Intelligence Review,* Vol. 13 (6), June 2002, p. 19.
69. Ministry of External Affairs Reports (Government of India), 1996-97, p. 32.
70. *Ibid,* 1995-96, p. 32-33.
71. Amit Baruah, No. 21.
72. EAM's Address at the Tajik National State University, 29 January, 2003 in *http://www.meadev.nic.in/speeches/eam-tajikuniv.htm*
73. Keynote Address by Mr. Yashwant Sinha, Minister of External Affairs of the Republic of India at Third India-Central Asia Regional Conference,Tashkent, November 6, 2003; Voice of the Islamic Republic of Iran, Mashad, BBC Global Monitoring-Central Asia, 6 January 2003.
74. Radio Free Europe/Radio Liberty (RFE/RL), Prague, Czech, Republic Central Asia Report, Vol. 3 (39), 21 November 2003.
75. *The Times of Central Asia,* May 1, 2003.

Notes on Contributors

Professor Abhai Maurya, formerly Head of the Department of Slavic and Finno-Ugrian Languages, University of Delhi, is now Vice-Chancellor of the English and Foreign Languages University, Hyderabad. He has held a large number of important administrative posts at Delhi University. He was formerly member of the UGC Panel of English and Western Languages and member of the Court, University of Delhi (1981–1985). He has also been member of several international organisations of Russian teachers and Slavists and President, Indian Association of Teachers of Russian (1998–2002). He has been member of the Editorial Committee for the 20-volume *Anthology of Russian and Indian Literatures*, Sahitya Akademi. His publications include, apart from teaching aids and dictionaries, *Confluence: Historic-Comparative Literary Studies* (1988), *India and World Literature* (ed.) for ICCR (1990) and *Yugnayika*, a novel in Hindi (2004). He has published many research articles and has presented several papers at national and international seminars. He was awarded the Pushkin Gold Medal, conferred by MAPRYAL, in 1986.

Dr Arup Banerjee is Reader, European History, in the Department of History, Delhi University. He was Associate Professor in the Eurasia Programme of the IGNCA, New Delhi for five years. During this tenure, he assisted in building India's first comprehensive collection of sources on Imperial Russian history, particularly material related to Central Asia, from Russian libraries. He conducted a Feasibility Study on documenting the valuable, but globally dispersed, remnants of ancient and medieval Central Asian civilisations for UNESCO and IGNCA on the basis of the award of a Hirayama Silk Roads Fellowship. He is author of the book *Merchants and Markets in Revolutionary Russia, 1917-1930.*

Devendra Kaushik, formerly Professor at Jawaharlal Nehru University (JNU) and currently at the Maulana Abdul Kalam Institute of Asian Studies, Kolkata, is a specialist on the erstwhile Soviet Union and Central Asia. He has published widely and is author of *Socialism in Central Asia, India and Central Asia, Indian Ocean: Towards a Peace Zone,* and *The Soviet Political*

System. He is Laureate of the Order of Friendship of the Russian Federation awarded in 2003 by President Vladmir Putin.

Dilorom Karomat is a musicologist and music critic. She has been a Fellow of the Khuda Bakhsh Oriental Public library (Patna, India, 1994-95, 1996-1998) and Fellow of The Asiatic Society (Kolkata, India, 2005-2006). She is at present Research Assistant on an AHRC-sponsored research project on 'North Indian Literary Culture: 1450-1650' in London. Her thesis 'Interrelations between Indian and Central Asian Music (11th-19th centuries)' was submitted in 2007 to the Bhatkhande Music Institute, Lucknow (India). She has presented papers at several international conferences and written extensively on Central Asian music.

Gulammohammed Sheikh is painter, poet, writer, and Professor at M.S. University, Baroda. He has lectured widely on art in India, Europe and the USA. He has been awarded the Kalidas Samman, (2002), the Padmashri (1983) and the National Award (1962). He was Visiting Artist, Art Institute of Chicago (1987–2002), Resident at Civitella Ranteri Centre, Italy, Artist-in-Residence at the University of Pennsylvania. He has had many solo exhibitions and participated in group shows in India and abroad. His recent exhibitions include his paintings on Kabir and work on mappings.

K.T. Ravindran is a well-known architect and urban designer. He is Professor, Head of the Department of Urban Design and Dean of Studies at the School of Planning and Architecture, New Delhi. He is Head of the Delhi Urban Arts Commission. He is an expert on several heritage and environmental committees. He is author of *The Ghats of Mathura and Vrindavan: Proposals for Restoration*.

Kalpana Sahni was Professor at the Centre of Russian Studies, Jawaharlal Nehru University, New Delhi till she took voluntary retirement in 2003. Her areas of specialisation include Russian and Soviet literatures and the cultures of the Caucasian and Central and Central Asian regions. She is author of, among other books, *A Mind in Ferment: Mikhail Bulgakov's Prose* (1984), and *Crucifying the Orient: Russian Orientalism and the Colonization of Caucaus and Central Asia* (1997). She has translated *The Ascent of Fujiyama* by Chingiz Aitmatov and K. Mohammejanov. She has been a consultant to UNESCO on the revitalisation of the old part of Samarkand and Bokhara, the collection of data in *mohallas* (in Uzbekistan) and the formulation of the National Museum Programme in Tadjikistan. She has taken part in the evaluation of Timurid Monuments in Kazakhstan for the Aga Khan Trust for Culture.

Meena Singh Roy is Research Officer in the Institute for Defence Studies and Analyses. Her area of specialisation is Central Asia. She completed her Ph.D. from the University of Delhi in 1994. She was associated with The Institute of Commonwealth Studies, SOAS, for her research work. She has presented papers in various national and international seminars and has several published research papers and articles. She is currently working on 'India-Central Asia Relations: Changing Dynamics and Future Prospects'.

Neelima Singh studied Russian at Jawaharlal Nehru University. She has taught Russian at Himachal Pradesh University and JNU and is currently teaching the language at Lady Shri Ram College. She has worked as lecturer and done research on Central Asia at the Academy of Third World Studies in Jamia Millia Islamia. She is a freelance translator and research facilitator. She is a business consultant to overseas companies from CIS.

Qamar Rais retired from Delhi University as Professor. He was deputed as Professor of Urdu at Tashkent University in 1962, 1965, 1970 and 1982. He has been Director of the Indian Cultural Centre at Tashkent (1997–2001). He is author and compiler of twenty-four books on literature and six books on Uzbek culture and literature, including translations of Uzbek poetry. The Government of Uzbekistan conferred two honorary doctorates in Fine Arts and Literature for his work on the cultures of Uzbekistan and India. He has served as Visiting Professor at the Academy of Third World Studies. He was the recipient of the Babur International Award in 2004 for his translations of Babur's poetry into Urdu and Hindi.

Radha Banerjee's areas of research include Chinese Buddhist and Central Asian Art and Iconography. The title of her doctoral thesis was 'A Comparative Study on Buddhist and Brahmanical Art Forms'. She has travelled and lectured widely. She has lectured at the Department of Inner Asian and Atlantic Studies, Harvard University and the Department of Central Asian Studies at Berkeley, University of California. She has participated in national and international seminars and has been supervisor and examiner of theses from Qaid-e-Azam University (Pakistan), Delhi University, National Museum, and Jawaharlal Nehru University. Dr Banerjee has been the recipient of the India-China Cultural Fellowship Programme (1996-1997) and the ICHR Fellowship. She is Senior Research Officer, East Asian Programme, Kala Kosa, IGNCA, New Delhi.

Rajeev Sethi, scenographer of the 36th Smithsonian's Silk Road Festival held in Washington D.C. in 2002, is noted internationally for his innovative contribution to preserving and celebrating South Asia's rich cultural heritage. For EXPO 2000/Hannover, Rajeev Sethi worked with environmentalists and craftspersons from 30 countries to create the seventy-thousand-square-foot, multicultural *Basic Needs Pavilion*. For this, Sethi was awarded the Order of Lower Saxony by the German government. He has also received the Presidential honour, the Padma Bhushan. He is founder of *Sarthi* and *The Asian Heritage Foundation*, and is goodwill ambassador and member of the Senate Committee of the Universal Forum of Cultures, 2004, Barcelona.

Romi Khosla is a known international architect as well as national consultant on urban planning issues. He has worked with The Aga Khan Trust for Culture (Geneva) in 2003 to prepare a Master Plan of the City of Kabul. He worked with UNESCO in 1997-1998 for the Revitalisation of Bukhara and Samarkand. He has worked on international projects in Nicosia, Romania, Cairo, Bulgaria and Jerusalem. He has worked with the Aga Khan Trust for Culture (1990–1999) on technical reviews of projects in Indonesia, Uzbekistan, Turkey, Singapore, Qatar and India. During 1972–1998, Romi Khosla was Senior Partner of a planning and architectural practice in Delhi with projects all over India and Nepal. He is the author of a standard reference book on Buddhist Monasteries in The Western Himalayas. He is Senior Consultant to The Indian National Trust for Art & Cultural Heritage as well as Vienna University, Australia, for cultural documentation and protection of monuments in the Himalayas.

Rta Chisti Kapur has studied the textile tradition, particularly natural and printing, in Rajasthan and Gujarat and *ikat* in Andhra Pradesh and Orissa and Gujarat. She has written scripts for films on Andhra *ikats* and Kanchipuram brocades by Dev Bengal and for 'Roti, Kapda aur Architecture', produced by the School of Planning and Architecture, New Delhi. She has lectured widely on textiles and put up exhibitions of textiles in India and abroad. She has been contributing author to the book titled *Arts and Crafts of Central India* published by Mapin and *Modern Indian Costume*, the 18-volume 'Dictionary of Art' by Macmillan Publishers. She is co-author of *Tradition and Beyond: Hand-Crafted Indian Textiles 1947-1990* and author of the publication of the 'Splendour of Indian Textiles' exhibition held in Beijing, China. She is member, governing body of 'Dastakar'. She has served on various juries and expert committees on textiles and fashion design. In 2003, she initiated the setting up of 'The Sari School' in New Delhi. In 1999, she received the PHD Chamber of Commerce award for Outstanding Contribution to Art, Craft and Culture.

Ruby Roy is a specialist in contemporary history and International Law. She has taught at Patna University. From 1998 to 2001, she was ICCR Visiting Professor at Osh State University in Kyrgyzstan. She was Visiting Fellow and Cluster Coordinator (Russia and Central Asia) at IDSA (2001–2004). Her particular field of interest is Russian Policy (in the Southern Periphery). She has published many articles and has translated the book *The Kyrgyz and the Kokand State.*

Saifullah Saifi submitted his doctoral thesis 'The Khanate of Bukhara from 1800 to the Russian Revolution' at Aligarh Muslim University. He is presently teaching at the Yasin Meo Degree College at Gurgaon. He has participated in many national and international seminars and has many publications to his credit.